W9-CNX-138

Praise for Andy Martino's

CHEATED

"In forensic detail, Martino describes the execution of the Astros' scheme and assesses the advantage it conveyed. More compelling, though, are his attempts to understand its perpetrators, especially Carlos Beltran, one of the ringleaders. . . . But Beltran's descent down the slippery slope from all-but-sanctioned espionage to reprehensible cheating gives Martino's narrative its compelling tragic arc." —*The New York Times Book Review*

"Well-reported and well-written. . . . It's all fascinating stuff, rendered all the more engaging by the context that Martino constructs. . . . A compelling look at what can happen to a team when they wade into the murky middle and allow their competitiveness to push them over the line." —*The Maine Edge*

"An interesting behind-the-scenes story. . . . Martino's history is both informative and amusing. Baseball fans will get a kick out of it." —*The News-Gazette* (Champaign, IL)

"What Martino's reporting reveals again and again is that technology— tiny cameras, smart watches, and especially monitors located near dugouts—led to paranoia that every other team was doing *something* to gain an unfair advantage. . . . Martino's book is the latest reminder that their sins will follow the Astros forever." —*Texas Monthly*

"Impressive. . . . Compelling. . . . Any baseball fan will enjoy Martino's look back at the prevalence of cheating in baseball, and how it developed over the past century. The thought-provoking threads Martino pulls on during the quick read will likely fuel bar arguments about cheating amongst baseball fans throughout this season, and in the next century of cheating to come."

—*The Washington Free Beacon*

"Sober, engaging, and freshly troubling. . . . [A] reminder that, whether or not Astro fans or anyone else like it, Astrogate will not disappear soon into history's recesses." —*Sports Central*

"Andy Martino delves, dissects, and masterfully delivers the high drama of the sign-stealing scandal that has rocked the baseball world since 2017." —Paul Auster, author of
The New York Trilogy and *4 3 2 1*

"Listen up. Here's a coded whistle, a bang on the nearest garbage can to let you know that a fastball is coming from Andy Martino with *Cheated*. This is a caper story about a plot to steal baseball's most coveted prize, the World Series, an outlandish scheme that works . . . until it doesn't. Fascinating, fascinating stuff."

—Leigh Montville, author of *The Big Bam* and *Ted Williams*

"Leave it to an old-school journalist like Andy Martino to get to the bottom of a modern-day baseball crime. With his intimate knowledge of clubhouse culture and ability to humanize the sport's most recognizable figures, Martino explains how an accepted form of gamesmanship gradually transformed into blatant cheating. This story couldn't be told in 280-character blocks on Twitter."

—Dylan Hernández, *Los Angeles Times* sports columnist

"With the eye of a keen reporter and the touch of a gifted story-teller, Andy Martino exposes the shadowy subculture of sign stealing in baseball. *Cheated* is the definitive story of the biggest baseball scandal of this era: how it was done, how it unraveled, and how the culture of the Astros—and the game itself—unleashed a full-blown crisis of paranoia, moral compromise, and broken trust on our national pastime."   —Tyler Kepner, author of
K: A History of Baseball in Ten Pitches

"I feel *cheated* by what the Astros did, as will anyone who reads this unbiased, fascinating, and detailed account of how an art form performed by the rarest of artists turned mechanical, forever tainting the internal beauty and magic of the greatest game in the world."
—MLB veteran Todd Zeile

"Sign stealing is as old as baseball and is viewed as either part of the game or a heinous infraction. The two viewpoints cross swords when they play out in the postseason, and the Houston Astros cheating scandal became the game's biggest since the 1919 'Black Sox' incident. Andy Martino delivers a high hard one here."
—Marty Appel, author of
Munson, Casey Stengel, and *Pinstripe Empire*

"Combining his reporting on a modern baseball scandal with an acute knowledge of the history of the game, Andy Martino intelligently dissects the Houston Astros scandal. A remarkable read about how much the game we love has changed—and how, in some ways, it has always remained the same."   —Ron Darling,
MLB veteran and award-winning analyst

"[Martino's] account of the unfolding, and undoing, of the Astros' plot is well covered and compellingly told."   —*Booklist*

"Martino craftily leads readers through the scandal, with all of its twists and turns. . . . The writing is engaging and casual throughout. . . . This disturbing tale will satisfy baseball fans, but will also be of great interest to many other sports followers."

—Library Journal

"Well-written . . . certain to appeal to baseball fans. Along the way, Martino documents countless jaw-dropping examples of moral laxity. . . . An entertaining account of one of baseball's sorriest chapters."

—Kirkus Reviews

"Martino makes the story accessible to casual fans, with enough detail to sate diehard fans of the sport. This account serves as a nice addition to the growing canon of books about sports scandals."

—Publishers Weekly

Andy Martino

CHEATED

Andy Martino has written about sports, culture, and entertainment, and has covered Major League Baseball for more than a decade. A former staff writer at *The Philadelphia Inquirer* and the New York *Daily News*, he is currently a reporter and analyst covering MLB for the SNY network in New York.

CHEATED

CHEATED

The Inside Story of the Astros Scandal and
a Colorful History of Sign Stealing

ANDY MARTINO

Anchor Books
A Division of Penguin Random House LLC
New York

FIRST ANCHOR BOOKS EDITION, MARCH 2022

Copyright © 2021 by Andy Martino

All rights reserved. Published in the United States
by Anchor Books, a division of Penguin Random House LLC,
New York, and distributed in Canada by Penguin Random House Canada Limited,
Toronto. Originally published in hardcover in the United States
by Doubleday, a division of Penguin Random
House LLC, New York, in 2021.

Anchor Books and colophon are registered
trademarks of Penguin Random House LLC.

The Library of Congress has cataloged the Doubleday edition as follows:
Names: Martino, Andy, author.
Title: Cheated : the inside story of the Astros scandal and a
colorful history of sign stealing / Andy Martino.
Description: First edition. | New York : Doubleday,
2021. | Includes bibliographical references.
Identifiers: LCCN 2020044983 (print) | LCCN 2020044984 (ebook)
Subjects: LCSH: Houston Astros (Baseball team)—History. | Baseball signs and signals—
United States—History. | Baseball—Corrupt practices—United States—History.
Classification: LCC GV875.H64 M27 2021 (print) |
LCC GV875.H64 (ebook) | DDC 796.357/64097641411—dc23
LC record available at https://lccn.loc.gov/2020044983
LC ebook record available at https://lccn.loc.gov/2020044984

Anchor Books Trade Paperback ISBN: 978-0-593-31143-1
eBook ISBN: 978-0-385-54680-5

Author photograph © Gene Mollica Studio, LLC
Book design by Michael Collica

anchorbooks.com

Printed in the United States of America
10 9 8 7 6 5 4 3 2 1

Contents

"I'M GONNA KICK HIS FUCKING ASS!"

"**T**ell your fucking hitting coach I'm gonna kick his fucking ass!" Yankees coach Phil Nevin screamed at Astros third baseman Alex Bregman.

It was not long after the Houston Astros and the New York Yankees began Game One of the 2019 American League Championship Series at Minute Maid Park in Houston.

The trouble had started a few minutes earlier, when the Astros were batting. As Yankees pitcher Masahiro Tanaka began his windup, he noticed a whistling sound but assumed it was coming from the stands. Opposing fans often tried to distract him, and Tanaka figured that's all that was happening here.

Inside the Yankees' dugout, the coaches knew better. They believed that Astros hitting coach, Alex Cintrón, was the whistler and that he was doing it to convey stolen signs. The exact tone and volume of the whistle would vary, depending on the pitch that Tanaka was about to throw.

Yankees manager Aaron Boone and a few of his coaches started yelling across at Cintrón, telling him to stop.

"What the fuck are you gonna do about it?" Cintrón called back from the Astros' dugout, dismissing Boone with a flip of his hand.

"I'll tell you what I'm gonna do," yelled Boone. "I'm gonna raise it with Bill."

As promised, Boone left the dugout between innings to notify home plate umpire Bill Welke of his concerns. Boone explained that in spring training, top MLB officials Joe Torre, Chris Young, and Peter Woodfork had visited his office during their annual rounds to all thirty clubs and explicitly said that whistling in the dugout to communicate with the batter was illegal and the rule was going to be newly enforced.

Welke told the Astros to knock it off. Coaches and players jawed at one another from across the field.

When Nevin jogged out to his position next to third base, he looked back at the Astros bench to see Cintrón sticking his middle finger in the air and pointing it at Boone: Fuck you, skip.

Nevin now turned to Bregman and barked the epithet about Cintrón. The Yankees were sick of suspecting the Astros, sick of having to change their sign sequences constantly, and sick of trying to beat a team they viewed as deeply unethical in order to advance to the World Series.

The Yankees won the game anyway. Afterward, general manager Brian Cashman walked into the clubhouse, smiling and ready to celebrate, only to find a current of anger rippling through the players and coaches.

"Those guys are fucking cheating," one of the coaches said.

Cashman's first thought? *Well, I'm not surprised.* After all, his own front office had asked MLB to search every crevice of the ballpark that same afternoon for clues of illegal activity.

Still, neither he nor anyone else in the ballpark could have guessed that this heated moment—a spat about whistling, of all things—would end up as one of the final on-field incidents in one of the worst scandals ever to befall American professional sports.

In a matter of weeks, it would all come apart.

—

The scandal that destroyed careers and left fans questioning the integrity of the national pastime began three full seasons earlier, but it was rooted deeply in baseball's traditions.

Cheating and sign stealing had been part of the game for more than a century, with many colorful examples sprinkled through its history. But beginning in 2017, the Astros incorporated technology in new ways to win illicitly, and that changed everything.

That year, they used a camera mounted in center field to steal signs and relay them to hitters in real time. The 2018 and 2019 seasons brought a wave of complaints from other clubs about increasingly advanced methods of cheating and resulted in MLB investigations into the Astros during that period.

During the 2019 playoffs, the era of electronic sign stealing began to crumble. First, the Tampa Bay Rays lodged several complaints with the league before the American League Division Series, hinting at the wilder charges later leveled against Houston—some that have never been reported, and some of which were later debunked. Then in the ALCS, the Yankees made their complaint about Houston's whistling. Five games later, the Yanks caught the Astros using flashing lights in center field. All through that series, whispers about the Astros' behavior in recent years—the garbage-can banging, whistling, wearable technology, hidden GoPro cameras, and more—spread through the Yankees clubhouse and executive suites. No one was yet sure what exactly was true and when it had happened, but suspicions ran hotter than ever.

Reporters were picking up on the gossip, too. What had long been a secret, the game-within-a-game that the world never heard about, percolated closer to the surface.

As the National League champion Washington Nationals prepared to face Houston in the World Series, they heard from contacts around the game about how to defend against the Astros. The Nats developed extra sign sequences and other preventive measures, and won the series. By now, everyone knew you had to be extra careful when playing in Houston.

That November, former Astros pitcher Mike Fiers went public, laying out the 2017 trash-can scheme in an interview with the online publication *The Athletic.* Innovative Twitter sleuths found video proving Fiers's claims, which went viral and lent a unique modern touch to this scandal.

The revelations shocked fans and led Major League Baseball to launch a major investigation. When it was over, three of the smartest managers in the game had lost their jobs, and America found itself talking about baseball more than it had in years—though not for reasons the league wanted. The sign-stealing fallout crossed over from ESPN to NPR, from MLB Network to the *Today* show and Fox News.

Even Congress would join the conversation, when Representative Bobby Rush, Democrat of Illinois, requested hearings on sign stealing. In his letter to the chair of the House Committee on Energy and Commerce, Rush called the Astros designated hitter Carlos Beltrán "the mastermind in the team's systematic cheating." Baseball had gone mainstream again.

When opposing players reported to spring training in February 2020, many launched stunning verbal attacks against their union brothers on the Astros. Ballplayers almost never speak out against one another, but anger over this issue was too intense to contain. Stars like Cody Bellinger of the Dodgers and the Yankees sluggers Aaron Judge and Giancarlo Stanton told the world that they had lost all respect for the Astros, and some called for MLB to strip them of their 2017 World Series title.

Players also openly questioned baseball commissioner Rob Manfred's ability to lead the sport. The union, for years the strongest in sports history, found itself torn between members who hated the Astros and those who played for them.

Players and the general public alike were able to sense that nothing less than the perception of fair play was at stake. Baseball was drowning in the problems of modern tech and needed to find a way forward to preserve its competitive integrity.

In order to buy into a sport—to invest time, money, and emotional capital—fans must believe that the game they are watching is an honest competition. They spend on tickets and cable TV and streaming packages because they love unpredictable drama and assume that the result is determined on the field, not off it.

When fans learned of the Astros' misdeeds, it led to a crisis of faith in the legitimacy of baseball itself. Once the competition isn't happening on the field of play, but in a tunnel or computer monitor out of sight, the air goes out of the fan experience. You can no longer trust what you are watching.

Sure, baseball teams had been stealing signs forever, but this felt worse. In Houston, a number of factors converged to create a uniquely troubling scandal.

The front office, led by general manager Jeff Luhnow, had long been questioning received wisdom and challenging what baseball people considered acceptable. Admirers saw Luhnow as a brilliant innovator. Detractors saw him as ruthless and amoral.

The team Luhnow assembled in 2017 employed two ravenous baseball minds in positions of influence: bench coach Alex Cora and DH Carlos Beltrán. A. J. Hinch, an otherwise brilliant manager, failed to muster the strength or leadership to stop what he considered wrong.

Add to those characters the fact that the team had access to technology that no other generation of cheaters could use. There was a video-replay room, iPads, smart watches, and phones, and allegedly wearable buzzers or devices activated remotely. This was a twenty-first-century scam, pulled off by a group of people with the right blend of intelligence and moral flexibility.

Houston won the World Series in 2017. The following year, Cora departed to become manager of the Boston Red Sox, and Boston hoisted the World Series trophy at the end of that season (the team was also later disciplined for a far less serious electronic-sign-stealing offense, in which Cora did not directly participate). The following year, 2019, the Astros won the American League pennant.

The scandal ran deep. Soon after, the game found itself in crisis.

In 1926, Ty Cobb summarized the sign-stealing issue in a succinct way that still applies:

"If a player is smart enough to solve the opposing system of signals he is given due credit. . . . There is another form of sign stealing which is reprehensible and should be so regarded. That is where mechanical devices worked from outside sources . . . are used. Signal-tipping on the fields is not against the rules, while the use of outside devices is against all the laws of baseball and the playing rules. It is obviously unfair."

Clearly, this wasn't new. The roots of the Astros scandal stretched back for the entire history of the game, but Houston—and to a lesser and more complicated extent, a handful of other teams—pushed the limits far enough to change the sport forever. Just as the 1919 Chicago "Black Sox" scandal forced the league to reckon with gambling, and the steroid era led to new rules about performance-enhancing drugs, the era of electronic sign stealing brought a reckoning on technology.

What follows is the story of how it happened—from the origins of sign stealing and pitch tipping more than a century ago, to the introduction of TV feeds in the clubhouse, to the scandal that shook baseball to its very core exactly one hundred years after the Black Sox conspired with gamblers to throw a World Series. It all started in the late 1800s, and its recent iteration ensnared the Astros and the Red Sox, and also had a deep impact on the Yankees and the Mets, largely innocent bystanders. The story is sordid, and at times ethically ambiguous. One thing, however, is clear: There is much that has not been told.

CHEATED

Chapter 1

HOW WE GOT HERE

Were the Astros part of a long tradition of sign stealing? Or were they outliers, worse than anyone else in history?

The answer is, well, both. What Houston did was the logical extension of more than a century of teams looking for an edge on the fringes of legality. But it was also new and different from anything that came before it.

It's important to understand the history.

The art of sign stealing stretches back at least to the days when Chester A. Arthur was president. It began with eyes, opera glasses, primitive buzzers, and scoundrels who sang in a cappella groups. As the twentieth century progressed, sign stealing claimed victims—most memorably, it rattled the gentle soul of Brooklyn Dodgers pitcher Ralph Branca—and expanded to include new tools. By the turn of the millennium, Branca's son-in-law Bobby Valentine would innovate the use of scouting cameras to decode opponents' signs. Later, the Astros pushed more advanced experiments with tech beyond the bounds of legality.

Those characters and teams would all emerge as important points on the continuum. But our story begins with the most notorious sign thief of baseball's early years, a man clever enough to pull off a scheme remarkably similar to what the Astros would execute a full 117 years later.

In the winter following the 1899 season, a lifelong reprobate and current Philadelphia Phillies utility man named Pearce Chiles, whose nicknames included "Petey" and "What's the Use," spent a day at the racetrack in New Orleans. When Chiles looked through a pair of field glasses to better see the horses, he noticed something else just past the track: a high school baseball game—and a clear view of the catcher's hands and signs.

Chiles had an idea.

This was a man always willing to bend rules, not to mention laws, in the name of personal gain. Born Pearce Nuget Chiles on May 28, 1867, in Deepwater, Missouri, he was a baseball vagabond by his teens, drifting for many years between minor league teams in cities ranging from Topeka to Little Rock, Scranton to Hot Springs. When opposing batters would hit pop-ups, Chiles often mocked them by shouting, "What's the Use?" before catching them with a flourish. By 1895 newspapers were using that as his nickname.

During that period, Chiles acquired more than just a memorable sobriquet. He also built a criminal résumé. On July 10, 1895, Chiles's mother died, and he likely traveled to Missouri for her funeral. The following February, when Chiles was in Phoenix for a winter league, the *Los Angeles Times* reported that he was "wanted in Missouri for illicit relations with a sixteen-year-old girl [in Deepwater]. As the age of consent in that State is eighteen years, the charge against him is constructive rape."

Chiles managed to escape Phoenix before the authorities caught up with him, and he played that summer in Shreveport and Galveston. Over the next few years he continued to get himself into and out of trouble with local law enforcement.

He also developed a reputation as a savvy baseball man. In 1898 he signed on as player/manager for the Atlantic League's Lancaster Maroons, and led the team to an 82-50 record. The following year, he received an invitation to the Phillies' spring training camp in Charlotte, North Carolina.

Chiles was a thirty-three-year-old bench player who had never reached the big leagues. But in Charlotte, he clicked with his new team, which included future Hall of Famers Ed Delahanty, Elmer Flick, and Napoleon Lajoie. Initially playing against the Phillies on an intrasquad team called the Yannigans, Chiles performed well enough to get reps with the varsity. He also fit in socially, earning the respect of his new teammates by knowing his way around a pool hall—and, of all things, an a cappella singing group.

That spring, first baseman Duff Cooley started a quintet with third baseman Billy Lauder, pitcher Red Donahue, and shortstops Monte Cross and Dave Fultz. The group serenaded local women with hits of the day like "The Bridge the Heart Burned Down" and "You'll Get All That's Coming to You."

Noticing that the ladies of Charlotte were sufficiently impressed, catcher Morgan Murphy wanted a piece of the action. He formed a rival group, harmonizing with Chiles, Delahanty, and Flick, and focusing more on comedic material.

Chiles broke camp with the team, and performed well that season in a reserve role, batting .320 in 356 plate appearances, with 76 runs batted in. He also contributed as a part-time baserunning instructor.

The Phillies invited Chiles back for the 1900 season, and used him as third-base coach on the many days when he was not playing. It was in that role that he would make his mark as one of the earliest known adopters of methods that laid the groundwork for the Astros' later trickery.

Thinking back to that winter day when he saw the high school catcher's hands through his field glasses, Chiles hatched a plan with his singing partner Murphy, who, as the backup catcher, did not often play. While Chiles coached third, Murphy would position himself beyond the center field wall, looking at the opposing catcher with a pair of opera glasses. The two wired up a system where Murphy could send a small electric shock to a device under the dirt in the third-base coach's box, indicating what pitch was coming. Chiles, feeling the pulses through his feet, would then relay it to the batter either verbally or through hand signals.

For months, opponents muttered about suspicious activity. Why was Murphy never in the dugout? And why did Chiles always stand in the same spot in the coach's box? And what, for that matter, was with all the twitching?

The gossip and innuendo escalated as the summer progressed, but no one could prove what Chiles and Murphy were up to. By mid-season, a Philadelphia paper joked that Chiles had the disease of Saint Vitus' dance, but only in his legs.

In September, suspicion boiled over during a doubleheader in Philadelphia between the Phillies and the Reds. In the third inning of the first game, Reds shortstop and captain Tommy Corcoran sprinted to the third-base coach's box and dug frantically at the dirt with his spikes.

The Phillies' groundskeeper quickly followed and confronted Corcoran, angry that someone was destroying his work. Both benches emptied, and soon police were on the field, trying to settle the commotion.

Corcoran had dug deeply enough to find a wooden board, which turned out to be the lid of a box containing a tangle of wires.

The Reds felt validated, but the Phillies continued to deny any sign stealing. Umpire Tim Hurst ordered the teams to resume play.

The day after the kerfuffle with Corcoran and the Reds, Phillies manager Billy Shettsline publicly denied any knowledge of a buzzer device. Opponents and reporters remained skeptical, and the papers began referring to Morgan Murphy as "the Thomas Edison of baseball."

On September 19, Chiles conceived a mischievous response to the Reds' accusations. Arriving at the ballpark early that day, he dug a hole in the first-base coach's box and buried a single piece of wood.

That day, coaching first instead of his usual third base, he began twitching and shaking his legs. That provoked Corcoran and several teammates to rush from the dugout and repeat their aggressive digging. But this time they turned up only the lone piece of wood, and Chiles had a good laugh.

Nevertheless, anger and suspicion followed the Phils. When the team played in Brooklyn on September 26, Brooklyn Superbas manager "Foxy Ned" Hanlon accused Shettsline of stationing Murphy in a tenement building beyond the center-field wall, using a newspaper to flash signs to Chiles.

"You're dreaming," Shettsline said.

"I know that Murphy was up in the room reading the catcher's signals with a field glass that cost seventy-five dollars," Hanlon said. "It is so powerful he can see an eyelash at two hundred and fifty yards."

Flustered, Shettsline accidentally conceded his team's guilt.

"There is where you are way off," he said. "The glass cost only sixty-five dollars."

Despite Chiles's puckish humor and Shettsline's clumsy denials, the Phillies did see a marked decline in their batting average at home after Corcoran discovered the box.

Before that game, the Phils batted .336 at National League Park, better known as Baker Bowl. After Corcoran and the Reds dug up the wires, the Phils' home batting average dipped to .292.

Though the Phillies were the most egregious sign stealers that year, they weren't the only team doing it. On September 29, the same Tommy Corcoran led teammates on a mission to center field in Pittsburgh's Exposition Park.

There, they found a corner that was fenced off. A Reds player mounted the fence and found a trap door on the other side—mission control for a cheating scheme less sophisticated than the one Chiles and Murphy had run with the Phillies.

The Pirates had stationed a person behind that fence who would use field glasses to steal signs, then operate the hands of a clock to replay the pitch to the batter: twelve o'clock for fastball, nine o'clock for outside curve, and three o'clock for inside curve.

It turned out that the Phillies and Pirates knew about each other's methods and had entered into a gentleman's agreement to not steal signs against each other. To prove their sincerity, the Phils agreed to keep Murphy on the bench during games against the Pirates.

The season ended amid rising tension over sign stealing in the league, with the Phillies a particular target of suspicion.

During the annual postseason meetings in October, owners argued about the issue. Brooklyn president F. A. Abell wanted the Phils' batting averages expunged from the record books, and their wins vacated.

On October 2, the Phillies' majority owner, Colonel John I. Rodgers, delivered his response in a defiant speech. Teams, he said, had been stealing signs to gain an advantage since the game began. There was nothing wrong with this, provided it was done with the naked eye.

Sure, there had been some talk of field glasses, Rodgers continued. But it was absurd to think that those could actually help.

As for the wooden contraption under Chiles in the coach's box, and the wires inside it? That was easy to explain, Rodgers said. An amusement company had used the field in July and brought electric lights. They must have left some equipment behind.

"It is absolutely too silly to further discuss the subject, and I therefore dismiss it," Rodgers said. "I will certainly not dignify the charge by pleading 'not guilty,' because *minimis non curat lex* (the law does not cure trivial matters)."

The issue did not strike Hall of Fame pitcher Christy Mathewson as trivial. In a book written years later, Mathewson asserted that the sign stealing had convinced opponents that the Phillies were an excellent fastball-hitting team—and as a direct result of that false perception, they were fed an inordinate amount of breaking balls for several additional seasons.

The team's denials did not prevent reporters from continuing to probe. Charles Dryden, a traveling beat writer covering the Phils, laid out the scheme in an October 8 article in *The North American* and traced its origins to Chiles's trip to the racetrack in New Orleans the previous winter.

Dryden reported that, with the Phillies, Murphy had first used a rolled-up piece of paper, holding it horizontally when a fastball was coming and vertically for a curve. Opponents soon began to notice, so Chiles thought back to a time earlier in his life when he'd been shocked by a live wire. That gave him the idea of adding electricity to the scheme.

It did not turn out to be Chiles's most serious infraction during this period. On a train bound for Hot Springs on February 15, 1901, Chiles and a friend named D. B. Sherwood ran a confidence game on a soldier named Benjamin F. Henry. After initiating a confusing wager and argument, Chiles and Sherwood made off with ninety-five dollars belonging to Henry. A state ranger apprehended them on the train and jailed them in El Paso.

As a contemporary press account described it soon after:

"Pearce Chiles, the famous coach and buzzer manipulator of the Philadelphia club, is now lost in the sea of despair. He has signed a new contract, but not for any $2400, nor will any American League team try to steal him away from his new employers. Chiles is to do two years on the Huntsville convict farm, and his uniform will be black and white, with the number 24876 across his back. He will not stop at the Fifth Avenue Hotel, but will sleep in an abandoned hog pen, and his daily menu will include sour bacon, hominy, corn bread and pure water. Incidentally, Chiles will be allowed to work from 6 a.m. to 6 p.m., and the work will be so different from that of last year that it will be an interesting novelty. . . . Such is the fate of Pearce Chiles. How this man ever got on the Philadelphia team is a mystery. He was run out of Kansas and Texas years ago for serious crimes, and now gets the two-year trick for working a flimflam game."

On August 19, 1902, Chiles escaped from the Huntsville prison. From there, he continued to float around the country and even play minor league ball.

Other than a few more newspaper mentions of his criminal behavior—the Portland Browns of the Pacific Coast League released him in 1903 after an arrest for punching a young woman in the face—"What's the Use" Chiles drifted into anonymity, his mark on baseball history already made.

Chapter 2

NO, THE 1951 GIANTS DON'T JUSTIFY THE ASTROS

In the spring of 1947, several Brooklyn Dodgers circulated a petition around the clubhouse stating their unwillingness to play with Jackie Robinson or any other black man. Pitcher Ralph Branca stood up and objected.

"If you don't want to socialize with Jackie," Branca told teammates, "at least work with him. Unless you're blind you can see he'll help us win the pennant."

The petition failed. Soon after, Branca was pitching for the Dodgers in an exhibition against their farm team, the Montreal Royals, of which Robinson was still a member. During the game, Robinson walked past the mound and muttered a quiet thank-you to Branca for his support. When it came time for the historic opening day a few weeks later, Branca stood next to Robinson on the field, signaling to white fans that the newcomer had his support.

He did the same in private. Noticing that Robinson was often alone in the locker room, Branca made sure, despite the objections of some others, that Robinson knew he could use the showers at the same time as his teammates. *If the Dodgers could play with Robinson,* Branca thought, *they could certainly share the showers with him.*

Branca extended many other gestures big and small to make Robinson feel welcome. They ate meals together—and once, when Robinson lunged into the Dodgers' dugout in St. Louis in pursuit of a foul ball, almost falling hard on the concrete floor, Branca reached out and caught him to prevent a nasty injury.

"That will help show the world this is a united team," Robinson told him after that subtle act of support.

When Robinson died in 1972, Branca was a pallbearer at the funeral. By then, he was into his third decade of being identified by the public not as the kind and generous person he was, but as the goat of perhaps the most famous home run in baseball history.

As Branca wrestled with hurt and anger, he also stood as the embodiment of the human cost of cheating via high-tech sign stealing.

Whatever players like Clayton Kershaw and Aaron Judge later felt about the Astros, Branca suffered through all those feelings first.

After the Astros' scheme came apart in the fall of 2019, many of the team's fans and defenders pointed to Bobby Thomson's 1951 "Shot Heard 'Round the World" home run against Branca as evidence that sign stealing had been part of the fabric of the game forever. What was the big deal about sign stealing? they asked. Even Bobby Thomson did it.

That was true, but misleading. At least as far back as Pearce Chiles's 1900 Phillies, plenty of ballplayers and teams have designed and executed electronic-sign-stealing schemes. But—and this is key—every time a player or team is caught, outrage ensues. Careers and lives are affected and people are hurt.

It has always been a big deal.

In other words, high-tech sign stealing has always been a part of the game, like, say, fraud has always been a part of business—it's persistent, but persistently wrong. And the world knows it.

The Yankees, for example, were first busted for sign stealing so long ago that they weren't even called the Yankees yet, and they ended up embroiled in a very public scandal. In 1910, New York's American League team still went by the Highlanders, because their ballpark was at one of Manhattan's highest points, Hilltop Park, on Broadway between 165th and 168th Streets. One afternoon that season, during a home game against Detroit, New York batters seemed so comfortable against pitchers Bill Donovan and George Mullin that the Tigers began to suspect their opponents knew what pitches were coming.

Detroit trainer Harry Tuthill took it upon himself to investigate, marching out to the scoreboard in distant left-center field. When he got there, Tuthill heard a rustling sound, as if someone had just hurried out of the area. Then he saw a half-eaten cheese sandwich and an unconsumed bottle of beer. He also found a handle that was connected to a shutter on the scoreboard. It turned out that the shutter shaded part of a letter *O* on the scoreboard in order to indicate the pitch: When the center of the *O* was open, a fastball was on the way. When it was closed, the batter knew to expect a curve. When partially shaded, a slow ball was coming.

New York sportswriters ultimately outed the sandwich eater as Arthur Irwin, a Highlanders scout. Irwin had been a player, manager, and friend of skipper George Stallings. Stallings, in turn, had once been a teammate in Philly of Morgan Murphy, one half of Pearce Chiles's sign-stealing scheme.

Also on the Highlanders' scoreboard was an advertisement for Young's Hats, which featured a large, movable derby. When a fastball was coming, the hat remained still—but it always managed to swing to the right or left to indicate a curveball or changeup.

As with the Phillies a decade earlier, these revelations hit baseball hard. American League president Ban Johnson threatened to suspend Stallings if he was caught again, and the team soon dismissed him as manager. This scandal, like the one involving the 1900 Phillies, would linger in the common memory for years. It would not, however, be anywhere near as notorious as the game's most famous pre-Astros sign-stealing story, the one that clouded the final sixty-five years of Ralph Branca's life.

—

Born in Mount Vernon, New York, in 1926, Branca was the fifteenth of seventeen children of John Branca, a trolley car conductor, and his wife, Katherine. As the only member of his sizable family to grow to be more than six feet tall, Ralph felt he could provide financial support for the others by pursuing a baseball career.

"Why me?" he would often ask one of his brothers, feeling the pressure brought on by his talent. "Why did God give me this gift of being big and strong?"

For several years, the Dodgers reaped the benefits of those gifts. In 1947, Branca went 21-12. He was a National League All-Star in 1948, 1949, and 1950.

In 1951, manager Chuck Dressen entrusted Branca with the most important spot of the year, in the ninth inning of a playoff game against their bitter crosstown N.L. rivals, the New York Giants. The game was the culmination of one of the wildest pennant races in baseball history. On August 11, the Dodgers had led the second-place Giants by thirteen and a half games. Then, from August 12 to August 27, the Giants won sixteen straight games, cutting the Dodgers' lead to six. The Giants finished the regular season on another streak, winning their last seven games. The Dodgers lost six of their final ten, and the teams closed the regular season with identical records of 96-58.

The rules then called for a three-game playoff series to settle the pennant. The Giants and Dodgers split the first two games, which set the stage for a winner-take-all contest on October 3 at the Polo Grounds, the Giants' home stadium in upper Manhattan.

A crowd of 34,320 packed the ballpark, and millions more watched around the world. The game was the first to be nationally televised and was also broadcast on Armed Forces radio to soldiers in Korea.

Behind ace Don Newcombe, the Dodgers led 4–1 after eight innings. In the ninth, Newcombe began to tire, allowing three hits and one run. With two on, one out, and Thomson coming up, Dressen called for Branca.

Branca's first pitch, a fastball, caught the inside corner. Strike one. He followed with another fastball, this one up and in. He expected it to be a ball, setting Thomson up for the next pitch, which was to be a curveball.

Branca never got the chance to throw his curve. Thomson drove the 0-1 fastball deep into left field. Branca spun his head around and watched. "Sink, sink," he begged, but the ball did not listen. It continued to rise, sailing over the left-field wall for a three-run homer.

Radio announcer Russ Hodges screamed, "The Giants win the pennant! The Giants win the pennant!" over and over. Manhattan partied. Brooklyn mourned.

As the Dodgers players left the field, dejected, Jackie Robinson was the only one who thought to look out for his friend. He stood alone on the infield, watching to make sure Thomson touched every base during his home-run trot. When Thomson made it home and Robinson finally walked toward the clubhouse, he found Branca sitting on the steps, sobbing.

"Hang in there, Ralph," Robinson said. "If it wasn't for you we wouldn't have even been here."

Branca cried through a cold shower, then met his fiancée in the parking lot. She stood there with her cousin, who was a priest.

"Why me?" Branca said.

"Ralph," the priest said, "God chose you because he knew you'd be strong enough to bear this cross."

Branca was strong enough, but three years later the cross became much heavier. Now a member of the Detroit Tigers, he heard a disturbing story from his new teammate Ted Gray. Gray had had a friend on the Giants who told him about an elaborate sign-stealing scheme New York had used in 1951: The team had an electrician wire a buzzer system between their clubhouse—which was located in center field—and their bullpen.

A coach named Herman Franks sat at a window in the clubhouse and looked at the catcher with a high-powered telescope. He would then hit the buzzer once for a fastball, and twice for an off-speed pitch. The bullpen catcher would toss a ball in the air to tell the batter that a breaking ball was coming or hold it to indicate fastball.

Hearing this, Branca couldn't help but feel bitter—and he held on to that feeling for many years. At an old-timers' event in 1962, he refused a journalist's request to pose for a photo with Thomson.

"It's taken years to live down that hurt," he explained. "If you want a picture, take one of the guy with the binoculars who was stealing our signs that day."

That year, commissioner Ford Frick heard of the allegations and considered them serious. He said that if they could be proven, he would vacate the Giants' win. But no conclusive proof emerged, and the scheme faded from the public consciousness.

Unfortunately for Branca, memory of his failure remained vivid to him and many who entered his life. Fans heckled him for the rest of his career, often with his young daughters in the stands. Grocery store clerks mentioned the home run to his wife while scanning her items. He never stopped hearing about it.

"A guy commits murder and he gets pardoned after twenty years," Branca once lamented. "I didn't get pardoned."

Publicly, Branca carried the pain with grace and humility. He warmed to Thomson, and in old age traveled with him, making money from appearance fees while discussing the classic game.

In 2001, a journalist named Joshua Prager convinced several Giants to admit to the sign-stealing scheme. In a groundbreaking story published in *The Wall Street Journal,* Prager described the operation in detail. Franks denied everything, but Thomson admitted to using the system—though he went to his grave in 2010 denying that he had had Branca's signs in that famous at-bat.

Reached at his home by *New York Times* columnist Dave Anderson after the story broke, Branca said, "I've known it since 1954, but I never said anything. I didn't want to cry over spilled milk. I became friendly with Bobby and I didn't want to demean his home run. I didn't want to cheapen a legendary moment in baseball."

But in candid moments with family, Branca made his hurt and anger clear. He relied on the memory of the home run and his relationship with Thomson for extra income but felt he had been wronged.

In 2009, Franks, now ninety-five years old and weeks from death, summoned Prager to his home in Salt Lake City. Now he wanted to admit it. Franks sat in his den, hooked up to an oxygen tank and surrounded by his wife and son, and made a startling confession: After spying the signal, Franks would look through his telescope at the batter's eyes, in order to make sure they looked toward the bullpen to pick up the sign.

Franks spent much of the afternoon of October 3, 1951, hiding in the clubhouse bathroom in between stealing signs. He had Branca's final pitch and relayed it via one buzz to the bullpen: fastball. Through his spyglass, Franks then homed in on Thomson's eyes. Sure enough, Thomson glanced toward the bullpen. He had the sign.

Late in Branca's life, he discovered that his mother had been born Jewish. That meant that Branca, a lifelong devout Roman Catholic, was technically Jewish, too. The writer broke this bit of news to Branca.

"Maybe that's why God's mad at me—that I didn't practice my mother's religion," Branca said, still searching for a way to understand his heartache. "He made me throw that home-run pitch."

Branca died in 2016 at ninety years old. The story of Thomson's "Shot Heard 'Round the World" dominated his *New York Times* obituary. Sign stealing wasn't mentioned until the twenty-seventh paragraph.

Chapter 3

THE ADVENT OF TV AND
SCOUTING CAMERAS

O ne night in 1968, when Bobby Valentine was an eighteen-
year-old phenom playing for the Dodgers' affiliate in Ogden,
Utah, he took his manager, Tommy Lasorda, to dinner at a
steakhouse.

For most of the evening, the two talked baseball. But as they
were leaving Lasorda asked if Valentine had any general questions or
problems.

"There is one thing," the youngster said.

"What's that?" asked Lasorda.

"I know this sounds sort of silly," Valentine said, avoiding eye
contact. "But . . . at my age, I think I should have hair on my chest."

Lasorda told Valentine that if he ate more of the fat on his steaks,
it would help him grow chest hair.

A few weeks later, Valentine approached Lasorda in the locker
room.

"Hey, skip—you were right," he said, beaming. "Look at this—
there's hair growing on my chest."

It was true: Tiny hairs were poking through the skin on Valentine's otherwise-bare chest.

Lasorda would remember the moment for years. He walked away
thinking that if this kid could summon the willpower to grow hair on
his own chest, he would end up making an impact in the big leagues.

Valentine did make an impact, though not in the way he initially hoped. A serious leg injury in 1973 forever altered his career, and he failed to achieve what his abilities as a top recruit and prospect seemed to promise.

But he developed as a heady player, one of the guys who could use his eyes to pick up on pitch tipping and decode sign sequences. While standing on second base, he would often give pitches or location to his friend and teammate Bill Buckner, who batted behind him in the order.

Because of this, people around the game began to speak of Valentine as a future manager. His playing career fizzled before he turned thirty, and he was soon coaching for the Mets. In 1985—at the nearly unheard-of age of thirty-five—he was named manager of the Texas Rangers.

This was only the latest entry on an already varied résumé. As a youth, Valentine had been a championship ballroom dancer. After he'd stopped playing and before he began managing, he opened a restaurant in his Connecticut hometown—and one day, when he was out of bread but well stocked with tortillas, he literally invented the wrap sandwich.

Later on, it was also Valentine who innovated the use of team-owned cameras to steal signs.

Though not nearly as aggressive as the Astros' later scheme—Valentine did not use the information from the cameras during those same games, and he was not looking for the opponents' pitches—his use of this technology served as a point on the continuum toward what Houston did with its internal video feeds in 2017.

The many stories of sign stealing during baseball's early days, from Pearce Chiles and the 1900 Phillies to Bobby Thomson and the 1951 Giants, revolve around telescopes, spyglasses, and other relatively low-tech pieces of equipment.

Then, in the middle of the twentieth century, the dark arts took a leap forward with the advent of baseball on TV. Suddenly teams had a far more convenient way to see the opposing catcher's signs.

The possibilities for this were immediately clear. In the leadup to the 1959 All-Star Game, NBC hyped a new eighty-inch camera lens in center field. As the Associated Press put it, the lens would "put the catcher practically into the living room."

The following week, the network used the camera for a nationally televised Yankees–Red Sox regular-season game.

In the broadcast booth, Mel Allen and Phil Rizzuto agreed that the new technology was eye-opening, and they used the shot to explain how one finger meant fastball, two fingers curveball, and so on. Throughout the game, they told viewers what pitch was coming, and never guessed wrong.

Commissioner Frick sensed how these tools could fall into the wrong hands. Saying that the new lens could "cause all kinds of trouble," he banned it from all future broadcasts.

Frick was right about the potential for trouble, though he seemed to have overestimated his ability to contain it. TV technology would only get better as the years and decades passed and monitors became more easily available. Naturally, teams saw an opportunity to get an advantage.

Of the handful of clubs accused of using TV to cheat in the twentieth century, the White Sox of the 1980s—and, some opponents insisted, the 1990s—were perhaps the most notorious.

During games at Comiskey Park on Chicago's South Side, a team employee would sit in the manager's office and pick up the catcher's signs from the broadcast. He would then use a toggle switch to activate a twenty-five-watt refrigerator bulb on the scoreboard, which told batters what pitch to expect.

Across town, the 1984 Cubs would assign a player to stand in the clubhouse and watch the tight shot from center field to decode sign sequences and relay them to the dugout verbally or in person.

These relatively primitive forays stretched deep into the 1990s and beyond. Once, the general manager of another club told Blue Jays manager Cito Gaston that he believed Toronto was using cameras to steal signs and warned Gaston not to try it against his team.

Gaston swore that his guys were not cheating, but simply skilled at getting pitches the legal way.

In 1996 the Baltimore Orioles heard about red lights blinking on cameras in the outfield at Jacobs Field, the Cleveland Indians' home ballpark.

Naturally, this struck the Orioles as suspicious, and they demanded that those cameras be covered before their playoff series in Cleveland. To this day, officials from that Indians team deny any tomfoolery, but Orioles alumni remain convinced.

Stealing signs via TV does have its limitations. A team cannot control when the broadcast will show the tight shot from center field, which is far more useful in obtaining the catcher's signs, or the wide shot, which is a more panoramic view. Network employees make those decisions, leaving teams reliant on the whims of a director. If he or she decides to shoot the catcher, great. If not, there is no way to get the sign from TV.

Scouting cameras, on the other hand, are wholly owned and operated by the ball club.

In 1995, between jobs in Texas and New York, Bobby Valentine spent a year managing in Japan.

There, he was startled to see scouts in the stands using cameras to film games. No one was doing this in the United States, but it struck Valentine as an effective way to gather information on your opponent.

He filed that away and returned to the Mets, first as a minor league manager and then as skipper of the big club in 1997.

During those years, teams began to experiment with using scouting cameras for internal evaluations. Unlike TV cameras, these could be used to home in on specific players to generate footage helpful to them. Pitchers could look at the mechanics of their windup, and hitters could analyze their at-bats.

In 1997, Mets general manager Steve Phillips purchased the team's first scouting cameras and had them installed in three locations at Shea Stadium: Next to the first- and third-base dugouts and on the screen behind home plate.

This was legal, but it didn't take long for Valentine, inspired by his time in Japan, to push the use of these cameras into new territory.

When he learned that the Mets' cameras could be moved with a joystick by a person in the clubhouse, he saw a clear way to adapt what he'd seen in Japan to an MLB setting.

When a base coach runs through a sequence of signs, calling for anything from a stolen base to a hit-and-run to a sacrifice bunt, he touches a sequence of body parts.

To steal signs from him, opponents historically looked for where the signs originated. Sometimes they came from the manager—but the manager's signs could also be decoys, with the real signs coming from the bench coach. The job was to figure out the true source of the signs in the dugout.

By using the cameras—primarily the one on the first-base side—Valentine conceived of a way to avoid looking at multiple coaches by decoding the third-base coach's signs, which went straight to the batter. He set to work devising what he called an algorithm to steal signs from base coaches.

In the clubhouse, he made a chart of the human body, and assigned a number to each part: say, 3 for the leg, 7 for the hat, 5 for the nose, and so on.

After games, Valentine stayed at the ballpark until four o'clock in the morning, watching the sign sequences and recording the numbers. If a coach went nose-hat-nose—5-7-5—before a stolen base, then Valentine had cracked that sign.

When the teams played next, he would know when a stolen base was coming, and could call for a pitchout.

In August 1997, Phillips was watching a game at Shea in his box with Philadelphia Phillies GM Ed Wade.

"Hey, come here for a sec," Wade said, gesturing to Phillips. "Do you know why the camera behind the plate, after each pitch, seems to go down the baseline and then comes back again? Do you think it's shooting our third-base coach?"

"I don't know," Phillips said. "Let me find out."

He called the dugout phone and asked Valentine if he was guilty of what Wade had accused him of. The manager said that he was.

"Well, don't do that ever again," Phillips said. "That's illegal."

"I didn't know, I didn't know," Valentine said, and agreed to stop.

By the time the Phillies noticed his system, Valentine had begun to lose enthusiasm for it anyway. It was too time-consuming to be worth the minimal payoff; it might take until the end of a three-game series to figure out the signs. And when the Mets saw the same team again later in the season, their sequences could be different.

For scouting cameras to be truly effective in sign stealing, they had to be able to provide feedback in real time, and not keep the manager in the clubhouse until the wee hours studying numbers on a chart of the human body.

Valentine assured Springer he would stop, and Phillips apologized to Wade. Both teams notified the commissioner's office, but the league took no action against the Mets.

"It wasn't a big deal," MLB senior vice president Katy Feeney told *The New York Times* in 1997, when the paper got wind of the investigation. Not a big deal this time, anyway. The league had no idea what was to come in the decades ahead.

Chapter 4

THE PATH TO BELTRÁN

Baseball is a game of oral traditions passed down from one generation to the next—and as such, one can draw a direct line between a locker room in Toronto in late September 1993 and the baseball scandal that shocked America twenty-six years later.

The Blue Jays were wrapping up a dominant regular season and preparing for October, where they would defend their 1992 World Series championship. The team summoned two top prospects from the minor leagues, hoping to give them a taste of their winning culture.

The prospects were friends, connecting over a shared curiosity about the world that stuck out among the other jocks in the Jays' farm system.

In their first hitters' meeting with the big club, manager Cito Gaston surprised them with a mandate: Every player on the team was required to pick signs and decode pitches while on second base, and then relay them to the batter.

Those rookies, Carlos Delgado and Shawn Green, would go on to become two of the most productive sluggers of the next decade-plus, combining for 801 home runs in the major leagues. Both players were wired to respond to an intellectual challenge. They were known in the clubhouse as guys who loved baseball but had a wider range of outside interests than most players.

While wrapping up his time as a baseball star at Tustin High School in Southern California, Green came across a book that altered the course of his life, *Zen and the Art of Motorcycle Maintenance* by Robert Pirsig.

"The book's Eastern perspective struck a resonant chord with me," Green would later write. "Particularly as I'd come to it wide open to exploring not only the world around me, but also the world within."

After devouring Pirsig's bestseller, Green sought out other books based on Eastern philosophy, such as *Way of the Peaceful Warrior, Zen in the Art of Archery,* and *Siddhartha.* He would later contribute his own volume to that canon, the 2011 book *The Way of Baseball.*

The Blue Jays selected Green out of high school in the first round of the 1992 draft, and he continued his self-education in philosophy, adding yoga and meditation to his routine. He already knew that the game as he experienced it then did not offer quite enough intellectual stimulation to keep him engaged.

Superficially, Delgado could not have been more different from Green, a skinny Southern California kid with a chill personality and hippie/surfer vibe. Delgado, a native of Puerto Rico, was intense, even surly at times. But like Green, his interests carried him beyond the baseball field.

Years later, Delgado would serve as baseball's version of Colin Kaepernick, more than a decade before the NFL quarterback's iconic national-anthem protests.

Objecting to the Iraq War and the U.S. government's treatment of Puerto Rico, he refused for several years to join his team on the field during the renditions of "God Bless America" that became a common element of the seventh-inning stretch after the terrorist attacks on September 11, 2001.

That was all ahead of him. In 1993, Delgado and Green were just two young buddies sitting in a hitters' meeting and wondering how in the world they were going to get the signs and pitches that their manager required.

The decoding of tipping in baseball has long been one of the hidden arts that operates under the game's deceptively placid surface.

Picking up on pitch tipping and stealing signs are separate activities, but closely related. The latter is the act of looking at a catcher's hand and attempting to decipher the number of fingers he is extending, and what they mean. If you can do that, you've stolen the sign, and know what pitch is coming.

The rule is simple: When a sign is stolen with the naked eye—say, by a runner at second base peering in at the catcher—it is legal. When done with the assistance of technology, whether a camera or binoculars, it is cheating.

Tipping is when a pitcher moves his body in a way that reveals his intention to throw a particular pitch. Those "tells" can be imperceptible to the untrained eye.

Expanding or flaring out the glove before a changeup is common. Babe Ruth, back when he was pitching for the Red Sox, used to curl his tongue whenever he was throwing a curveball. Those are tips.

Tipping was made possible by a rule change in the National League in 1883 that lifted a prior ban on overhand pitching.

This major alteration created a path toward pitching mechanics as we know them today. And once pitchers could choose from a variety of pitches—there was the fastball, the changeup, the curve, and the "dinky curve," which resembled the modern-day slider—they could also inadvertently tip which one they were about to throw.

By the early twentieth century, examples of pitch tipping were well documented. Ty Cobb took pride in knowing when Walter Johnson was about to throw the occasional curveball and when Cy Young was going to throw to first for a pickoff attempt.

Legendary manager Connie Mack's 1911 Philadelphia Athletics developed a reputation as masters of picking up on tips and tendencies, led by pitcher Chief Bender. Cy Morgan, another pitcher on that team, described tipping in a way that rings true more than a hundred years later:

"There are lots of little things almost unnoticeable about the motions different pitchers use in their delivery, and most of these motions have a meaning. We sit there in a row on the bench and study the pitcher, and if we detect any difference in his motion we watch to see what kind of a ball it means. Bender gets up on the coaching lines for a while, and if there is anything in it back he comes and tells us what kind of a ball that motion means. . . .

"Before I joined the Athletics they used to hit me. I did not know why. When I joined them [first baseman] Harry Davis came to me and told me. He said some other team might discover the little thing they had figured out, and then I changed my delivery so as to cut it out. The Athletics had not been able to hit me because they had my catcher's signs, but because they had my spitball figured out. That is all there is to any signal-tipping bureau, as they call it."

Through many more decades, hitters continued to look for pitch tipping, and every generation featured a handful of hitters known as particularly smart about it, and pitchers sloppy about tipping.

In the 1960s, the Dodgers' Maury Wills developed a system for decoding every pitcher's tell for when he was throwing the ball to home rather than to first base for a pickoff attempt. This helped Wills lead the league in stolen bases for six consecutive seasons, from 1960 to 1965.

In 1967, a player came into the league who was far less talented than Wills, but perhaps just as savvy.

Cito Gaston ultimately played eleven seasons for the Atlanta Braves, San Diego Padres, and Pittsburgh Pirates. His lifetime batting average was an unremarkable .256, but he developed a reputation as being one of the best at helping teammates pick up on pitch tipping.

Later, as a coach for the Blue Jays in the 1980s, Gaston continued to refine and share those skills, and he made them a priority upon becoming manager in 1989.

A trade the following year delivered to Gaston a player who would become known as his own generation's master of decoding pitchers, future Hall of Fame second baseman Roberto Alomar.

On October 11, 1992, the Blue Jays trailed the Oakland A's 6–1 at the end of seven innings in Game Four of the American League Championship Series.

The stakes for Toronto could not have been higher. Oakland had been an American League powerhouse for years, winning the pennant each season from 1988 to 1990, and the World Series in 1989. The Blue Jays, an expansion team created just fifteen years earlier, had never appeared in a Fall Classic.

Toronto was ahead in this series two games to one, but their lead—and their momentum—was at risk.

In the top of the eighth, the first three Toronto batters reached base. That sent A's manager Tony La Russa jogging out of the dugout to raise his right arm in the air and call for his closer, the great Dennis Eckersley.

Eckersley had long established himself as the most feared reliever of his time. He intimidated opponents not only with a dominant repertoire of pitches, but with a cocky, gunslinger persona.

That attitude was evident after Eckersley entered and allowed base hits to John Olerud and Candy Maldonado, cutting the Jays' deficit to 6–4. He followed by striking out Ed Sprague to end the inning, staring into the Toronto dugout and firing a fake pistol in the players' direction.

Incensed, the Jays started screaming and banging on the dugout railing. But behind the anger of the moment, they had a secret weapon calmly preparing for his shot at Eckersley: Roberto Alomar. He knew that when Eckersley slowed his delivery ever so slightly, he was preparing to throw a breaking ball.

Few on the Toronto bench were surprised when, in the ninth, Alomar swung at a high fastball like he knew it was coming and drove it for the biggest home run the franchise had yet seen. Alomar's blast tied the game; the Blue Jays went on to win it and capture the next two world championships.

Alomar's skill in picking up pitcher tendencies followed him for many more years.

On September 28, 1996, he was playing for the Orioles against the Blue Jays. With the game tied 2–2 in the top of the tenth inning, Toronto brought in left-handed reliever Paul Spoljaric.

As Spoljaric warmed up, Alomar walked from the on-deck circle back to the dugout, grabbed a massive thirty-six-ounce bat, and said, "Boys, I got this."

He stepped into the box and homered off a fastball he knew was coming.

When Shawn Green and Carlos Delgado arrived in Toronto in 1993, they could not have had better mentor in learning how to pick up on tipping. Alomar, along with another veteran, Joe Carter, were masters at carrying out Cito Gaston's mandate.

It didn't click immediately. When Alomar first took Delgado aside to point out what he saw in an opposing pitcher, Delgado shook his head and thought that his teammate might as well be speaking Chinese. Within a few months, he started to see what his teacher saw.

Green, who was still cultivating his spirituality by reading and practicing meditation, initially found that when he knew what pitch was coming, it would clutter his mind. If a pitcher tipped a fastball, Green would get overanxious and swing at a bad one.

For a few seasons, as he worked to establish himself as an everyday player in the big leagues, Green tried not to pick up on the pitches.

Then one day, he was facing a lefty who had always given him trouble. The guy had a good changeup, a pitch that Green often struggled with.

Delgado approached Green on the bench and told him to watch the pitcher's glove. When he was throwing a changeup, it flared out and became slightly bigger.

From there, Green saw how much easier it was to hit when he knew what was coming. He began to work on the skill in a way that was compatible with his meditation practice. Rather than isolating particular moments in a pitcher's delivery, he would imagine the entire windup and swing as a movie and try to lock in to its flow.

If he saw a bigger glove and knew a changeup was coming, for example, he would automatically look for a pitch up in the strike zone because a changeup typically starts high and then drops. Remaining in the flow of the film in his mind, he would drop his hands and wait back a little longer than usual.

This allowed him to practice the art of decoding without shifting into the analytical side of his brain. It also helped him get outside himself and his own mind by focusing on another person—the pitcher—rather than his own hitting mechanics. These were the techniques he would later pass on to others.

While still learning, Green had another breakthrough with Kansas City right-hander Kevin Appier, a pitcher who had always given him trouble.

Appier threw a fastball at ninety to ninety-two miles per hour that would run either down and in or belt-high and inside. He also threw a slider that would break straight down. If you didn't know which to expect, it was easy to be fooled, because both pitches started from the same spot before breaking differently.

Then something clicked: Appier's tip came very late in his delivery. In the middle of his windup, when he was kicking his leg and his glove was in the air, he would pop his glove open to indicate a slider. Now Green could hit Appier just fine.

Working with Delgado, Green soon felt that he had something on roughly half of the pitchers in the league, and that tipping could raise his batting average at least a hundred points against a given pitcher.

His list included several future Hall of Famers. Before throwing the nastiest slider in the game, Randy Johnson would flare his glove. Green batted .303 off Johnson, with a whopping .576 slugging percentage. Curt Schilling's delivery started the same for every pitch, but when his hands went over his head, his fingers rounded on the forkball and remained flat on the changeup. Green batted .333 against Schilling and slugged .556. In the middle of John Smoltz's windup, the glove would go horizontal on a forkball and diagonal on a fastball. Green batted an incredible .593 in his career against Smoltz, slugging .815.

As for the craftiest and most admired ace of his time, Greg Maddux? When the glove went over his head, Green could see an inch of the palm of Maddux's throwing hand emerging from the heel of his glove. That meant a fastball or cutter. Green batted .316 against Maddux, and slugged .579.

Green became obsessed. He would position himself at the front of the dugout, so he could watch the pitcher as closely as possible. When he was on deck, he would stand as close to the plate as the umpire would let him.

He and Delgado used the Jays' rudimentary video system—the team had just two VHS recorders in the clubhouse, a far cry from what the Astros would use a quarter-century later—to study film of pitchers before and after games. They decided to each buy a small notebook that they would keep in the dugout and use to jot down information on the pitcher from each at-bat.

After about two years, Green switched to a higher-tech method, building a database on a program called FileMaker Pro and entering information on each pitcher. Before each series, he would print out what he had on the opposing team and hand it to his hitting coach.

The Jays also engaged in legal sign stealing. The process went like this for Green: When batting ahead of Delgado, he would often try to steal second base.

This wasn't typically advisable with a power hitter batting, because it opened up first base for the pitcher to walk the batter rather than risk a home run. But the friends were so into the challenge of sign stealing that they deemed it worth the risk.

Once at second, Green would peer in. A lot of catchers, trying to conceal the signs, would fall into patterns more predictable than they realized. Sometimes the first sign after the number two was the true sign. On other occasions, it was the first sign after the last pitch.

Green would figure this out, then signal to Delgado that he had the pitch. He did this by touching his helmet, placing his hands on his hips, or looking into the outfield. Finally he would give the actual sign with his first step—often to his right if a fastball was coming, to his left for an off-speed pitch.

The casual viewer could be forgiven for thinking that baseball contained extended lulls in its action, that nothing happened for minutes at a time. But with players like Green and Delgado, there was always complex and covert action just under the surface.

After the 1999 season, Green signed with the Los Angeles Dodgers. He and Delgado kept in touch, and missed their collaboration. Both remained feared sluggers well into their thirties.

In 2006, Green, after a stint in Arizona with the Diamondbacks, was traded to the Mets. The move reunited him with Delgado, who had since gone from Toronto to Miami to New York.

It also introduced him to a young star so naturally talented that he did not show a significant interest in the hidden arts that Green and Delgado offered to teach—at least not yet.

That player's name was Carlos Beltrán.

Chapter 5

THE EDUCATION OF A. J. HINCH

When Andrew Jay Hinch, manager of the Houston Astros, first heard the dull echo of a baseball bat crashing into a plastic trash can in the tunnel behind him in 2017, he did nothing.

All through the season, as the banging continued, Hinch would mutter about it, shake his head, tell friends he was angry—but still, he took no decisive action to stop his players from cheating.

How, Hinch's many friends in the game later wondered, did a principled person end up complicit in an historic scandal? It occurred to some of them that the seeds of his reluctance may well have been planted in another dugout tunnel eight years earlier, on May 15, 2009.

On that date Hinch turned thirty-five years old and found himself at the center of a scorching controversy. Arizona Diamondbacks general manager Josh Byrnes had fired his manager early in the season and selected Hinch to succeed him. Hinch had never managed or coached at any level.

Players were not ready to accept a leader so inexperienced, and several more seasoned coaches grumbled that they should have gotten the job. The bad vibes quickly boiled over.

On May 15, the Diamondbacks trailed the Atlanta Braves 3–2 in the seventh inning. Starting pitcher Doug Davis, one of the veteran players who disapproved of Hinch, grabbed his bat and prepared to walk to the on-deck circle.

"You're up, no matter what," Hinch said.

Minutes later, Hinch motioned for Davis to return from the on-deck circle in favor of a pinch hitter. Davis stormed back into the dugout and confronted the manager. He had thrown only eighty pitches and wanted to continue.

The two exchanged words in full view of cameras before disappearing into the tunnel to hash it out. It was a clear challenge to Hinch's status as leader of the team, a show of disrespect for players and fans to see.

The dispute itself stemmed from a simple misunderstanding. When Hinch said "You're up, no matter what," he had meant, "You're going up there on deck, no matter what."

Davis had understood the comment as, "You're batting, no matter what."

But Davis's anger wasn't really about semantics, or even pinch-hitting. He and many other Arizona veterans simply could not accept Hinch as their manager.

The televised mutiny, and the drama that occurred behind closed doors before and after it, left Hinch wounded and conflict-averse, just as he was working to develop as a leader.

The effects of that trauma would percolate underneath Hinch's confident surface for many years and follow him all the way to Houston. They would affect the development of the leadership skills that he began to hone as a teenager on the prestigious fields of Stanford University.

Hinch's time at Stanford seemed at first like it would be charmed, but he surmounted steep challenges from the very beginning. During a practice in Hinch's freshman year, hitting coach Dave Esquer approached him on the field.

"Hey, Nine wants to see you," Esquer said, referring to veteran head coach Mark Marquess, who wore that number on the back of his uniform.

Mindful of Marquess's rule prohibiting players from walking while between the foul lines, Hinch sprinted toward the dugout. Marquess walked about fifty feet to meet him on the grass. Appearing shaken, the coach put his arm around Hinch.

Marquess led Hinch to his office. When they were both sitting, he finally spoke.

"I don't really know how to say this to you," Marquess said. "I've never had to say this to a player. But you just lost your father."

Dennis Hinch had died from a heart attack at age thirty-nine. His son's All-American career had now been disrupted by tragedy, leaving young A.J. in need of a mentor.

Prior to this shock, Hinch's was an upbringing of talent and privilege. He was the kid whose dad was his best friend—who built a batting cage for him in the yard, and who brought him along on weekend trips to his softball tournaments. He was the kid whose mom drove him countless hours and miles to games and practices.

As one of the country's top high school catchers, Hinch was recruited by top colleges, and he won the 1992 Gatorade National Player of the Year Award for high school athletes, beating out a shortstop from Michigan named Derek Jeter. The Chicago White Sox drafted him in the second round out of high school, but he decided to forgo that opportunity to play college ball. When your athletic life had been a series of one break after another, it was easy to assume that another pro opportunity would come.

Once Hinch arrived at Stanford, he pledged a fraternity, batted second and third in a stacked lineup, and made friends for life on the baseball team. He was as famous as a freshman baseball player could be, having appeared on the cover of *Baseball America* magazine before even arriving as the top recruit at a top program.

Now he found himself traveling home for his dad's funeral, adjusting to a new reality that was no longer as stable as the one he'd always known.

While Hinch was gone, his roommate and best friend, right fielder Brodie Van Wagenen, played a Friday-night game wearing every piece of Hinch's uniform but the jersey. Van Wagenen hit the game-winning home run.

When Hinch returned to school, Van Wagenen presented him with a Pac-10 ball with a note on it that said the homer had been for him. The two had already become extremely close in the accelerated way that college freshmen bond, and they would forever remember not only the intensity of that time, but how it changed the course of Hinch's life and determined the type of leader he would become.

Hinch's relationship with Marquess grew as a result of the tragedy. The two had already shared a bond derived from Hinch's status as a top player, but now Marquess was the most prominent older male in Hinch's life.

Soon after Dennis Hinch's death, A.J.'s mother moved to the Bay Area to be closer to him. For a college kid this brought the additional task of needing to be strong and present enough to help a grieving widow. Most players called their parents once or twice a week; Hinch's mother was suddenly at every game. It was a lot, and Marquess knew to check in.

"Hey, you okay?" he'd ask. "How are you handling everything?"

Marquess was already a legendary coach, having been in his position since 1976. He would ultimately last in the job for forty-one years and became the fourth-winningest head coach in Division I baseball history.

Marquess was tough but caring. Hinch would later describe himself to friends as "just enough of a prick to be a manager," and Marquess was no different: gruff and able to get on a player when necessary, but also capable of flattering with empathic individual attention, as he did when delivering the news of Dennis Hinch's death.

Hinch was deeply influenced by Marquess's energy and intensity. Though decades older than his players, the coach would not allow himself to be outworked or outhustled. He never missed a day, sprinted all over the field, and ran drills like he'd just finished two pots of coffee.

But Marquess could easily shift into other personas. In addition to the hard-ass coach, he could also be the recruiter and face of the program—charming, engaging, and easy. And still another version of Marquess would look a player in the eye and offer life advice that had nothing to do with baseball. "How are we gonna get you to graduation in three years?" he would say.

The young Hinch filed all of this away for future use—the energy, the public-facing charm, the ability to forge personal connections with players.

Not all Stanford players enjoyed the access to Marquess that Hinch had. But those who did looked back on their time there and believed it had made them better people. Later on, Hinch wanted his players to feel the same way about teams that he managed.

As Hinch moved through Stanford, he remained an MLB prospect and earned Pac-10 player-of-the-year honors in 1995, his junior season. But in a trend that foreshadowed his pro career, his stock was falling, if almost imperceptibly.

When you're on the very top as a teenager, as Hinch had been when beating out Jeter for the Gatorade award, it doesn't take much of a comedown to feel that you've disappointed.

Hinch played well but his draft position fell after his junior year, when he was selected by Minnesota in the third round—one round below the one he'd been picked for in high school. Rather than turning pro, he played in the 1996 Olympics and returned to school.

Teammates noticed that the draft seemed to register a small dent in Hinch's self-assurance. But despite all the inner turmoil that his college years brought, he remained outwardly confident. This fit with the environment he was in. Stanford ballplayers were always known around baseball as either confident or arrogant, depending on who was judging.

Some of this was the anti-intellectual strain in the game—if a minor league teammate spotted a Stanford alum reading a book on the team bus, he was likely to mock it. But baked into the way Stanford athletes viewed themselves was also a whiff of superiority. It came in part from the school's rigorous recruiting process, which encouraged candidates to feel that they were joining an exclusive club.

Stanford alums who made it to the big leagues even seemed to share a common walk: shoulders back, chin thrust in the air, elbows pointed out. The Stanford strut.

Hinch still had it in Houston a quarter-century later, though friends saw hints of insecurity underneath. As far as most people knew, he fit in with a culture of alums that ended up successful and influential in all aspects of the big leagues, from executive suites to agencies to the field.

Stanford's Rubén Amaro Jr., a utility player who later became GM of the Phillies, was known within his own clubhouse in the 1990s as "The Total Package"—a name sometimes intended as a compliment, other times an amused assessment of how Amaro felt about his own skills.

Hinch's friend Van Wagenen ascended to the highest ranks in the cutthroat world of baseball agents before talking his way into a GM job with the Mets in 2018. Whether working alongside Jay-Z during the hip-hop mogul's brief agent phase to negotiate a $240 million deal with the Seattle Mariners for second baseman Robinson Canó, or convincing Mets ownership he could handle their top job, Van Wagenen dipped into endless reserves of charm and self-assurance to propel himself forward in the world.

One Stanford product whom Van Wagenen represented as an agent and later brought to the Mets, infielder Jed Lowrie, married a

State Department diplomat and willed himself to become an All-Star despite his diminutive stature.

There was no denying that Stanford guys were smooth, cerebral, and outwardly confident. But that did not prevent Hinch from wrestling with insecurities and the pressure to maintain the star status that had led the school to recruit him in the first place.

Hinch did not disappoint. He graduated with a .351 batting average, seventh highest in the history of Stanford's program. He was sixth in runs scored with 219, fourth in hits with 305, sixth in doubles with 58, fifth in triples with 15, and seventh in runs batted in with 191. He also completed a bachelor's degree in psychology. Later, the NCAA named Hinch the top catcher in Stanford history.

The Oakland Athletics selected him in the third round of the 1996 draft. After rising through Oakland's minor league system, Hinch made his major league debut in 1998. That alone was an accomplishment that only a tiny fraction of ballplayers are able to achieve. But playing at the highest level, he never approached numbers as robust as those he'd produced in college.

In nine seasons in the A's, Royals, Tigers, and Phillies systems, Hinch hit a respectable .286 in the minor leagues, with 54 home runs; and .219 in the big leagues, with 32 home runs. It's a success to hold on that long, but Hinch was far from a star.

In 2004, at age thirty, he played 4 games for the Phillies, and 77 for the team's Triple-A affiliate in Scranton/Wilkes-Barre, Pennsylvania. The next year he played 85 games for Scranton and did not sniff the big leagues.

That fall, Hinch faced a pivotal decision. The Phillies were willing to have him back as their Triple-A catcher, but he was also mulling a future as a front-office executive. In fact, he'd been smart enough to plant those seeds while still playing, traveling to industry meetings in 2003 to network and make his intentions known.

As it happened, Hinch's longtime agent, Jeff Moorad, became

CEO of the Arizona Diamondbacks in 2005. He hired Josh Byrnes, a bright young assistant GM in Boston who had been part of the Red Sox brain trust the year before, when that team broke an eighty-six-year championship drought.

In the fall of 2005, as Byrnes was settling into Arizona and assembling a staff, he interviewed Hinch. The two had met years before but did not know each other well. Sitting down now and seeking a deeper understanding, Byrnes found himself immediately impressed by Hinch's openness.

"Should I keep playing, or should I go on to the next phase?" Hinch mused aloud, displaying a capacity for self-analysis beyond what Byrnes was used to hearing from ballplayers.

Byrnes felt an instant connection. He didn't know why yet, but felt on a gut level that he was speaking to a person with integrity. He also sensed that, while Hinch already possessed a deep knowledge of the game, he was eager to listen to others and learn more. His confidence did not block his curiosity.

Byrnes offered Hinch a job as Arizona's director of minor league operations, and Hinch accepted. Just like that, his playing career was over.

Almost immediately, Hinch realized how challenging, yet intellectually stimulating, this new path would be. At the winter meetings in 2005, Byrnes and his top lieutenants stood at the front of a hotel suite while more than a dozen staffers sat at a group of tables.

The group brainstormed potential deals, scribbling ideas on a whiteboard. Before long, they had whipped themselves into a controlled frenzy and written the framework of eight or ten possible trades.

Sitting in his chair, silent and more than a little overwhelmed, Hinch saw that front-office work was going to be more complex than he'd expected. How did these guys know so much about the players in every organization?

Many others in the meeting believed that, though Hinch was green, he would one day be the boss in a room like this. He was sharp, curious, and looked as much at home in his new uniform—khakis and a polo shirt—as he had in baseball pants and a chest protector.

Over the next few years, it became clear to those who worked with him that he was destined to become a GM.

One May night in 2009, Byrnes was in South Carolina preparing for the upcoming draft by scouting two top prospects facing off against each other, outfielder Jackie Bradley Jr. and pitcher Mike Minor.

Afterward, Byrnes drove down to Jacksonville, Florida, where the Diamondbacks' Double-A affiliate was set to play the next night. He asked Hinch to meet him there.

This was a standard request. Hinch had by then been promoted to director of player development and was working closely with Byrnes on plans for all prospects in the organization. They spoke often, at ballparks and on the phone.

But unbeknownst to Hinch, Byrnes had different intentions for this meeting. He wanted Hinch to sit with a young outfielder named Gerardo Parra and speak to him as a manager would. Byrnes was eager to see if that felt as natural as he suspected it might.

Now in his fifth year on the job, Byrnes had experienced some success—the team won ninety games in 2007—and some challenges, including two seasons with losing records and a regression to eighty-two wins in 2008.

He was also, in a way that proved several years ahead of its time, beginning to rethink the very role of the big-league manager.

There is in baseball a longstanding stereotype of the manager as the team's general, wielding absolute power over his players and game strategy. For many years, this was an accurate view of the job.

From the Giants' John McGraw at the turn of the twentieth century to Baltimore's Earl Weaver and the Yankees' Billy Martin seven or eight decades later, managers ruled their teams, often holding more power than their ostensible bosses in the front office.

Early indications of a shift occurred in Oakland in the 1980s, when Sandy Alderson was GM of the Athletics. A former marine and local attorney with no prior experience in the game, he took the job at a time when nearly all his counterparts were ex-players, managers, or scouts.

In order to compensate for his lack of field experience, Alderson became the Johnny Appleseed of advanced statistics in baseball, starting what was later popularized as the *Moneyball* movement, named by the popular book and movie.

That approach required significantly more input from a front office. Now game strategy relied on the insight of data and analysts, not merely the hunches of an all-powerful manager.

When Alderson began working for the team as general counsel in 1981, the manager was Billy Martin, most famous for five separate tenures as skipper of the Yankees. Martin was as old-school as they came, a brawler always falling in and out with Yankees owner George Steinbrenner.

In between stints with the Yankees, Martin had brought his high-octane brand of "Billy Ball," which emphasized speed and defense, to Oakland. Martin was also technically the general manager, a dual title that showed just how much power a field manager once held. He had no use for Alderson and his ideas and would try to shout him off the field and out of the clubhouse. He wanted to run his own game and keep the geeks far from his office.

Martin was not alone, and his habits hung around in the game for decades. More than thirty years after Martin left Oakland, most managers still expected to retain their traditional level of power. Change happens slowly in baseball.

There were some exceptions. Organizations like the A's, the Red

Sox, and the Indians gradually came to pursue a modern approach in which front offices were more influential, and managing was collaborative rather than autocratic.

During Boston's championship year in 2004, Byrnes was part of a staff that delivered advanced information to manager Terry Francona and encountered minimal resistance. Francona just wanted tools that would help him win ballgames and was rarely defensive about who offered them.

In Arizona, Byrnes found a different dynamic. For several years, he bumped up against his skipper, Bob Melvin. Melvin was more progressive than some in the game, and would later enjoy a successful run as manager of the *Moneyball* A's.

But as Byrnes saw it, Melvin still expected the traditional division of power. The GM was looking for collaboration, and too often found struggle.

In Boston, Francona had been open to creative bullpen roles, which could be more effective than the traditionally rigid assignments of particular relievers to the sixth, seventh, eighth, and ninth innings.

When Byrnes told Melvin and his pitching coach, Bryan Price, that he wanted to follow that model in Arizona, the pair objected.

"We can't do that," they scoffed. "Players want to know their roles."

"What if their role is to be ready for anything?" Byrnes responded, incredulous.

In December 2007, he made an outside-the-box trade, sending a successful closer, José Valverde, to Houston for three players, including infielder-outfielder Chris Burke. The idea was that saves, the stat used to evaluate closers, were overvalued, and the defensive versatility that Burke offered was undervalued.

Byrnes planned to use Burke at many positions, including shortstop, but encountered a strong headwind from Melvin.

"Well," the manager told his boss, "Burke has never played shortstop."

And that was that. Burke got two games at short that year. Why, Byrnes wondered, was it so crazy to try something new? Especially if it was something that could work?

Interactions like these left a term rolling around in Byrnes's mind, one used often in the business world: *siloed.*

It felt like GMs and their staffs operated in one silo, while managers and their coaches occupied another. Instead of sharing information in an open exchange of ideas, these silos viewed each other with suspicion and hostility.

From the managers' side, these attitudes could be understandable. Afraid of being automated out of existence and feeling that their age-old skills were being devalued, many skippers retreated into a defensive position. Not every new-school executive was sensitive to this.

At home, describing the Diamondbacks to his wife, Byrnes recalled the broken dynamics that the couple had seen in the delivery room during their child's birth. The nurse did not seem to be talking to the anesthesiologist, the anesthesiologist didn't seem to be talking to the obstetrician, and so on. Everyone just remained in his or her separate silo. This was how a baseball team worked.

Surely, Byrnes thought, *there must be a better way.*

After a disappointing 2008 season, the Diamondbacks stumbled in April 2009, going 9-13. By the end of the month, the team's owner and CEO, Ken Kendrick and Derrick Hall, were angry and pushing for change.

Kendrick, Hall, and Byrnes met several times to brainstorm possible replacements for Melvin. Before long, Hinch's name crept into the discussion.

Everyone was impressed with his work in the farm system, and everyone believed he had a bright future. But he was thirty-four years old and had never managed or coached anywhere. Was this too big a leap?

The owners were treating the idea like a bombshell, but one that could have appeal. "This is a legacy hire for you," Hall told Byrnes.

Byrnes didn't see Hinch that way. This wasn't an idea intended to shock the industry. He simply suspected that Hinch might be the best person for the job, especially the version of it that Byrnes wanted to see.

When he met Hinch in Jacksonville, Byrnes was still thinking it over, eager to see Hinch work with Parra.

This was a good case study for how he wanted to rethink a traditional model. For years, the typical meeting between a big-league manager and a minor leaguer lasted maybe thirty seconds and was superficial. The player would enter the manager's office, learn he had been sent down, and then be dispatched with a few quick, generic words.

Byrnes wanted his organization to sit with players, listen to them, and tease out a road map to success. He wanted feedback to be caring and specific.

"I want to see you talk to Parra as if you're the manager," Byrnes told Hinch on their way into the ballpark that night. "Let me see what it looks like."

Parra was a talented player who sometimes swung at too many pitches out of the strike zone. When he'd met with Byrnes earlier that spring, the GM said he was sending him to Double-A and wanted to see a .400 on-base percentage when he visited in May.

When they walked into the clubhouse in Jacksonville, Parra approached with a big smile on his face.

"My OBP is .426!" he said. "What do you want me to do next?"

Byrnes stepped aside and let Hinch take over. He watched as Hinch articulated goals for Parra's defense and provided specific information about his throwing.

"Here's what we see," Hinch said, sitting and making eye contact with Parra. "And here are some adjustments we could make." Hinch was warm, engaged, and clear about his expectations.

Byrnes was sold on him as the next Diamondbacks manager. Problem was, Hinch wasn't sold on taking the job. His ambitions had been clear since his playing days—he wanted to be a GM. His time in uniform was over.

But as Byrnes laid out his vision for a new type of dynamic between front office and field staff, Hinch bought in. In the same way that Hinch challenged players, Byrnes was gently challenging Hinch to prove he could take a leap.

In the end, Hinch was far too confident, curious, and ambitious to turn down the unexpected opportunity. Byrnes fired Melvin, named Hinch as manager—and then watched, stunned, as the clubhouse exploded.

It began with a tense news conference on May 8 at Arizona's Chase Field.

Fans and media were already wondering why Byrnes hadn't chosen Kirk Gibson, the iconic former slugger and current bench coach. National columnists were running stories with anonymous quotes criticizing the hire.

Bryan Price, the pitching coach, resigned immediately, then told a newspaper reporter that Byrnes had made "a poor decision" in hiring Hinch.

"A.J. has worked hard to get his credibility in the business in that [player development] side of things," Price went on to say. "But he doesn't have any credibility between the lines as a manager. That, for me, just wasn't going to work."

Behind the scenes, third-base coach Chip Hale sulked, disappointed that he didn't get the job. This was the beginning of a troubling trend; the following season, new third-base coach Bo Porter would loudly tell players and writers that he should be manager.

By the time Byrnes held a news conference to introduce Hinch, he was already on the defensive.

"He brings unique leadership and perspective to the job," Byrnes told the assembled media. "We're not here to reinvent the wheel, but to change the nature of the job a little bit? Okay, we'll do that. A.J. is a leader. He connects with people. He gets things done."

In the seats, one reporter turned to another and said, "He's talking down to us."

Back in the clubhouse, the reaction was even worse. Melvin had been popular among players, who perceived that he had backed them in debates with a proactive front office.

In the news conference, Byrnes had used a phrase that echoed around the locker room and ended up mocked by players and media alike: "organizational advocacy." Most people took that to mean that a member of the front office had put on a uniform and moved into the clubhouse, essentially eliminating the traditional manager position.

Hinch remained characteristically confident in his own abilities but was surprised by the strength of the blowback. From the first day, several veterans and coaches worked to actively undermine him. Publicly, catcher Chris Snyder complimented Melvin. Privately, he criticized Hinch to teammates. Davis, and other veteran pitchers loyal to Price, refused to accept Hinch as their leader.

One day not long after taking over, Hinch posted a lineup that began with shortstop Stephen Drew leading off, followed by outfielders Chris Young (no relation to the MLB vice president) and Justin Upton. Before the game, he revised the new lineup to flip Drew and Upton.

The clubhouse buzzed with a conspiracy theory: The GM must have written the new lineup.

Just a few years later, this would have been a nonissue. By the middle of the next decade, the Dodgers would install a research-and-development department near the clubhouse, churning out data that determined lineups and matchups. The Yankees would have more than twenty analysts doing the same. GMs would routinely meet with managers before and after games to provide strong input on all matters of game strategy. The power dynamic would be totally different.

But in 2009, no one was ready for this, and few in Arizona handled it well.

On one occasion, veteran infielder Felipe López hit a ground ball and failed to run hard to first base. Typically in that situation, a manager will wait for the player on the top step of the dugout and, out of the corner of his mouth so as not to make a scene or embarrass the player, order him not to do it again.

When López returned to the dugout, Hinch was waiting on the top step. One player in the dugout at the time recalls that instead of slowing down or stopping, López accelerated and rammed into Hinch's shoulder with his own. Hinch was left hanging.

Another time, reliever Jon Rauch started screaming at Hinch about not receiving enough opportunities to close games, and they had to take the argument into Hinch's office, where everyone in the clubhouse could hear.

Not every player resisted Hinch. Some of the youngsters, in particular, like Young and catcher Miguel Montero, both bright and curious, appreciated Hinch's listening skills and caring approach.

Snyder, the other catcher, ramped up his complaining about Hinch to teammates when he lost playing time to the promising Montero. Hinch couldn't win.

When Davis disrespected Hinch in public, Byrnes felt that he should intervene. But that was a situation without a palatable option: If Byrnes backed Hinch, he would be once again accused of running the team through a puppet manager.

Byrnes decided to speak with Davis and his agent, and emphasize that Hinch was willing to be a supportive, players-first manager, if only Davis would let him.

Davis resisted, and the conversation became heated.

"Doug," Byrnes yelled. "You're not a guy who throws ninety-five. You're not a first-round pick. You're kind of an acquired taste. And you were just an asshole to a guy that's in your corner," meaning that Hinch was the type of manager who would work with and help Davis, if only Davis would give him the chance.

At the end of the dismal season, Byrnes convened the only team meeting of his long career in baseball. He ripped into the players.

"I expect us to win here," he said. "Playing out the string in September doesn't work for me and it starts with effort level. Give a shit."

He and Hinch left the room feeling like the talk hadn't landed. There was just no way for Hinch to connect with this group.

The next season began with marginal improvements. Hinch had the benefit of a winter to prepare. He designed and ran spring training for the first time. He brought in a few coaches—though Porter, the new third-base coach, criticized Hinch to anyone who would listen.

Hinch started to remark to those around him that people like Porter were out to get him. That was true to a degree, but friends also worried that the pressure was making the manager edgy and paranoid.

To those who were willing to see it, Hinch's strengths continued to poke through. Veteran infielder Kelly Johnson signed with the team in the off-season, and immediately felt that the anti-Hinch contingent was acting small and petty.

Johnson saw Byrnes and Hinch for what they were: progressive, player-friendly club officials ahead of their time in their style of collaboration.

Hinch wanted to use his youth as an advantage, making him more relatable to the guys on the team. His idea was to empower players, not lord over them like an old-school manager. Once, when Johnson made a mistake on the field, Hinch quietly summoned him into the office, where he went over the play in a respectful manner and facilitated a discussion about how to improve.

Having seen managers go out of their way to call out and embarrass players in team meetings, Johnson strongly preferred this approach. He also saw in Hinch a manager interested in the X's and the O's of the game, not the drama that had come to surround his very presence in the job.

Unfortunately, that drama would soon swallow both Hinch and Byrnes. The Diamondbacks sank to last place in the early months of the 2010 season, and the controversial Hinch hire became an easy scapegoat. In June, owners Hall and Kendrick began pushing Byrnes to make another managerial change. They pointed to a ten-game losing streak from May 23 to June 2 as a reason for doing so.

Byrnes, trying to take a long view, asked his bosses if their opinions would be different had the team gone 2-8 in those ten games.

Yes, the owners said. It would. This seemed like no way to run an organization.

Believing that firing Hinch would deepen the team's problems, Byrnes dug in. At some point in June, he began to sense that if he insisted on keeping Hinch, ownership might just fire both of them.

On July 1, that's exactly what happened. The Hinch hire had cost Byrnes his own job.

At the time, many in the business viewed Hinch's time in the Arizona dugout as one of the more disastrous managerial tenures in recent memory.

But those who were really watching, from Byrnes to Johnson to Montero, thought that they had seen the beginnings of a great leader.

Longtime friends saw how this affected Hinch: Prior to managing the Diamondbacks, he had been like many young men who think of their own needs above others. After discovering he could help people, Hinch began to mature, turning away from pure ambition and incorporating a measure of altruism.

Once angling to be a GM, Hinch was too competitive to return to that goal now. He had failed in his first try as a manager, which had activated his ego, curiosity, and competitive energy. He now had to prove to himself and the world that he could do the job well.

Indeed, Byrnes's ability the year before to coax Hinch back into uniform had fundamentally altered the course of Hinch's career.

He had also been humbled. The Stanford grad had now disappointed himself twice, first with a playing career that did not meet expectations, and then by failing as a manager.

Without that miserable stint in Arizona, Hinch never would have been an Astro, or a champion. But his takeaways from the experience weren't all good—without the internalized trauma brought on by a veteran mutiny against him, he might have said something about the cheating, too.

Chapter 6

THE EDUCATION OF CARLOS BELTRÁN

On a Sunday morning in April 2014 in St. Petersburg, Florida, a group of reporters gathered around the locker of Yankees pitcher Iván Nova and pumped him with questions about the news from the team that he would need elbow surgery and miss a year.

The interview turned awkward when Nova did not seem to know about his diagnosis. He said he didn't think the injury was too major, and he asked for a bilingual reporter to explain what the Yankees had announced.

Sitting at his locker across the clubhouse, veteran outfielder Carlos Beltrán glared. He saw injustice.

Later that same day, the Yankees flew to Boston for a series against the Red Sox. In the second game there, another young Dominican pitcher, Michael Pineda, started for New York, but was ejected for having too much pine tar on his neck. The game's unwritten rules allowed for a pitcher to use some pine tar in order to improve his grip, but it had to be subtle. Pineda had gone too far.

Beltrán believed that Pineda had misunderstood advice given in English from a teammate about how much pine tar to apply.

Between what he had seen with Nova and Pineda, Beltrán had had enough. He simply wasn't going to stand by and allow another young player to endure what he once had, and it was time to take action.

By the time Beltrán signed with the Yankees prior to the 2014 season, his fifteenth in the league, he carried himself with what nearly everyone around him called "presence."

In physical terms, that meant he walked with his back straight, head tilted slightly back, and lips curled at the ends into a knowing grin.

Many teammates arrived at the ballpark wearing a polo shirt and khaki shorts; Beltrán reported in white skinny jeans and shirts adorned with bright pastels and paisley cuffs, or a similarly loud ensemble.

Out in the world, when Beltrán walked into a room, the people already in it might not know that an MLB star had entered, but they could usually tell that they were looking at *someone*. Beltrán was just one of those people who commanded attention.

It wasn't always like that. Twenty years earlier, as a teenager in Manatí, Puerto Rico, Beltrán was already in possession of some of the qualities that would give him that presence—intelligence, curiosity, a certain exterior stillness—but he was yet to develop a key piece, the confidence.

As a seventeen-year-old high school senior in the fall of 1994, Beltrán drew interest from many MLB teams. With speed, athleticism, and a smooth swing, he had emerged as one of the year's top prospects. He was capable of excelling as a pitcher, shortstop, catcher, and outfielder, and he possessed more natural speed and athleticism than nearly any other prospect.

The Kansas City Royals were one of several clubs taking an especially close look. That fall, they sent one of their most trusted scouts, Allard Baird, to watch Beltrán in a workout.

Baird, a thin, businesslike native of New Hampshire, was a cross-checker for the Royals, meaning that his job was to take a second look at players already identified by the team's scouts as possible draft picks.

Baird and his wife had no children, and he would come to develop a deep affection for Beltrán. Their relationship, which would stretch across multiple decades and organizations, began quietly at that autumn workout in Manatí.

Arriving to scout Beltrán, Baird shook the young man's hand. Beltrán offered only a shy nod before he trotted out onto the field and showcased his skills.

Not long after, Baird found himself at the Beltrán family home, representing the possibility of generational wealth.

The Beltráns were middle class, but that term was relative in Puerto Rico, where the median income was well under $20,000 a year. Carlos's father, Wilfredo, was a former amateur ballplayer who worked on an assembly line for a pharmaceutical company. He supported his wife and four children without much left over.

When Carlos and his older brother Nino played in the streets, they used a rolled-up wad of tape for a ball, a broomstick for a bat, and cardboard boxes or T-shirts for bases.

The lack of supplies did not deter Carlos from playing endlessly. Nino was five years older, and when he lost interest in hanging out with his little brother, Carlos would walk for half an hour, alone, to the nearest baseball field. There he would throw a ball in the air, swing, and play entire ballgames in his imagination.

After recording three fanciful outs, he would trot to the outfield and make plays, throwing ghost runners out at home. He did this for many hours at a time, until it was too dark to see.

When Baird visited, Carlos did not speak English, or at least not enough English to engage in conversation. But every time anyone else spoke, whether in English or Spanish, the young man narrowed his eyes and leaned his head in to listen.

Baird could see the wheels turning, and he could tell that Beltrán was working hard to process and understand. The deep reserves of intelligence and curiosity that would later define him as a star player were already evident.

Around that time, Beltrán injured his hamstring in a tryout for the Montreal Expos and fared poorly in a separate showcase for the Boston Red Sox. He underperformed in a winter league as a result of the injury and slipped to the second round in the June 1995 draft.

The Royals snagged him there, leaving Baird to believe that his team had stolen a top-ten gem.

When Beltrán reported to his first professional team, the Gulf Coast Royals in Fort Myers, Florida, he might as well have been dropped onto another planet. Baird, keeping tabs on Beltrán, thought that the eighteen-year-old perfectly embodied the cliché "fish out of water."

Nowadays, some organizations provide everything from English-language classes to United Nations–style earpieces for real-time translations during meetings.

But in 1995, players from Latin America could only listen to the English spoken all around them and learn as quickly as they could. The extent of the services offered was—at best—one Spanish-speaking coach per minor league affiliate.

Beltrán was at least fortunate to have a bilingual manager, Bob Herold. Other than that, there was little to help him acclimate.

Beltrán hadn't been especially garrulous in Manatí, but his new teammates considered him one of the most introverted people they'd ever met. They didn't realize that he was also prideful, embarrassed, and more than a little frustrated by his inability to make friends with the many teammates who spoke a language he did not understand.

Life away from the field was even harder. Beltrán would go to the mall, try to order food in a restaurant, buy clothing—all of the little things that a person needs to do to get by. At best, he was greeted by Florida locals with blank stares. At worst, hostility.

Before long, Beltrán asked a teammate, Ricky Pitts, to tutor him in English. In return, he taught Spanish to Pitts. It was here that he began charting his own long course to fluency.

When he was home in Puerto Rico during the off-season, Beltrán developed a crush on Jessica Lugo, a college student and the sister of his best friend, Hector. He would hang around their house, even when Hector was not around, but he could not muster the confidence to speak to Jessica.

One day, he devised a solution. Still too shy to make his feelings known, Beltrán scribbled his phone number on a piece of paper, left it on a table, and went home.

The strategy worked. Jessica called, and she kept calling when Carlos left the following season to play again. Too reserved to forge close bonds with most of the people in his life, Carlos found himself comfortable opening up to this new companion about baseball, his ambitions, and all of his experiences in the mainland United States.

The two married in 1999 and would remain a tight unit, often so tight that others in the business felt they could not break through.

Jessica acted as a fierce advocate for her reserved husband, willing to express herself—loudly, if necessary—to everyone from Scott Boras, Beltrán's high-profile agent, to team officials who she felt had crossed her husband.

By 1996, Beltrán's second year in professional baseball, the struggles of playing in an unfamiliar place had begun to impair his progress. He batted .249 in the low levels of the minors, with just seven home runs. He ate too much fast food because it was the easiest thing to order, and he cried at night when the language barrier became too much to bear.

One week, a scout would see him play and report back that Beltrán was a future All-Star. A different scout watching the following week would write up Beltrán as nothing more than a backup.

He had more natural speed than anyone on the team, but in his first two minor league seasons he was caught stealing five times in just twenty-five attempts. When he was thrown out, he would hang his head and sulk while leaving the field.

He would do the same after swinging and missing at a breaking ball, the pitch that confounded him. Determined to improve, Beltrán worked with a Royals minor league coach, Kevin Long, on becoming a switch-hitter. He also played winter ball in Puerto Rico alongside major leaguers.

Baseball in the Caribbean is intense, and when Beltrán returned from the experience, Baird and other members of the Royals' front office noticed that he was walking differently—a little more upright, a little more confident. He seemed to have internalized his ability to compete with the big boys.

That season brought more struggle, but improved composure. Though he hit just 11 home runs and had a .229 batting average, he began to flash power in batting practice.

The Royals saw a player who no longer sulked after he struggled, and who had begun to show field awareness—a sense of what was happening in the entire game, outside of his own responsibilities as a hitter and fielder.

At the end of the 1998 season, the Royals gave him a quick look in the big leagues. By 1999 Beltrán was not only there to stay but earned American League Rookie of the Year honors. He batted .293, hit 22 home runs, stole 27 bases, and played an aesthetically stunning center field.

Beltrán achieved this without knowing much about how to steal signs, decode sequences, or determine when an opposing pitcher was tipping. That all came later. As a youngster, he succeeded because the raw tools that had made him a top prospect—speed, power, arm strength, fielding, hitting for average—had evolved into repeatable skills. He won that Rookie of the Year award on athleticism, helped along by increased confidence and the beginnings of what would become his presence.

—

"Carlos, I can't let you stay here and work out on your own," Allard Baird told his young star. "I can't put you or the organization in that position."

In the summer of 2000, Beltrán's defiant streak, which would later work both for and against him, emerged in a conflict with his team.

In July, he suffered a bone bruise in his right knee and needed to go on the disabled list. When it came time to rehabilitate the injury, Baird—now the Royals' general manager—followed standard procedure and asked Beltrán to report to the team's spring-training complex in Davenport, Florida.

Beltrán and his agent, Scott Boras, did not believe that was necessary, and they asserted that a player had the right to remain with his teammates.

Teams already granted this permission selectively, with stars like Atlanta's John Smoltz and San Francisco's Barry Bonds receiving the courtesy. Why should a young player be treated differently?

Baseball City, the complex where the Royals trained in Davenport, stood in the middle of an abandoned amusement park. This was really better than a big-league stadium?

With the Royals about to leave for a long road trip, Baird told Beltrán that he was not permitted to either travel with the team or use the facilities in Kansas City, which Baird said were inadequate.

This did not sway Beltrán. He and Boras thought the same about the Florida complex. In the end, Beltrán didn't think he should have to report to Florida, so he refused. The team suspended him without pay, and the Players Association filed a grievance on his behalf.

Beltrán didn't return for two months, but never held it against Baird. This was about principle, not a personal issue, and the two remained close.

The incident itself set a lasting precedent favorable to players.

From then on, teams were more careful about constructing better rehab facilities at their spring-training complexes, often at significant expense. Players felt forever emboldened to challenge rehab plans and locations.

Much later, when the commissioner's office made an aggressive move against Beltrán for his role in the Astros scandal, more than a few of his friends in the game theorized (admittedly without evidence) that the league's grudge went all the way back to the rehab case of 2000.

Over the next several seasons, Beltrán's confidence continued to grow. As he approached free agency in 2004, he was still not the leader he would later become—his stature and presence in Kansas City were based more on performance than obvious leadership skills—but he had begun to develop some of the necessary traits.

Almost never vocal in larger groups, he started to take aside younger players and teach them about the game. More confident with his own English now, he helped rookies from Latin America acclimate to the new language and culture.

He was also starting to notice things about pitchers that had previously eluded him. He was able to stand in the dugout, nod toward the mound, and suggest to a teammate that a fastball was coming. Or a changeup or a breaking ball. Beltrán was so physically gifted that he didn't yet need this skill, but he was acquiring it anyway.

In 2007, when Mets star David Wright found himself on second base in a game against the rival Phillies, one of two annoying things usually happened.

Phils shortstop Jimmy Rollins would engage Wright in meaningless conversation, distracting him from his job preparing for the pitch. Or, when the catcher was giving signs, second baseman Chase Utley would step between Wright and the pitcher's mound and blow a bubble too close to Wright's face.

"I wish I could pick up on what they're doing," Wright would yell at Utley. "But I can't."

Rollins and Utley suspected that Wright was stealing signs—and while they were wrong about the particular player, they were wise to believe that the Mets were up to something. This was the year that Carlos Delgado and his old friend Shawn Green reunited and joined forces to help Beltrán take his skills to the next level.

Since they had learned the dual arts of pitch decoding and sign stealing from manager Cito Gaston and teammate Roberto Alomar in Toronto more than a decade earlier, Green and Delgado had gone on to enjoy highly productive careers. Delgado had stuck in Toronto for many years before signing with the Florida Marlins, and Green went on to star for the Dodgers.

Prior to the 2006 season, the Mets traded for Delgado. That August, the team acquired Green. It was the first time that the two friends had played together since 1999, Green's final year on the Blue Jays.

Coming to New York, they joined a ball club on the upswing. Prior to the 2005 season, new general manager Omar Minaya had made a pair of dramatic free-agent signings, which combined to herald a new age for New York's perennial also-rans.

First, Minaya lured Boston Red Sox ace Pedro Martínez to Queens. Then he snagged the year's biggest free-agent prize, the twenty-seven-year-old Beltrán, who had launched himself from stardom to super-stardom in October 2004.

Baird, knowing that his small-market team was not going to be able to afford Beltrán going forward, had traded his friend to Houston in June 2004. Beltrán proceeded to set a major league record by hitting at least one home run in five consecutive postseason games. He tied Barry Bonds's mark of eight playoff homers and batted .435 in twelve October games.

He could not have timed his national coming-out party any better. Minaya, looking to establish the Mets as a winning team again after several down seasons, mounted an aggressive pursuit. He ultimately landed Beltrán for seven years and $119 million.

At first, Beltrán embraced his role as a high-profile savior. At an introductory news conference attended by nearly 250 media members, he smiled and spontaneously rebranded his team as the "New Mets."

Privately, he reached out to Wright, a homegrown player who was on his way to becoming the face of the franchise, and proposed that they begin working out together. The two met up and began to bond.

But it didn't take long into the 2005 season for the new level of scrutiny to bring out the old introvert lurking inside. Beltrán performed well at first, but fell into a slump in June, batting .198 that month.

This was normal in baseball—even the best players endure down periods during the long season—but when you're a big-money import in New York, you find your every move scrutinized.

At the ballpark, Beltrán heard boos. On the streets, people would walk right up to him and tell him how to fix his swing. This did not happen in Kansas City.

Beltrán became more withdrawn in the clubhouse, and he stopped calling Wright to work out. The two would maintain a level of mutual respect over the next seven years as teammates but would never again be close.

After that season, Minaya acquired Delgado to play first base and, as another veteran slugger, to take some of the pressure off Beltrán. Both were proud natives of Puerto Rico, and they quickly became inseparable.

When Green joined the group in August 2006, the Mets were storming through the National League, on their way to ninety-seven wins and a division title. Beltrán was back to being the player the Mets had thought they'd acquired in 2005, ultimately hitting forty-one home runs and making the All-Star team.

Still, the season ended in a way that would come to embody what many fans mistakenly saw as his passivity.

In the bottom of the ninth inning of Game Seven of the National League Championship Series, Beltrán was up with the bases loaded, two outs, and the Mets trailing St. Louis by a run.

Cardinals rookie pitcher Adam Wainwright dotted the outside corner with a perfect 0-2 curveball, and Beltrán took it for a season-ending strike three.

For many years after, Mets fans wondered why Beltrán hadn't swung the bat. Failing to realize that Wainwright had simply thrown a perfect pitch, many in New York viewed the take as an indictment of a quiet player who remained largely a mystery to them.

The next year began with Delgado, Green, and Beltrán together from spring training on. Delgado and Green provided tutorials to anyone interested in how to tell what a pitcher was planning to throw.

"I've got the signs," Green would say. "Just let me know if you want them from second."

At first, few players did. Some, like Wright, never would. He'd had a bad experience thinking that a fastball was coming and getting a breaking ball instead. He geared up for a big swing and ended up embarrassed by nearly twisting himself to the ground. The whole process just cluttered his mind.

But Wright watched as many other teammates signed on to the Green/Delgado plan. The 2007 Mets became the most active sign-stealing team for which he had ever played.

Back then, there was no replay room in which players could scrutinize video. Teams were allowed to use portable DVD players to study pitchers. For veterans like Green and Delgado, this was an improvement from the 1990s, when the Blue Jays used VHS tapes.

The two would huddle over one of the DVD players, watching footage of an upcoming opponent. If a pitcher's glove was a fraction of an inch one way or another, they could tell what pitch he was going to throw. Delgado would scribble it in his notebook.

Wright would laugh.

"There is no possible way you can see what you're claiming to see," he'd say.

But other players, including Beltrán, bought in. He had already begun to develop an eye for the techniques in Kansas City, and with proper teaching he quickly became advanced.

Before long, he joined the roster of others in his generation, from Delgado to Green to Boston infielder Alex Cora to Yankees third baseman Alex Rodriguez, as the premier guys at picking up signs and pitch tipping.

What Roberto Alomar and Joe Carter had once done for Green and Delgado, Green and Delgado had now finalized for Beltrán. He would soon begin to pay it forward himself.

This wasn't the only way that Beltrán was looking to help others. A few years into their time in New York, he and Jessica began discussing how they could allocate their considerable wealth to fulfill their social conscience.

Nearly any ballplayer growing up in Puerto Rico regarded public service as an essential component of stardom. Roberto Clemente, the icon of the island, had modeled this in the most meaningful way imaginable when he was killed in a plane crash while en route to Nicaragua to deliver supplies to earthquake victims.

Carlos and Jessica had established the Carlos Beltran Foundation in 2002 and focused on providing funding for sports and education for low-income children. Once he hit the jackpot with his Mets contract, Beltrán began donating 10 percent of his annual salary to the foundation.

Nearly every well-paid athlete has a charity, and many do it mostly for appearances or tax purposes. Beltrán saw his as an opportunity to follow Clemente. He had never forgotten the trauma of those early years in the Royals organization and wanted to find a way to save others from similar experiences.

With the Mets, he stepped up his work with young players. In

2011, with Beltrán's speed beginning to decline, the team wanted to move him from center field to right and replace him in center with the younger Ángel Pagán.

Rather than protecting his territory, Beltrán embraced the chance to teach. Soon Pagán, a fellow Puerto Rican, was following Beltrán everywhere. All the veteran had to do, no matter where he was in the clubhouse, was shout, "Pagán!" and his protégé would appear.

But Beltrán was still searching for a signature contribution. He and Jessica hit on the idea of education, which dovetailed perfectly with his one-on-one work with teammates.

Wanting to better prepare players for pro ball, and educate those who would not make it, they decided to start a school where young Puerto Rican athletes could learn both on- and off-field skills.

The Carlos Beltran Baseball Academy opened on August 11, 2011, in the town of Florida, in Puerto Rico. At the ribbon-cutting ceremony, Beltrán wept. Heading into the final leg of his career, he had merged the two things about which he felt most deeply, baseball and mentorship.

That helped him to settle into a more self-assured phase, as did a long-overdue parting with the Mets. Beltrán's relationship with fans in New York had never quite recovered from his slow debut in 2005, or the Adam Wainwright curveball in 2006.

His dynamic with the front office had soured, too. After the 2009 season, Beltrán underwent arthroscopic surgery on his right knee. The Mets claimed that he'd had the procedure without their consent.

The situation erupted into public and private hostilities. On a conference call with reporters, Mets assistant general manager John Ricco described the team as "upset" with Beltrán for failing to notify them of the surgery.

Beltrán responded with a statement that said, "Any accusation that I ignored or defied the team's wishes [is] simply false."

It was getting to be time for everyone to move on.

The team traded Beltrán to San Francisco in July 2011, months before he was set to become a free agent again. He moved on from there to the Cardinals, then the Yankees and Rangers—all while settling into a role as one of the game's venerated elder statesmen.

In 2014, after watching his Yankee teammates Nova and Pineda struggle during the same week to express themselves to both the team and the media, Beltrán called the Players Association.

He reached Leonor Colon, the senior director of international and domestic player operations, and an ally to Latin American players. For several years, the two had discussed a rule that would require teams to employ interpreters for Spanish-speaking players.

"Enough already," Beltrán told Colon. "Get it done."

When Beltrán decided to throw the full weight of his star power behind the idea, it provided the needed momentum. He spoke to several media outlets about the need for interpreters, prompting Players Association executive director Tony Clark to issue a statement saying that he was "very interested."

Negotiations commenced and became drawn out. Some teams were reluctant to pay for the new position. Advocates noted that during a March 2016 trip to Cuba, English-speaking MLB officials had access to interpreters. Why, Beltrán and others wondered, was this an automatic for the American suits but something that Spanish-speaking athletes had to fight for?

By the beginning of the 2016 season, an agreement was in place: All thirty teams would be required to employ a full-time Spanish-language translator.

To Beltrán, this was nearly as meaningful an accomplishment as the opening of his academy. He remembered being a rookie in Kansas City, when all he could offer the media were stock phrases like "I feel good," "I had a good game," and "I'm happy I helped the team."

Back then he'd had a head full of sophisticated ideas about the game and the world, and simply could not express them to the public, let alone many teammates.

Now, confident both with his English skills and his stature as a man-in-full with valid opinions, he was finally ready to open up.

Before games, late-career Beltrán sat in front of his locker, availing himself to the media for one detailed conversation after another. When the reporters left, he was an undisputed leader to all players in the clubhouse, white and Latino alike.

Without knowing it, he was preparing for one final adventure as a player: a return to Houston as a mentor to another highly talented young group.

Chapter 7

LAST STEP TOWARD THE ASTROS: ADVENT OF THE REPLAY ROOMS

On June 2, 2010, a journeyman named Armando Galarraga, pitching for the Detroit Tigers, took a perfect game into the ninth inning.

After retiring twenty-six consecutive Cleveland batters, Galarraga induced a soft ground ball from Jason Donald. First baseman Miguel Cabrera scooted to his right, fielded it, and tossed it to Galarraga, who was covering first. Cabrera's throw beat Donald to the bag. The perfecto should have been complete, Galarraga's place in history secure.

But instead, umpire Jim Joyce shocked everyone in the ballpark by spreading his arms to signal that Donald was safe. It was a blown call, a brain fart, an inexplicable moment. When Joyce returned to the umpires' room and watched the replay, he yelled, cursed, and tore off his uniform. He cried on and off for days and endured threats, abuse, and depression.

Galarraga had lost his perfect game, and Joyce—one of the game's most respected veteran umpires—had forever tainted his own reputation. Fans, umps, and league officials surveyed the carnage from this moment of human error and concluded that it was time for change.

MLB already had an instant-replay system in place, but it lagged far behind any of the other major American sports. Beginning in 2008, home-run calls were subject to review, but that left many other potential holes. Over the next few years, blown calls accumulated in other areas of the game, and baseball's refusal to utilize available technology to review them left the sport looking increasingly antiquated. Fans loved a good old-fashioned argument between a manager and umpire, and instant replay would severely reduce those. But as time passed, it became harder to justify choosing inaccuracy over tradition.

The emotional impact of Joyce's error helped to accelerate the conversation. Change moved at a deliberate pace, as advances in the national pastime often do, and other umpire mistakes added up. But by 2013 the league announced that it would implement a system of manager challenges for the following season.

In order to do this, MLB ordered the construction of a replay-review room in every clubhouse. Typically just a few steps from the dugout but sometimes farther away, these rooms contained multiple monitors that offered several angles of every play. When a manager suspected that the umpire had gotten a call wrong, he signaled for a halt in the action and directed one of his coaches to call the replay room.

In that room, a team employee designated as the replay coordinator quickly reviewed the play in question. Using the replay phone, he then advised the coach whether or not to tell the manager to challenge the play.

If the manager did challenge, the umpires would don a headset to communicate with another crew stationed at the Replay Operations Center in New York City. That crew would look at the play from every angle and decide whether to overturn it. They would then notify the umpires at the ballpark of their decision.

This was an innovation intended to improve the integrity of competition and the accuracy of results. But as sometimes happens with the best of intentions, it would end up leading directly to one of the worst cheating scandals in the history of the game.

—

It was the summer of 2015, and Carlos Beltrán, Alex Rodriguez, and outfielder Chris Young were in the replay room at Yankee Stadium.

Some teams built their rooms far from the dugout, making it inconvenient for players to use them to watch in-game video of their own at-bats or opposing pitchers. Not the Yankees, who carved out a space not far behind the home bench.

This was Beltrán's second year living a childhood fantasy of playing in the Bronx. He had dreamed of being a Yankee since he was a kid, rooting for center fielder Bernie Williams, a fellow Puerto Rican.

In the final hours before signing with the Mets in 2005, Beltrán had instructed Scott Boras to tell the Yankees he was willing to accept less money to play for them. It wasn't a fit at the time, but in December 2013, when the club offered him a three-year, $45 million contract, Beltrán jumped.

In Beltrán's second year with the Yankees, Rodriguez re-joined the team after missing the entire 2014 season while serving the longest suspension for performance-enhancing drugs in the history of the game. His rule-bending skills extended beyond just steroids. A-Rod had always been a baseball nut, long regarded as one of the elite in his generation at using his eyes to steal signs and pick up on pitch tipping.

He was a longtime acquaintance of Beltrán's, another of the best in the business at those skills. Since playing on the Mets with Carlos Delgado, Shawn Green, and later Alex Cora, Beltrán had sharpened his already well-practiced eye. Now in the latter stages of his career, he was as good at it as anyone, and loved to pass along what he learned.

Late in the 2014 season, the Yankees had also signed the veteran outfielder Young, recently released by the Mets. Young was a soft-spoken native of Texas who had developed a keen eye. Over the course of a thirteen-year career in the big leagues, he'd learned how to stand at second base, look in at the catcher, and figure out the sequences. He liked to call it "breaking the code."

Young was well liked in the Yankee clubhouse, but far from influential. This was a team loaded with stars, from A-Rod and Beltrán to Ichiro Suzuki, Brian McCann, and CC Sabathia. Young was the last man on the roster, a backup.

But he, Beltrán, and A-Rod did share a common enthusiasm for decoding sequences.

To the casual fan, sign sequences represent one of baseball's most impenetrable mysteries. What exactly happens between the pitcher and the catcher in the moments before every pitch is thrown?

Here's what we see: As the pitcher stands on the mound, holding the ball and looking in at the plate, the catcher flashes a series of fingers in rapid succession.

The pitcher either shakes his head, sending the catcher into another sequence, or nods and begins his windup. Sometimes, if he shakes a few times in a row, the catcher trots out to the mound to resolve their disagreement.

It takes a highly trained eye to understand any of it.

The most basic form of signs works like this: One finger calls for a fastball, two fingers a curveball, three fingers a slider, and four fingers a changeup.

With runners on base, especially second base, the equation becomes much more complicated. Smart players like Delgado and Green made it a regular practice to stand on second and peer in at the catcher.

The base runner would pick up the sign and set about relaying it to the batter. First, he'd make a subtle gesture to indicate he had the pitch—say, sliding a hand across the letters on his jersey.

If the batter wanted the sign, he would respond with a gesture of his own, like touching the brim of his helmet.

The base runner would then indicate the pitch by looking into the outfield, stepping to his right or left, touching his leg—whatever the team had agreed on beforehand.

Because of this practice, catchers complicated their sequences when runners were on base. You couldn't make it easy on a Delgado by simply flashing one finger and telling him that a fastball was coming.

There are many different sign sequences, but three of the most common are called "chase the two," "outs plus one," and "ABE."

In "chase the two," the catcher flashes several fingers, but the real sign comes immediately after the number two. If he goes 1-3-2-4, he is calling for a changeup, because the 4 followed the 2.

"Outs plus one" means that the number of outs in the inning dictates the actual sign. If there are zero out, the first sign is the true sign. If there is one out, it's the second sign. If there are two outs, the third sign.

"ABE," or ahead behind even, is even more complex. If the pitcher is ahead in the count—meaning he has thrown more strikes than balls to the batter—the true sign is the first one. If he is even in the count, it's the second sign. If he's behind, it's the third sign.

If a catcher wants to switch from one sequence to another, he communicates that by rubbing a hand across his chest protector, adjusting his mask, or using another gesture that he and the pitcher have agreed on before the game. Those are called indicators.

Smart base runners used their eyes to figure out the indicators, decode the sign sequences, and pass the intel along to their hitters.

This practice was completely legal—but, as one might expect, frowned upon by pitchers. For decades, teams caught stealing signs from second were subject to retaliation.

By the second decade of the twenty-first century, MLB was far more aggressive in issuing ejections, fines, and suspensions to pitchers who threw at batters. It became much harder to retaliate against a hitter for any perceived offense.

And then, in 2014, every team installed a replay room in its clubhouse. This treasure trove of video offered easy looks at what players had long been squinting at from second base.

What was a heady player like Carlos Beltrán going to do, not look at it? For Beltrán, A-Rod, and Young, the work started before and after games, when they would scrutinize video of upcoming opponents.

If the Red Sox were coming to town and Rick Porcello was starting the first game, what sequence did he typically prefer? Chase the two? ABE? Did he switch up his sequences during games in any sort of discernible pattern? Once you figured that out, you stood a decent chance of getting his signs from second base.

Naturally, that pregame preparation drifted into in-game work. The location of the Yankee Stadium replay room made it possible for a player or coach to watch footage in real time, then walk into the dugout armed with information—or to just yell it from the room to teammates on the bench. Someone in the dugout would then signal to a base runner what sequence the pitcher and catcher were currently using.

Communication would also flow in the other direction. Beltrán, Young, or another Yankee would know from their pregame study which sequences an opposing pitcher typically used. From the dugout, they'd ask a runner on second if those sequences were currently in effect. The runner could peer in at the catcher and confirm or deny.

Not everyone considered this method effective. Yankees first baseman Mark Teixeira found that by the time the signs got from the replay room to the base runner to the batter's box, it was too late to benefit. Teixeira's turn at bat would be over, and the pitcher might switch to a different sequence by the next inning.

"You are not good at this," he would say, according to an interview he later did with reporter Joel Sherman of the *New York Post*. "You are trying to give signs, then you get mad at me because I am not good at it either. We are not that good at it." To be sure, this was an in-game sign-stealing system, and it would soon be illegal. The Yankees were far from the only team that passed sign-sequence information from the replay room to the dugout in 2015, 2016, and 2017. The Red Sox and Dodgers were among the other clubs clever enough to use the new tool this way. Those clubs sometimes used dugout phones to pass the information, too.

The rule on the books at the time made clear that the behavior of the Yankees and others at least pushed into a gray area. It read: "No equipment may be used for the purpose of stealing signs or conveying information designed to give a Club an advantage."

At the time, sign stealing was generally fair game, part of a long tradition. Lifers hadn't been forced to think much about what the rapid influx of new technology, from scouting cameras to replay rooms, could do to alter the integrity of the sport. If anything, they interpreted the above rule to mean no texting signs during games. It was one of those rules, like pitchers' use of pine tar, that went largely ignored and unenforced.

Beltrán, A-Rod, and Young believed they were simply putting in the hard work to stay current on technology and remain students of the game. It was an intellectual challenge, and it did not feel like cheating. True cheating would have meant decoding the sequences in the replay room and conveying them directly to a hitter, without needing a runner on base as the middleman. There was no way to do that.

Well, there was one way. But it would require a far more aggressive technique.

Chapter 8

THE CONSTRUCTION OF THE ASTROS

L ate in the 2016 season, a Houston Astros intern named Derek Vigoa approached a superior in the team's offices at Minute Maid Park.

He had a spreadsheet in his hands, and he was excited.

"Hey, look," Vigoa said. "We've got sign stealing."

The Astros already had an innovative research-and-development department and were looking into the use of sophisticated scouting cameras to help pitchers and hitters with their mechanics. Staffers worked directly with players on how to translate and implement analytics. The Astros had so much information obtained through legal means that the official's first response to Vigoa was to shrug. Sign stealing? Do we really need that?

Despite running into initial apathy, Vigoa continued to push his system. On September 22, 2016, he debuted the idea to general manager Jeff Luhnow in a PowerPoint presentation.

He gave the system a dramatic name, "Codebreaker," but the actual details of the proposal were fairly simplistic—far less sophisticated than anything the Astros' actual analytics department would have devised, had they been pursuing sign stealing.

Vigoa had built an Excel spreadsheet that used some of the software's basic functions to log and decode catcher signs.

In the plan he laid out, a member of the front office would watch a live feed of the game and input the signs and sign sequences into the spreadsheet. That was it.

Essentially, it was a computer version of what players had engaged in on second base for decades. It took what smart men like Carlos Beltrán, Chris Young, and Alex Rodriguez were doing with their eyes in the replay room and added an element that was hardly cutting-edge.

In his presentation, Vigoa was not specific about whether or not Codebreaker would be used during or before games. If done pregame, Codebreaker was legal.

If used in-game, a member of the staff could get the decoded sequence to the dugout, where it could be relayed to a runner on second base, who could then relay it to the batter. Under 2016 rules, this was a bit of a gray area—technically banned, but not emphasized or enforced.

Luhnow expressed an interest in the system and asked follow-up questions. With help from Tom Koch-Weser, who worked in the replay room, Vigoa implemented Codebreaker, though players and senior members of the analytics department would question its usefulness.

Much later, when Codebreaker became public in the wake of the broader scandal, many people inside and outside the game viewed it as evidence that a culture of sign-stealing was deeply embedded in every level of the institution in Houston. In reality it was the work of a few relatively new employees striving to impress their boss— and that is actually where Codebreaker tells the most about how the Astros' intense culture under Luhnow led to cheating.

Every season ended with pointed meetings, where the GM singled out department heads and asked, "What's your department going to look like in five years? Ten years?"

Luhnow would often lean especially hard on pitching coach Brent Strom, demanding that every year bring fresh and revolutionary ideas about pitching.

Once, in a meeting like this, an Astros employee who felt extreme pressure to come up with a new idea or lose his job turned to another.

"We're just dots on a page to this front office," the employee said.

Under these circumstances, it's easy to understand why a young staffer would tinker with Excel to come up with something he could slap a fancy name on. It's also easy to see how people could slip into cheating in order to feed the organization's endless appetite for innovation.

During Luhnow's second full season in baseball, working for the St. Louis Cardinals in 2005, he became intrigued by Michael Witte, an illustrator in his early sixties with graying hair and no experience working in baseball.

Witte was friends with some of the team's minority shareholders, and for several years had been sketching pitchers in their windups. Through the study of their movement that came from executing these sketches, Witte developed a theory of successful pitching mechanics.

Luhnow made Witte a consultant and sent him DVDs of several pitchers that the team was considering for the upcoming draft. A few of those whom Witte flagged as injury risks did indeed get hurt, leading Luhnow to believe that the artist knew what he was talking about.

Then he made a decision that some of his colleagues in the Cardinals organization would still be chuckling about fifteen years later: He invited Witte to lecture a group that included pitching coach Dave Duncan and general manager Walt Jocketty.

Duncan, a rough-edged Texan and former marine, was widely regarded as one of the top pitching coaches in the history of the game. Jocketty was a silver-haired baseball lifer who had enjoyed a long run of success with the Cardinals. These were men confident in their own success and knowledge.

Armed with sketchbooks and a presentation called "Classic

Mechanics: A Throwing Model Based on the Construction of the Motions of Great Historic Pitchers," Witte pulled out VHS tapes labeled DRYSDALE!!! and SEAVER!!!

Duncan seethed at having to take time from his day to listen to a neophyte. Jocketty rolled his eyes and thought, *When is this going to be over?*

It's not that Luhnow was wrong to think creatively and seek input from an unusual source. But by misjudging the openness of his colleagues, he guaranteed that the Cardinals would not benefit from Witte's presentation. Duncan and Jocketty needed a gradual nudge into modernity, and Luhnow offered a hard shove.

Thin, graying, and often soft-spoken, Luhnow gave the impression in public of a data-driven technocrat. He was actually an engaging conversationalist, a fun guy to have a beer with. His friends swore by him. But his lack of outreach often left old-school baseball guys in the cold.

To those who knew Luhnow's employment history, his management style made a bit more sense. His jobs before baseball included six years as a consultant at McKinsey & Company, the top consulting firm in the world—and an institution as controversial in business as Luhnow became in baseball.

At different junctures, McKinsey worked with Enron (coincidentally, the original owner of naming rights to what became Minute Maid Park) and the Kingdom of Saudi Arabia, whose government would later be implicated in the murder and dismemberment of journalist Jamal Khashoggi.

McKinsey also helped President Donald Trump's administration carry out its aggressive crackdown on illegal immigration by proposing that the government cut spending on food and medical care for detainees.

In a 2019 op-ed for *Current Affairs,* an anonymous McKinsey employee wrote:

"McKinsey has done direct harm to the world in ways that, thanks to its lack of final decision-making power, are hard to measure and, thanks to its intense secrecy, are hard to know. The firm's willingness to work with despotic governments and corrupt business empires is the logical conclusion of seeking profit at all costs. Its advocacy of the primacy of the market has made governments more like businesses and businesses more like vampires."

Luhnow was not implicated in the worst of McKinsey's work; he was not even at the company for most of it. But the firm's management style was evident in the way he operated in baseball.

McKinsey subscribed to the "up or out" mentality, in which employees could lose their jobs if not promoted. This was not much different from the pressure placed on Astros officials to innovate or move on.

And Luhnow's team mirrored the McKinsey principles of advising companies to be lean, ruthless, and—in the view of critics, if not conceded by Luhnow and his allies—morally flexible.

Luhnow's relationship with the firm stretched deep into his Astros years; in 2017, he brought in a team of McKinsey consultants shortly before executing mass firings in the scouting department.

Throughout his years at McKinsey, and in his other business ventures before or after, Luhnow was always following and thinking about baseball. Born in 1966 in Mexico City, where his father had moved for work and where the family remained, Luhnow traveled to attend Astros and Dodgers games as a kid. He later earned dual bachelor's degrees from the University of Pennsylvania in engineering and economics, and an MBA from Northwestern. But he always felt the pull of the game.

While in grad school, Luhnow often found himself in the bleachers at Wrigley Field, dreaming of what he would do to turn around the long-suffering Cubs. He ultimately wrote a paper on that topic, and devoted considerable energy to his fantasy baseball team.

In 2003, Luhnow received an inquiry from a young man whom

he'd once recruited to McKinsey and turned out to be the son-in-law of Cardinals owner Bill DeWitt Jr. The Cardinals GM, Jocketty, was successful but old-school, and DeWitt wanted to modernize the team with data and analytics.

This was a trendy pursuit in the year of Michael Lewis's hit book *Moneyball*, which detailed the low-cost success of the analytically inclined Oakland A's. DeWitt wanted his own *Moneyball* guy, especially to improve his club's performance in the amateur draft. That September, he hired Luhnow as vice president of baseball development.

DeWitt's internal memo announcing the hire went out of its way to mention Luhnow's most famous employer.

"I think he presents a unique opportunity for us to bring to the Cardinals a high level McKinsey talent at a below market price to fill a very challenging and important position," the owner wrote.

The move immediately caused tension in the organization. Luhnow ranked below Jocketty but had a direct line to DeWitt. This was a recipe for employee insecurity and the makings of a power struggle.

Over the next few years, Luhnow accumulated more influence with the owner, and two distinct silos developed: those loyal to Jocketty, who pointed to his long record of success and wondered why the team needed a fresh voice; and the newer hires who worked with Luhnow.

Iconic manager Tony La Russa was firmly in the former camp. He often reacted with anger and hostility when Luhnow offered lineup suggestions and other ideas. Cardinals officials aligned with the GM and manager began calling the bespectacled Luhnow "Harry Potter" behind his back.

Before long, assistant GM John Mozeliak became a bridge between the two factions, and most of Luhnow's team didn't even feel comfortable talking to La Russa.

Luhnow kicked around ideas years ahead of their time, like extreme defensive shifting and the use of openers, or relievers who started games and pitched an inning or two to save mediocre starters from facing the heart of the lineup more than once or twice.

"We could never get Tony to do that," Luhnow would say.

He was right, though the issue was more the dynamic between manager and messenger than manager and idea. La Russa did employ shifts based on the hunches of José Oquendo, one of his trusted coaches. That he and Luhnow could not discuss the same concept was a mutual failure of communication.

The Cardinals won the World Series in 2006 after defeating Carlos Beltrán and the Mets in the infamous National League Championship Series that ended with Beltrán looking at Adam Wainwright's curveball.

DeWitt continued to back Luhnow, and Luhnow continued to push for more efficient methods of running a baseball organization, and to do it tactlessly.

Turning his attention to scouts, Luhnow wanted to test their accuracy and expose those whose projections proved unreliable. Traditionally, a scout might watch a pitcher and say, "I don't like his arm action. He's going to get hurt."

Luhnow thought that was too generic.

"Rate how much more likely he is to get hurt than the average pitcher," he would say. "Is he fifty percent more likely? Sixty percent more likely?"

When a scout would say that a batter had "sixty power," using the traditional scouting scale where a tool is measured on a scale of 20–80, Luhnow would answer, "Don't tell me he has sixty power. Give me a more statistical projection. Is he going to hit twenty home runs in Double-A? A lot more? A lot less?"

Luhnow and his team not only pushed their scouts to make more specific predictions, but they recorded and saved the guesses. The idea was to revisit each scout's body of work in a few years and determine how frequently they were correct or incorrect.

"You've got to give me a reason to trust you," Luhnow told one scout.

Again: a reasonable expectation, and an overly blunt way of conveying it.

One move that even Luhnow came to realize went too far came after he scrutinized the form that Cardinals scouts filled out on each player they watched. At the bottom of the sheet was a box that asked the scout for a simple recommendation regarding the player he had evaluated: acquire or don't acquire.

"What the fuck does that even mean?" Luhnow asked a colleague, correctly noting that the choice was too reductive.

The decision whether or not to acquire a player involved roster and payroll considerations, among other factors. It wasn't useful to simply vote yes or no without a discussion of context.

Luhnow had the box removed from the form, and scouts flipped out. It turned out that they liked to feel that they had some influence over these decisions, even if it was false. Luhnow restored the question and admitted to his inner circle that he should have just left it on and ignored the answers.

In October 2007, less than a year after the Cardinals' first World Series title since 1982, DeWitt fired Jocketty and named Mozeliak GM. Luhnow had fully secured his power base, and he continued to push the Cardinals and their scouts toward what he saw as a smarter approach to player procurement.

Evaluators who had worked for other organizations noticed a seriousness of purpose during Luhnow's drafts that they had not seen elsewhere. Even in the later rounds, when many teams lose focus, Luhnow and his staff bore down, searching for hidden value.

The 2009 amateur draft was a highlight that defined his time in St. Louis. Luhnow selected five players who would go on to contribute to the team that reached the 2013 World Series: pitchers Shelby Miller, Trevor Rosenthal and Joe Kelly and infielders Matt Carpenter and Matt Adams. Adams came out of the twenty-third round and hit seventeen home runs in 2013.

Luhnow would go on to earn widespread praise in the industry for that draft, as the Cardinals advanced through October in 2013 and ultimately lost in the Series to Boston in six games.

But Luhnow would enjoy those accolades from afar, for by then he was running the Houston Astros.

Houston's National League franchise opened for business in 1962, the same year as the New York Mets.

While the latter team hired an aging Casey Stengel to manage, dropped a record 120 games, and developed a brand identity as baseball's lovable losers, the Houston Colt .45s—renamed the Astros in 1965—were simply bad for many years and with little redeeming charm.

Houston didn't make the playoffs until 1980, and though they fielded some excellent teams in the eighties and nineties, didn't see a World Series until 2005.

That pennant-winning club, led by veterans like Roger Clemens, Andy Pettitte, Lance Berkman, and Craig Biggio, lacked the high-end farm system that would have rendered their success sustainable. By 2009 the Astros were back in fifth place.

In May 2011, a group led by businessman Jim Crane purchased the team for $680 million from the previous owner, Drayton McLane. Crane, who had pitched for Central Missouri State University in the 1970s, was a successful but controversial figure in the business world.

The company he built, Eagle USA Airfreight (later Eagle Global Logistics), had been the subject of a lengthy critical report issued by the Equal Employment Opportunity Commission, and had also been sued for war profiteering.

As the *Houston Chronicle* reported, the EEOC found that Eagle paid "female and minority employees less than white men who do similar work; did not investigate employee complaints of sexual harassment; and destroyed evidence that the company was instructed to retain as part of the two-year EEOC investigation."

Crane himself was accused of advising managers not to hire African Americans, saying, "Once you hire blacks, you can never fire them." The company paid $8.5 million in settlements related to the claims.

In 2006, the U.S. Justice Department brought the war-profiteering suit, claiming that Crane's company had jacked up the prices on military shipments to Iraq. Eagle paid a $4 million settlement.

As part of Crane's deal with Major League Baseball to buy the Astros, he agreed to move the team to the American League. This was important to the commissioner, Bud Selig, because it evened the leagues at fifteen teams apiece—important enough, in fact, that MLB and McLane reduced the purchase price by $65 million because Crane agreed to the move.

On November 17, 2011, the league's other twenty-nine owners voted unanimously to approve Crane's purchase of the Astros.

Almost immediately, Crane fired general manager Ed Wade and set about remaking the organization on every level. He was looking for cost-effective, repeatable success.

Three weeks later, at the industry's winter meetings at the Hilton Anatole hotel in Dallas, Crane offered the GM job to Luhnow.

After accepting, Luhnow called an ally from the Cardinals' front office and said, "Now we're going to do all the things we always talked about doing."

He started by bringing a few key people with him, including Strom, the pitching coach, whose willingness to try creative ideas cast him as a crackpot in the Cardinals organization, but endeared him to Luhnow.

Luhnow also poached Sig Mejdal, a former NASA engineer who had left that career to pursue his dream of working in baseball and ended up as an analyst for Luhnow in St. Louis.

With the Astros, Luhnow created for Mejdal the title "Director of Decision Sciences." One can imagine how older baseball folks reacted to that one.

Rounding out his team, Luhnow hired Mike Fast, an expert at advanced statistics, a writer for the innovative analytics website *Baseball Prospectus,* and a former semiconductor engineer.

He brought in Kevin Goldstein, another mild-mannered *BP* writer, who reported to work wearing the type of fedora that was trendy in 2010-era Brooklyn, but rarely seen at ballparks.

"Scouting games in a fucking fedora?" one veteran scout sneered upon seeing Goldstein at a ballpark during his first year, unwittingly demonstrating just how hostile the industry could be to even the smallest unfamiliar detail.

Luhnow also hired a young Harvard graduate named David Stearns as assistant GM; Stearns would go on to enjoy a successful run as GM of the Milwaukee Brewers. Yale grad Mike Elias was a special assistant for scouting; he would later be hired to run the Baltimore Orioles.

It was a group marked by Ivy League degrees and real-world experience, and an uncommon quantity of former media members. Luhnow, true to character, had assembled a front office that looked different from anyone else's.

The group inherited several young players who would later prove impactful, from outfield prospect George Springer to second baseman José Altuve to pitcher Dallas Keuchel.

Springer was a large man—six feet three and all muscle—but a kind soul. A Connecticut native who hailed from a tight family, he fought shyness caused by a childhood stutter. He was Ed Wade's final first-round draft choice in 2011.

Altuve signed out of Venezuela in 2007 and made his major league debut in 2011. Listed generously at five feet six, he overcame extreme skepticism that a player his size could make it in the big leagues. He would go on to become a batting champion, MVP, and perennial All-Star.

Keuchel, a seventh-round pick in 2009, had yet to find his way—but he would. Pitching with a Mennonite-style beard and cerebral approach, Keuchel utilized data from the Astros front office to help him win the American League Cy Young Award in 2015.

Those successes were far away in 2011, when the Astros finished with 106 losses, the most in baseball. That meant they had the first overall selection in Luhnow's first draft, an occasion that he used to supplement Springer, Altuve, and Keuchel with two additional big pieces.

In the first round, the Astros chose Carlos Correa, a seventeen-year-old shortstop from Ponce, Puerto Rico. Correa was known for stunning but raw talent, and a smooth personality that seemed polished beyond his years.

When scouts or reporters spoke to him, even at that age, he looked them in the eye and addressed them in a manner more typical of a big leaguer in his mid-twenties.

With their next pick, the forty-first overall, the Astros selected Lance McCullers Jr., a right-handed pitcher out of Jesuit High School in Tampa, Florida, and the son of a big leaguer.

Houston's farm system was already on the mend, though the big-league team remained years away from winning. That was partly by design, as Luhnow had proposed to Crane a style of rebuilding that looked exactly like tanking, the strategy of completely sacrificing the present in order to accelerate the return to success.

With a typical lack of concern for appearances, Luhnow reasoned that as long as the Astros weren't going to contend for a championship, they might as well trim payroll, lose as many games as possible, and enjoy the savings and high draft picks that resulted. What was the difference between winning seventy-five games and winning sixty-five, anyway?

Of course, that thinking didn't account for the visceral difficulty that players, fans, and even executives had to endure during the long and boring years of losing.

One April night in 2014, an Astros game registered a 0.0 Nielsen rating—essentially no one in Houston, not old fans and certainly not youngsters cultivating a love for the game, could be bothered with the Astros. The team wasn't trying to win that year, so why should anyone spend any time or money to watch them?

Crane surely didn't mind the cost-cutting aspect of this plan. During the 2012 season, Luhnow traded his highest-paid veterans, pitchers Brett Myers and Wandy Rodriguez and slugger Carlos Lee. The Astros opened the 2013 season with a $26 million payroll, lowest in the league.

In August 2012, Luhnow had fired inherited manager Brad Mills. That winter, he made his own selection for that important job, settling on the boisterous and self-assured Washington Nationals coach Bo Porter, one of the coaches who had undermined A. J. Hinch in the Arizona clubhouse in 2010.

During Porter's first spring training with the Astros, Luhnow boasted to a reporter that his new manager could last in the job for "decades"—quite a few years longer than even the most lauded contemporary skippers tended to remain employed.

Like many of Luhnow's ventures in Houston, Porter's tenure did not go quite as hoped. By 2014, the two had fallen out and Luhnow fired him.

In several other ways, that season represented the worst of the pre–sign-stealing Astros. For the first time, many of the darker aspects of Luhnow's culture bled into public view.

Houston again had the top pick in the June draft, and used it to select Brady Aiken, a left-handed pitcher out of California. Aiken and the Astros agreed to a $6.5 million signing bonus and scheduled the standard physical exam.

Because $6.5 million was less than the recommended slot value for a first overall pick, the Astros used the savings to offer $1.5 million—way above slot—to fifth-round pick Jacob Nix. Nix was a friend of Aiken's, and both traveled to Houston with their agent, Casey Close.

But rather than unveil their two new prospects in a celebratory news conference, the Astros waited several days, then reduced their offer to Aiken to $3.1 million.

That number was significant, because it represented exactly 40 percent of the slot value for a first overall pick. By MLB rules, 40 percent was the threshold at which the Astros could get a compensatory pick the following year if they didn't sign Aiken.

It turned out that the physical exam, which included an MRI of the left elbow, raised significant concerns about Aiken's long-term health. Luhnow determined that the team was better off losing him and taking the compensation pick.

A wave of public criticism, stronger than Luhnow had ever experienced, hit the Astros. Close, an agent who almost never spoke to the media, condemned the team in a pointed interview with Fox Sports reporter Ken Rosenthal.

"We are extremely disappointed that Major League Baseball is allowing the Astros to conduct business in this manner with a complete disregard for the rules governing the draft and the twenty-nine other clubs who have followed those same rules," Close said.

"Brady has been seen by some of the most experienced and respected orthopedic arm specialists in the country, and all of those doctors have acknowledged that he's not injured and that he's ready to start his professional career."

Tony Clark, head of the Players Association, accused the Astros of "manipulation"—essentially using Aiken as a pawn to acquire another pick and try again in a year.

Media condemnation was swift and widespread. Sensitive to criticism, Crane told Luhnow to up his offer. But it was too late. Close and Aiken did not want to do business with the Astros and did not even respond to Luhnow's $5 million olive branch.

Nix was collateral damage, because once the Astros lost Aiken's slot money by failing to sign him, they could no longer allot a piece of it to pay Nix. The two friends went home unsigned.

The following year, Aiken announced his intention to enroll in the IMG Academy's postgraduate baseball program, in order to reset his draft status. During the first inning of his first start there, Aiken left the game with elbow discomfort. Shortly after, he underwent Tommy John surgery. He would never pitch in the major leagues.

The Astros' medical opinion had been validated; they had been right to reject Aiken.

It wasn't until years later, with the benefit of the sobering hindsight caused by a different ethics scandal, that members of Luhnow's inner circle thought, Maybe we were right on principle but screwed up the human side of it.

The Aiken mess was only the beginning of the trouble that 2014 brought. On June 30, *Deadspin* published leaked contents of the Astros' internal database, which was called Ground Control.

The leaks contained information embarrassing to both the Astros and other clubs. Among the many revelations, it showed that the Miami Marlins had been willing to trade their star slugger, Giancarlo Stanton, for Carlos Correa and George Springer, and the Astros were trying to dump pitcher Bud Norris.

Luhnow was forced to apologize to the players of his who were named, and to the teams that saw private discussions aired out on the Internet.

When he found out the following summer who was responsible for the leak, it was another shock. Chris Correa (no relation to Carlos), an analyst under Luhnow with the Cardinals, had hacked into Sig Mejdal's Astros email account and obtained full access to Ground Control.

Correa had apparently been motivated by an old interoffice rivalry with Mejdal, in addition to media coverage praising Luhnow and Mejdal's work with a Houston team that hadn't even won anything yet.

Correa claimed that the Astros had hacked first, and he was looking through Ground Control for information stolen from the Cards' database, Redbird Dog.

"On December 21, 2011, the Houston Astros employee accessed proprietary data on a St. Louis Cardinals server," Correa would claim in a statement.

"Later I would learn—through unlawful methods—that Cardinals data were used extensively from 2012 through 2014. Houston Astros employees used the data to replicate and evaluate key algorithms and decision tools related to amateur and professional player evaluation. Many individuals throughout the Houston organization, including the General Manager and Assistant General Manager, were included in e-mail discussions about these efforts."

In 2016 a judge sentenced Correa to forty-six months in federal prison and ordered him to pay $279,000. Major League Baseball banned him for life. The issue of whether anyone from the Astros got away with hacking remained a he said/he said proposition.

The Astros' problems in 2014 did not stop with front-office drama. This was also when clubhouse unrest over the Astros' data-driven approach boiled over into public view.

On May 23, beat reporter Evan Drellich of the *Houston Chronicle* published a story headlined RADICAL METHODS PAINT ASTROS AS "OUTCAST."

Drellich wrote of "pockets of internal discontent and a potential reputation problem throughout baseball," and quoted pitchers Bud Norris and Jarred Cosart.

Norris, a veteran, was the one to use the word "outcast," and said that agents and other players around the league held the Astros' front office in low regard.

An anonymous Astros player added, "I don't think anybody's happy. I'm not. They just take out the human element of baseball. It's hard to play for a GM who just sees you as a number instead of a person. Jeff is experimenting with all of us."

Luhnow defended his tactics and continued to believe that the organization was on a path to success. But he did need a better voice for the players, a manager who could help to translate the front office's ideas to change-averse athletes.

Doing diligence on one of the potential candidates, Luhnow called Josh Byrnes, now an executive with the Dodgers.

"You need A.J.," Byrnes told him, "even more than A.J. needs you."

Chapter 9

THE YANKEES AND THE DODGERS OPEN THEIR WINDOWS

In July 2016, Yankees general manager Brian Cashman finally executed an idea he'd been entertaining for several years: He traded away star players and stopped trying to win.

For the Yankees, this counted as a revolutionary decision. Throughout his previous two decades on the job, Cashman had operated with the burden of George Steinbrenner–size expectations, and that left no room for rebuilding.

Steinbrenner believed that the Yankees were supposed to win a championship every season. He considered any other outcome a failure, and since he was the owner, that pressure trickled down.

Though the Yankees benefited from Steinbrenner's willingness to spend money, they suffered from his impatience, which had practical consequences. He wanted championships so badly that he was almost always willing to trade away young players for veterans.

Cashman had long yearned to pursue a more sustainable approach. He wanted a farm system that produced homegrown talent, so he didn't have to chase free agents every year, many of whom failed to provide value.

He had been there for the previous Yankees dynasty, and knew that it had happened only as a result of the player-development model to which he sought a return.

In the early 1990s, Major League Baseball suspended Steinbrenner for two years for hiring a gambler to dig up dirt on one of his own players, Dave Winfield. In the Boss's absence, general manager Gene Michael, a legendarily hawk-eyed evaluator of players, was able to run the team without interference.

Rather than trade away prospects for veterans, Michael identified players who would help in the future, and he kept them.

The Yankees watched as Derek Jeter, Bernie Williams, Andy Pettitte, Mariano Rivera, and others rose through the farm system.

During the Michael years, Cashman enjoyed the benefit of a close-up view. With help from a business connection between his father and Steinbrenner, he'd started with the Yankees as a college intern in 1986. When he graduated from Catholic University, he took a low-level job in baseball operations.

Studious and politically savvy, Cashman worked his way up. While learning the finer points of the game, he leaned on Michael and scouting director Bill Livesey, another lifer with a sharp eye.

The Yankees under Michael were early adopters of the offensive approach later popularized in *Moneyball,* in which walks and on-base percentage were more important than batting average and stolen-base attempts. Using his eyes and instincts, Michael arrived at many of the same conclusions as Sandy Alderson and Billy Beane did using data in Oakland.

Within a few years the Yankees had recovered from a fallow period and were on the verge of dynasty. They reached the playoffs in 1995 for the first time in fourteen years.

MLB reinstated Steinbrenner in time for that playoff run, and the subsequent championships in 1996, 1998, 1999, and 2000—all with the core built and held together while Michael was GM.

Michael and Steinbrenner were usually on their last nerve with each other, and Michael's final year as GM was that 1995 season. By then Cashman was assistant GM, and he remained in that job under Bob Watson, who succeeded Michael.

Watson lasted just two seasons with Steinbrenner. When he

stepped down in 1997, Steinbrenner made the thirty-year-old Cashman the youngest GM in the game.

Michael had built a strong foundation, and Cashman was doing what he could to maintain it, though that was not as easy as it should have been. By the early years of the twenty-first century, Steinbrenner again began to undermine his team's success.

The owner's addiction to big-time free agents resurfaced, leaving Cashman and manager Joe Torre to watch the slow evaporation of the special chemistry that had defined their finest seasons.

After losing the 2004 American League Championship Series to Boston in historic fashion—the once-unstoppable Yankees had led in the series 3–0 before collapsing—Jeter stood in a mournful clubhouse and told reporters, "It's not the same team."

Through these years, when the Yankees were still winning division titles but losing every year in the playoffs, Cashman began to see more clearly that the Yankee way needed to change.

He noticed that the best front offices, like Theo Epstein's in Boston and Billy Beane's in Oakland, based their decisions on data more often than emotion.

In 2005, the Yankees lost in the first round of the playoffs to the younger, cheaper Los Angeles Angels. Steinbrenner raged to his baseball operations staff.

Cashman's contract was up. He was losing sleep over the organization's messy chain of command, where some people reported to him and others tried to undermine him with a direct line to Steinbrenner. Unlike the A's, the Red Sox, or other smart teams, the Yankees lacked a unifying baseball philosophy or vision.

Steinbrenner and Cashman argued, and both began to suspect that the GM might find a better fit elsewhere. Cashman had no shortage of other opportunities and wondered if he should leave the Yankees to pursue one. Finally, Steinbrenner softened and offered Cashman more power.

Cashman signed a new contract and devised a flowchart in which every baseball department reported to him. Within two years, he had a new manager, Joe Girardi, who was more receptive to data than the iconic but increasingly disengaged Torre had been.

Still, it wasn't easy to build a team the right way in New York. Internal distractions persisted, like when Alex Rodriguez opted out of his ten-year, $252 million contract during the 2007 World Series. Cashman did not plan to pursue a reunion, and he began to dream about all the ways he could spread around that money to improve the organization.

Then team president Randy Levine and ownership worked around him, cutting a side deal with a few Goldman Sachs bankers representing A-Rod. The third baseman ended up with a brand-new, record-setting ten-year deal.

A-Rod starred in the 2009 postseason, leading the Yankees to their only off-dynasty championship. But from then on, his descent into injury and scandal served as symbols of the club's dreary decline.

In order to win in 2009, Cashman had supplemented his aging core with veteran big-money free agents CC Sabathia, A. J. Burnett, and Mark Teixeira. It worked, but it wasn't the model he needed long-term.

George Steinbrenner died in 2010, and his son Hal assumed control of the team. Hal was marked by two characteristics that his father did not possess, patience and relative financial restraint.

While still willing to flex on free agents when Cashman deemed them essential, Hal was uninterested in throwing good money after bad—and he was open to giving Cashman the time to build a winner from within.

The vision that the GM had laid out for George Steinbrenner back in 2005 could finally become fully real under Hal, who was not only willing to grant Cashman power but had the temperament to hang back and let him fully exercise it.

By 2013, the Yankees were only half-trying to make the playoffs. With veterans like Jeter, A-Rod, and Teixeira either retiring or slowed by injuries, Cashman plugged their spots with journeymen, not stars.

Privately, he made the case to Steinbrenner that the team should go into a full rebuild, like the Astros were currently doing under Jeff Luhnow. But the Yankees were too reliant on their winning brand, not to mention attendance and TV ratings.

Cashman was granted a compromise: Prioritize the farm system over championships for a few years but remain competitive on the major league level.

Now the pressure was on Cashman to build the next Yankees dynasty. He had already assembled a front office as loyal to him as he once was to Gene Michael and Bill Livesey.

Former Red Sox infielder Tim Naehring was the Yankees' top evaluator, possessing the only scouting eye that Cashman had ever regarded as comparable to Michael's. Naehring was the rare ex-player in a front office who was not only open to new data, but skilled at translating it to reluctant coaches.

Most of that data came from Michael Fishman and his team. Fishman joined the Yankees in 2005 as their first analyst. A decade later he was an assistant GM, overseeing a staff of more than twenty number crunchers, one of the largest analytics departments in the game. He had played a major role in transforming the Yankees into one of the game's most analytically inclined teams.

Jean Afterman was Cashman's assistant GM for legal issues, contracts, and general advice. An attorney who once worked on the agency side of the business, Afterman was now one of the highest-ranking female executives in the game.

She could outthink, out-yell, and out-curse most of her male counterparts. Her office at Yankee Stadium shared a wall with Cashman's, and the GM used her as a frequent sounding board for ideas.

This group toiled for several years to reconstruct the Yankees from the bottom up.

That project had actually started all the way back in 2009, while the expensive veterans were busy winning the World Series, and the team's international scouts signed a sixteen-year-old catcher out of the Dominican Republic named Gary Sánchez. Sánchez was left untouched as he developed through the minor league system; Cashman had no intention of trading him.

The same went for Aaron Judge, a towering outfielder drafted thirty-second overall in 2013. And for Luis Severino, a right-handed pitcher signed out of the Dominican Republic in 2011. And Greg Bird, a promising first baseman drafted in the fifth round in 2011. The Yankees simply weren't going to part with players of this caliber.

Meanwhile, the plug-and-play approach to the big-league team had proven surprisingly effective. The Yankees somehow snuck into the wild-card game in 2015, a year when they held no illusions about being a championship-caliber club.

They lost to a dominant Dallas Keuchel and an Astros team enjoying its first trip to the postseason under Luhnow.

The following summer, the Yankees took an even bigger leap into the unfamiliar. Knowing his team was not a serious contender, Cashman for the first time decided to act as a trade-deadline seller.

In July, rather than chasing deals that could help him squeak into the playoffs, he flipped star relievers Aroldis Chapman to the Cubs and Andrew Miller to the Indians, both in exchange for prospects. He traded Carlos Beltrán to Texas, also for minor leaguers.

In return for Chapman, Cashman had found a franchise-altering return in top infield prospect Gleyber Torres. That winter, the Yankees re-signed Chapman as a free agent, securing the ninth inning for years to come.

By then, the team's fans were already enjoying the fruits of this rebuild. In 2015, Bird exploded onto the scene, hitting 11 home runs in 46 games. Severino arrived the same year, posting a 2.89 earned run average in his first 11 starts.

The 2016 season brought even more excitement for a fan base that hadn't seen this much homegrown talent in two decades. Judge made his debut in August, and Sanchez stunned all of baseball by hitting 20 home runs in 53 games.

Another championship window had opened. Now Cashman had to prove he had designed his own dynasty.

He knew that in baseball, windows remain open for only a few years.

Clayton Kershaw stood in the middle of a swarm of reporters, his voice quiet, his eyes on the floor.

"There's no way to explain it," he said, nearly vibrating with frustration.

Kershaw was twenty-five years old and about to win his third Cy Young Award for the Los Angeles Dodgers. He seemed on his way to joining the short list of the greatest pitchers in the history of the game.

But in Game Six of the 2013 National League Championship Series, a series in which he had already lost once, Kershaw found himself embarrassed by the St. Louis Cardinals. In the fourth inning, Cards batters mauled him for four runs. In the fifth, Kershaw allowed three more without recording an out.

The Cardinals won the game 9–0, eliminated the Dodgers, and moved on to the World Series. Carlos Beltrán was on that St. Louis team, and scouting circles buzzed with gossip that the Cardinals had figured out how Kershaw tipped his pitches.

That January, accepting his Cy Young at the annual Baseball Writers' Association of America dinner in New York, Kershaw thanked the Cardinals "for reminding me that you're never as good as you think you are."

The ghastliness of Kershaw's October failure planted the first ominous seeds of a burden that he was about to start carrying, the question of whether he could win when it mattered most.

One year and one more playoff loss later, the Dodgers took a significant step toward surrounding Kershaw with a perennially contending team and providing opportunities for redemption: Ownership poached the highly sought-after executive Andrew Friedman from the Tampa Bay Rays.

For nine seasons, Friedman and his group had dazzled the industry by fielding competitive teams in Tampa, including a pennant winner in 2008, despite some of the lowest payrolls in the game.

Friedman arrived in Los Angeles with a mandate of breaking a championship drought that had lasted far longer than the one currently frustrating Brian Cashman and the Yankees. One of the game's storied franchises, the Dodgers hadn't hoisted a banner since Kirk Gibson made his triumphant limp around the bases in 1988.

The recent past had been ugly, as owner Frank McCourt went through a bank-breaking divorce and lost control of the team. In March 2012, Guggenheim Baseball Management LLC, a group led by CEO Mark Walter and NBA great Magic Johnson, purchased the team for more than $2 billion.

The Guggenheim group quickly commenced a spending spree, signing or trading for stars like pitcher Zack Greinke and sluggers Adrián González and Hanley Ramírez. These were temporary measures to restore competitiveness; like the Yankees, the Dodgers knew that the best systems were rooted in player development and organizational stability.

When Friedman arrived to replace deposed GM Ned Colletti, he assumed the title of president of baseball operations and assembled his front-office dream team.

He made the highly regarded Oakland A's executive Farhan Zaidi his GM. He brought in Josh Byrnes as his director of player personnel, and within a few years would have former Toronto GM Alex Anthopoulos on his staff, too.

Operating like a West Coast version of the Red Sox or the Yankees, the Dodgers combined big data with big spending, and devoted considerable resources to beefing up analytics and research and development.

The Dodgers made the playoffs again in 2015 but lost in the division series. Friedman fired manager Don Mattingly and brought in Dave Roberts.

Roberts was a steady, self-assured former speedster who understood what a contemporary manager was supposed to do: serve as a conduit between the front office and players, shaping the baseball operations strategy in ways that athletes could understand and buy into.

Like the best of his contemporaries, Roberts focused on establishing a strong presence in the clubhouse and understood that decisions were collaborative.

Meanwhile, Kershaw's postseason troubles continued to accumulate. In 2014, the year after the Cardinals first stunned him, they did it again, punishing him for eight runs in Game One of the National League Division Series.

In Game Four, Kershaw pitched with his team facing elimination. The Dodgers led 2–0 in the seventh inning, but Kershaw allowed a three-run homer to Matt Holliday, spoiling another season.

It happened yet again in 2016, when he lost to the Cubs in Game Six of the NLCS, costing the Dodgers yet another chance at a World Series appearance.

As 2017 began, Kershaw and the Dodgers were as hungry as the Yankees and Cashman, maybe hungrier. While the Yanks were coming out of a down period that felt extreme to them, they had been able to celebrate five championships in the time since the Dodgers had last captured one of their own.

Kershaw was rounding into his late twenties, when most pitchers begin to fall off their physical peak. Like Cashman, he was facing increased urgency to prove he could win while his own window was still open.

Chapter 10

THE ELECTRONIC-SIGN-STEALING ERA KICKS INTO HIGH GEAR

E arly in spring training of 2016 in Fort Myers, Florida, Red Sox outfielder Chris Young called a meeting with the pitching staff.

This was unusual for a number of reasons.

One, Young was a position player. Hitters and pitchers interact as little as possible, and certainly don't tend to hold meetings for one another. Two, Young was a soft-spoken fourth outfielder, not a vocal leader or a star. Three, he was brand new to the team, having arrived as a free agent after a stint with the Yankees.

But while in New York, Young had spent many hours in the replay room with Carlos Beltrán and Alex Rodriguez, scrutinizing video of opposing pitchers and catchers to decode sign sequences and pitch tipping.

While doing so, he learned of an important weakness in Boston. When he signed with that team, he brought the information as an urgent message to Red Sox pitchers.

"It's too easy to pick your signs from second base," Young told them in the meeting. "You need to change your signs more often."

Naturally, discussions about that soon came to include talk of how the Red Sox could themselves figure out an opponent's sequences. Soon Young was doing with teammates what Beltrán and A-Rod had done with him in New York over the previous few years.

Boston's early forays into sign stealing were old-school and legal. Whenever Young reached second base, he would get to work looking in at the catcher and figuring out what sequence he was using.

Was it "chase the two," when the real sign came after the catcher flashed the number two? Or "outs plus one," when the sign followed the number of outs in the inning? Or another pattern?

In 2016, before electronic sign stealing became widely suspected and teams defended against it by making their sequences far more complicated, it wasn't particularly difficult to break an opponent's code from second base. Most teams used only one or two sequences, and even that was more than many pitchers wanted.

Oftentimes, catchers would find themselves frustrated by batterymates who asked to stick with the same sequence for an entire game—or, worse, to go with the Little League–level signs of one finger for fastball, two for curveball, and so on, without any variation.

As one catcher told his pitcher in a mound conference in 2015, after the pitcher asked him to use 1-2-3, "Why don't you just go ahead and tell the runner at second what you're going to throw?"

It was understandable that pitchers wanted to avoid cluttering their minds with the need to remember indicators and complex sequences. But that mentality made it much easier for a player like Young to break the relatively simple codes from second base.

After he figured out the signs, Young would signal to the batter by hopping on the base, looking into the outfield, or taking a step to his right or left.

The Red Sox won their first of three straight American League East titles that year and were swept in the division series by Cleveland.

In 2017 they started slowly, finishing April with a 13-11 record. But by the end of July they were ten games over .500, well on their way to squeaking past the Yankees to win the division by two games.

They were also building camaraderie by huddling in the Fenway Park replay room, looking at catchers' sign sequences and figuring them out. In his quiet way, Young had emerged as a leader on the team, teaching and bringing people together.

The Red Sox started holding meetings in the clubhouse before games, during which they would present information gathered from the video room.

"This is what the starter uses," they would tell one another. "These are his patterns."

Players would take that information to second base, knowing what to look for and making it easier to get that sign to the batter.

Not everyone was convinced. Just as Mark Teixeira had done with the Yankees over the past few years, several Red Sox players and coaches criticized the process as not accurate enough to be reliable.

"You guys are wrong like three-quarters of the time," one coach said to a group of players that summer.

But many Red Sox felt differently, believing that they had found a way to gain an advantage over pitchers.

It was a short but significant leap from there to the use of Apple Watches.

As spring turned to summer in 2017, teams around baseball became more attuned to the possibility that opponents might be using increasingly sophisticated methods to steal their signs, perhaps even electronics.

No one seemed to know exactly what was happening—were there hidden cameras? Were the TV networks helping?—but more hitters than ever seemed to be swinging with too much confidence, like they knew what was coming.

It was the fourth season of the instant-replay room, and teams seemed to be pushing further into an ethical gray area in their use of that resource.

The Yankees and Red Sox were especially suspicious of each other. This was not surprising, given their longtime rivalry, which rendered anything that the two teams touched more intense. In this case, both clubs knew about Chris Young's skills, meaning that both were well aware of what the other was capable of doing.

For several months, the Yankees chased a strong inkling that the Red Sox were getting their signs. They were sure it was happening but couldn't find proof.

During an August series in New York, the Sox developed their own suspicions, when they believed that the Yankees were shooting footage of manager John Farrell as he passed signs from the dugout to third-base coach Brian Butterfield.

Teams often designated a coach to give decoy signs for strategies like stealing, bunting, and hit-and-run, and one of the challenges for an opponent was to identify the chain of command for the real signs. For the Red Sox that year, it was Farrell to Butterfield, and they began to think the Yankees were on it.

That led to paranoia about the dugout, and the materials in it.

Red Sox coaches typically taped sheets of paper containing information from their advance scouts to the wall behind the bench. That week they had sheets showing catchers who tip pitches—Yankees backstop Gary Sánchez was known to telegraph the fastball by rising up in his crouch when expecting one—and how to position infielders. There was also a sheet about how the Yankees pitchers tipped.

Farrell instructed first-base coach Rubén Amaro Jr. to remove all papers from the walls. He and his staff suspected that the Yankees were using cameras from their rights holder, the YES Network, to zoom in on the details.

The Yankees would always strongly deny this, and on that charge had logic and history on their side.

No club had ever been credibly accused of coordinating with its TV network to spy on an opponent. It was just too difficult: The broadcast was run by a director out of a truck, and he or she worked for the network, not the team.

The same went for camera operators. They didn't coordinate or even interact with baseball operations personnel. A club and a TV network might have a business affiliation, but rank-and-file employees did not function as coworkers.

But while the Red Sox were wrong about the method, they were right to think the Yankees were watching, considering it their duty to monitor the opponent.

Footage available to the replay rooms could be rewound and rewatched after games. Yankees replay coordinator Brett Weber, like many of his counterparts around the league, would review the tape to see if he could pick up anything interesting.

The way his Yankees bosses viewed it, if the Red Sox were dumb enough to attach advance scouting reports to the dugout wall during games, it was fair game for Weber to look at them.

The Yankees had a nagging sense that the Sox were doing even more and going way beyond picking signs from second base with their eyes. For months, they stewed about it, believing that something was off.

On Friday, August 18, they were finally able to prove it.

It's part of any replay coordinator's job to play defense against possible cheating by the opponent, and on this night Weber was paying particular attention.

Nine different times in the game, the Red Sox had a runner on second base. They had a hit in five of those at-bats.

The first came with two out and nobody on in the second inning, when Xander Bogaerts doubled off Yankees starter Jordan Montgomery. Rafael Devers followed with a home run.

In the replay room, Weber had fourteen or fifteen different camera angles available to him at all times, coming from TV cameras all over the ballpark.

It was similar to what the director viewed in the truck, when he or she chose which of the many available shots to air. The difference for Weber was that he did not control the camera operators and was at the mercy of what they and their director chose to shoot.

At Fenway, there were two cameras positioned in a way that could help Weber as he tried to prove that the Red Sox were cheating.

One was called the "high third," which was on the upper level of the third-base side. The other was the Monster Cam, which was stationed on the tall left-field wall nicknamed the Green Monster. Both would occasionally point into the home dugout, which was on the first-base side.

Looking closely at the feeds from those two cameras when a runner was on second, Weber finally caught it.

Red Sox assistant trainer Jon Jochim would look at an Apple Watch, and then walk quickly over to a player. Second baseman Dustin Pedroia and utility man Brock Holt were among the players whom Jochim approached.

Once he reached the players on foot, Jochim would engage in a whispered conversation—not normal behavior for members of the same team in the dugout.

Then Holt or Pedroia would make a hand signal to the runner on second, who would relay the pitch to the batter. One of the shots showed Chris Young as the runner on second.

Weber gathered evidence over the course of two games, and then presented it to manager Joe Girardi in the replay room.

Girardi agreed that the evidence was damning. He shot a video of the replay monitor with his phone and sent it to general manager Brian Cashman.

"I want to show you the things that stood out to us," Girardi told Cashman, walking him through the evidence.

Cashman forwarded the video to Peter Woodfork, MLB's senior vice president of operations, and the league commenced an investigation that would change the rules of the game forever.

Robert D. Manfred Jr. became commissioner of baseball on January 25, 2015. Long the heir apparent to his predecessor, Allan H.

"Bud" Selig, Manfred had spent decades as the league's point person on labor issues and negotiations with the union.

His personality suited that role: He was blunt, shrewd, and pragmatic.

With hair only slightly longer than a military commander's, Manfred looked and sounded the part of a hard-nosed dealmaker. A native of Rome, New York, about forty miles west of Syracuse, he spoke with the sharp western New York accent that recalls the movie *Fargo:* The name Bob becomes "Bahb" and the city of Rochester is "Rahchester."

Often sarcastic in a way that could read as cutting or dismissive, Manfred spat his accented words through a gap between his two front teeth.

As MLB's chief operating officer in 2013, Manfred, as one of his final duties before replacing Selig, coordinated the league's investigation of Alex Rodriguez's PED use.

A-Rod had been a client of Biogenesis, an "anti-aging" clinic run out of a Coral Gables, Florida, strip mall by a PED supplier named Tony Bosch. Manfred sought enough evidence to issue a long ban.

The lessons that Manfred drew from that experience reveal much about how he would later handle the intense pressure brought on by the Astros scandal.

The fight between MLB and A-Rod was a bare-knuckle affair. Selig's view on the issue was black and white: Steroids had tarnished his legacy as commissioner, and he wanted to bring down A-Rod as a symbolic trophy that would prove how tough he had become on the issue. Doing so would burnish his case to make the Baseball Hall of Fame.

At Selig's direction, Manfred unleashed the league's Department of Investigations on South Florida. Selig had created the DOI on the recommendation of former U.S. Senator George Mitchell's 2007 report on PEDs in baseball. To run it, he'd appointed former NYPD detective Dan Mullin, who staffed it with other ex-cops.

Down in Miami, Mullin and his crew hunted for concrete evidence that A-Rod had used PEDs supplied by Biogenesis.

In March 2013, Manfred authorized Mullin to spend $100,000 to purchase four flash drives containing Biogenesis records from a shady character named Gary Jones. Mullin made the transaction by sliding an envelope stuffed with hundred-dollar bills across the table to Jones at a diner in Pompano Beach.

A few weeks later, Mullin spent another $25,000 of MLB's money on Biogenesis ledgers and photos.

MLB had purchased stolen documents, though the league would later strongly deny knowing that their source had obtained the material illegally.

On January 12, 2014, CBS News reporter Scott Pelley asked Manfred on *60 Minutes* if A-Rod had tried to have a man killed.

"Are you saying that Alex Rodriguez and/or his associates were involved in threatening to kill Tony Bosch?" Pelley said.

"I don't know what Mr. Rodriguez knew," said Manfred, then MLB's chief operating officer.

"I know that the individual involved has been an associate of Mr. Rodriguez for some time."

That "individual" was convicted steroid dealer Jorge "Ugi" Velazquez, a former liquor store owner, A-Rod acquaintance, and well-known figure in the Miami underworld.

Velazquez had sent a text message indicating that Bosch would not live to see the end of the year.

During that time, MLB and A-Rod lobbed allegations back and forth about threats of violence, stolen evidence, and improper investigative techniques. A-Rod felt unfairly persecuted; MLB thought that goons working on his behalf engaged in intimidation tactics, including threats of murder.

What Manfred did next showed that he was more pragmatic than Selig, and more capable of understanding the complexity of cheating in his sport.

First, he began listening to Bosch, the man who had caused him so much trouble. As MLB's chief witness against A-Rod, Bosch was in New York for an extended period as the appeal hearing dragged on.

Bosch and Manfred had many detailed conversations about the latest PED trends, and why players would always try to cheat. Where Selig threw around the term "post-steroid era" in an attempt to imply that PED use had stopped, Manfred demonstrated to Bosch a far better understanding that drugs were a perennial threat.

Bosch came to admire Manfred as someone who realized that players in the game he oversaw would always try to cheat, and that he would always be in need of updated information about how they did it.

Later, after becoming commissioner of baseball, Manfred would make another calculation that one could read as savvy, cynical, or both: He decided to welcome A-Rod back into the game's good graces.

Toward the end of his suspension, Rodriguez and his attorney had quietly slunk into Manfred's Park Avenue office and apologized, then solicited advice on how to rehabilitate A-Rod's image and career.

Manfred saw that Rodriguez was popular among segments of baseball's fan base and had a knack for cultivating interest and intrigue—even in retirement, when he reappeared on the covers of supermarket tabloids by dating Jennifer Lopez.

Where Selig had ordered that Manfred unleash his DOI to ruin A-Rod, Manfred decided to forgive old grievances and move forward with a public alliance. Rodriguez would soon make a well-reviewed debut as an analyst on the Fox network, launching a broadcast career.

Manfred's actions made clear that he saw his job as that of a businessman, not a moral arbiter.

In a move that would become crucial to later investigations into sign stealing, Manfred also decided to fire Mullin and his crew of detectives at the DOI, alleging improper use of expense reports and other offenses that the league said were unprofessional (the people fired strongly denied these charges).

Among those were allegations, backed by an affidavit, that Mullin had entered into a sexual relationship with a witness in the Biogenesis case. Mullin would deny it, but Manfred wanted wholesale changes in the DOI anyway. He didn't want another investigation to embarrass MLB the way he felt that this one had.

The commissioner did not replace Mullin with another ex-cop, but with former assistant U.S. attorney Bryan Seeley. It was a departure from the style of investigations that Senator Mitchell had initially recommended, as a lawyer's methods would naturally differ from a detective's. It was Seeley's team that would investigate during the sign-stealing era.

MLB's belief was that Seeley would spend more time probing what it called "club-on-club" crime instead of running around places like Miami, negotiating with low-level criminals and allegedly bedding witnesses.

The Yankees' Apple Watch complaint was the new DOI's biggest early example of a club-on-club infraction. The Yanks submitted three of the videos that Girardi shot off Weber's screen, and Seeley and his group set about interviewing Red Sox players, including Chris Young, and the team's trainers.

Other members of the Red Sox organization believed that Young had taught players how to use technology to engage in real-time sign stealing, but Young would always strongly deny participating in an Apple Watch scheme. He would maintain that he helped teammates learn to pick signs from second base, and that was it.

The investigation took another dramatic turn in early September, as MLB was preparing to punish the Red Sox.

On September 5, *New York Times* reporter Michael S. Schmidt published a story headlined BOSTON RED SOX USED APPLE WATCHES TO STEAL SIGNS AGAINST YANKEES.

The story summarized the evidence that the Yankees had gathered, revealed that MLB had questioned Young, and noted that the Red Sox had logged a counter-complaint against the Yankees that very day.

None of this was supposed to be public yet. Neither Manfred nor Red Sox leadership was pleased.

At a news conference at Fenway Park, president of baseball operations Dave Dombrowski condescended to both the Yankees' complaint and the *Times* story.

"Do I think sign-stealing is wrong?" Dombrowski said, literally chuckling. "No, I don't. I guess it depends how you do it. But no, I never thought it was wrong. I guess everybody in the game has been involved with it throughout the years. People are trying to win however they can. It's an edge they are trying to gain. Sometimes your sophistication of signs can make a difference. So no, I never felt like it's wrong. Put it this way, I was never brought up that it was wrong."

Dombrowski was also not brought up in the era of replay rooms and Apple Watches. He could deflect all he wanted, but the sign-stealing issue was evolving rapidly.

Manfred happened to be at Fenway that day for a previously scheduled event. Sitting at a table in the cramped Fenway interview room, he fielded questions about the *Times* story. He seemed to echo Dombrowski's dismissiveness—though he did note that the high-tech aspect of the accusations cast the violation in a more serious light.

"We actually do not have a rule against sign stealing. It has been a part of the game for a very, very long time," Manfred said. "To the extent that there was a violation of the rule here, it was a violation by one or the other that involved the use of electronic equipment. It's the electronic equipment that creates the violation."

Despite Dombrowski's public laughter, the Red Sox privately seethed about the Yankees and their complaint.

When the *Times* story filtered down to the clubhouse, the Boston coaches reacted with genuine outrage. The team had already told investigators that Farrell and Dombrowski knew nothing about the Apple Watch use, and the league had found that credible. And of course they all had their own suspicions.

"What about the Yankees?" one coach exclaimed.

But Seeley and his investigative team did not find evidence of any serious violations by the Yankees. Boston's specific complaint stemmed from the coaches' earlier belief that the Yanks had filmed their dugout, Farrell and Butterfield specifically.

On September 5, Boston formally complained to MLB that the Yankees had used the YES Network camera to spy on them. They made this complaint on the day of the *Times* report, and several weeks after learning of the Yankees' accusation.

In his news conference, Dombrowski couldn't help but let slip his anger with the Yankees, whom he believed had leaked the story.

"The Yankees decide they want to give [the story] today, for whatever reason," Dombrowski said. "I think maybe because it just so happened the commissioner is in town today. I'm not sure [if] there is a direct correlation to that."

Media coverage of the allegations struck a decidedly more aggressive tone than the one put forth by Dombrowski and Manfred.

"Cheating in baseball," wrote *Boston Globe* Red Sox beat reporter Peter Abraham. "There's apparently an app for that."

Globe columnist Dan Shaughnessy referenced the New England Patriots' pair of ethical scandals, "Spygate" and "Deflategate," and wrote that "Boston's reputation in sports [had taken] another hit."

The New York *Daily News* took it further, writing "First, Spy-Gate. Now, iGate. The Boston Cheat Party is back at it again."

For the first time, the media and public had a glimpse of high-tech sign stealing. If this was a new element for fans to process, it was the same for Manfred and the league.

In the weeks that Seeley conducted his investigation, Manfred pored over the details of sign-stealing incidents in decades past, looking for precedent. He found that the game had typically treated the issue as Dombrowski had, with a dismissive chuckle.

Manfred could tell that with the introduction of new technology, the seriousness of the offenses had changed. It didn't seem adequate to apply 1950s judgment to a twenty-first-century problem.

He set about trying to thread a needle by punishing under the old rules but establishing a new precedent that would make it easier to hammer sign-stealing teams in the future. As he had on the PED issue after getting to know Tony Bosch, he saw the need to make an adjustment on an important cheating issue.

On September 15, 2017, Manfred announced the results of the investigations into the Yankees and the Red Sox.

The lengthy news release included these significant paragraphs:

"At the outset, it is important to understand that the attempt to decode signs being used by an opposing catcher is not a violation of any Major League Baseball Rule or Regulation. Major League Baseball Regulations do, however, prohibit the use of electronic equipment during games and state that no such equipment 'may be used for the purpose of stealing signs or conveying information designed to give a Club an advantage.' Despite this clear Regulation, the prevalence of technology, especially the technology used in the replay process, has made it increasingly difficult to monitor appropriate and inappropriate uses of electronic equipment. Based on the investigation by my office, I have nonetheless concluded that during the 2017 season the Boston Red Sox violated the Regulation quoted above by sending electronic communications from their video replay room to an athletic trainer in the dugout.

"In assessing the significance of this violation, the investigation established three relevant points. First, the violation in question occurred without the knowledge of ownership or front office personnel. Second, when the Red Sox learned of the Yankees' complaint, they immediately halted the conduct in question and then cooperated completely in my investigation. I have received absolute assurances from the Red Sox that there will be no future violations of this type. Third, our investigation revealed that Clubs have employed various strategies to decode signs that do not violate our rules. The Red Sox' strategy violated our rules because of the use of an electronic device."

Manfred fined the Red Sox and announced that his investigators had found no evidence that the Yankees had used YES Network cameras to cheat. But Manfred did include the following judgment against New York:

"We learned that during an earlier championship season (prior to 2017) the Yankees had violated a rule governing the use of the dugout phone. No Club complained about the conduct in question at the time and, without prompting from another Club or my Office, the Yankees halted the conduct in question."

Manfred fined the Yankees what he called "a lesser amount" than he fined the Red Sox. But the most important statement in his lengthy news release did not involve either club, but the broader issue of precedent and a way forward on the issue.

"Moreover, all 30 Clubs have been notified that future violations of this type will be subject to more serious sanctions, including the possible loss of draft picks."

It's impossible to overstate the importance of that sentence. Those twenty-seven words transformed electronic sign stealing from gamesmanship to serious, punishable cheating. It set rules that Manfred could apply to all future violators.

The commissioner had been especially intentional about his inclusion of the phrase "draft picks." Clubs valued the inexpensive, controllable players acquired through the draft more than any other asset; when Manfred threatened to strip those, he knew he was signaling his newfound seriousness on sign stealing.

Had that language been on the books in 1900, when Pearce Chiles received a small electric shock in the third-base coach's box to indicate an off-speed pitch, the Phillies would have been severely penalized. Same for Bobby Thomson's 1951 Giants, Bobby Valentine's 1997 Mets, and many others.

On the sign-stealing issue, there were two eras: before September 15, 2017, and after.

But Manfred had left one small loose thread. Brian Cashman was extremely angry. In several phone calls with officials at the commissioner's office, Cashman screamed that Manfred's penalties and statement had been unfair—the Yankees were victims of the Red Sox, not fellow rule breakers.

Furthermore, hadn't the DOI cleared the Yankees of using the YES Network cameras to steal signs?

But by this time, there was nothing the Yankees could do about the perception that both teams had engaged in some form of cheating, even if Manfred had fined the Yanks "a lesser amount."

Cashman's fears proved true. Over the next few years, as sign stealing became more and more prominent in the news, both the media and fans would casually lump the two teams together, referring to both the Yankees and the Red Sox as being guilty of something in 2017.

But Cashman and MLB had access to an important detail that the public did not, because Manfred had referred to it only in generic terms in his statement: The Yankees' violation had not involved sign stealing.

In fact, Manfred had fined them for a single incident, when pitching coach Larry Rothschild, the sexagenarian who was hardly a tech whiz, picked up the phone in the dugout that connected to the replay room and asked if a particular pitch had been a ball or a strike.

Quickly remembering that he wasn't supposed to use the phone for that purpose, Rothschild hung up, self-reported, and didn't do it again.

That was it. That was the sole violation for which the Yankees were punished. They had decoded signs in the replay room in earlier seasons, but that wasn't the issue here.

For the next several years, Cashman would carry around his anger about that. Whenever he felt victimized by a team—and soon the Houston Astros would render the Red Sox and their Apple Watch a mere footnote in the era—he felt it bubble up again.

Chapter 11

ENTER HINCH AND CORA

The 2014 season was a miserable one for the Houston Astros, with one notable exception.

Underneath all the turmoil—an ex-Cardinals colleague hacking their database, a failure to sign their top draft pick that led to an outcry about ethics, and players openly complaining that general manager Jeff Luhnow saw them as faceless pawns—the team posted a nineteen-win improvement over the previous year.

Granted, the jump was from 59-111 to 70-92, but Luhnow could at least now demonstrate that his teardown was trending in a direction that suggested success.

Bo Porter, Luhnow's first managerial choice, had failed, and the GM knew he needed a collaborator willing to help sell his ideas to players. He also needed a human touch during games, a manager capable of adjusting to situations and knowing when to occasionally go against the data.

Typically when a team seeks a manager, the search drags into the first month or two of an off-season, as the front office interviews upward of a half a dozen candidates or more. Naturally, Luhnow did not care about this convention.

The day after the season ended, he announced that his new skipper would be the same guy who had struggled in Arizona several years earlier, A. J. Hinch.

In a statement, Luhnow touted the diversity of Hinch's experience, and highlighted the particular needs of his team:

"Throughout our process, we searched for a person with previous Major League experience, who could effectively lead our young, growing nucleus of talented players. I have no doubt that A.J. is the right person to do that. He brings experience as a Major League player, Major League manager and player development executive. His skillsets and leadership abilities will be enormous assets in our clubhouse and to our entire organization."

More than one member of the local media read this and rolled their eyes. It seemed clear that Luhnow was simply bringing in a puppet to carry out his ideas in the clubhouse and on the field.

But the Hinch who reported to work in Houston was, at forty years old, stronger and more focused than the one who had struggled to create buy-in in Arizona. His vision of his own purpose had fundamentally changed: He now burned to be a manager.

Back in Arizona, GM Josh Byrnes had had to sell Hinch on the idea of putting on the uniform. At that time, Hinch had seen himself as a future general manager.

After the Diamondbacks fired him in 2010, Hinch had returned to front-office work, taking a job as vice president of pro scouting for the San Diego Padres. He worked there under Byrnes, who had joined that team as a top executive and soon ascended to the same position he'd held in Arizona.

But this front-office job was different for Hinch than the one he held in Arizona. While committed to the work in front of him, he was waiting for the right managerial opportunity to arise. The failure in Arizona had changed him, leaving a need to prove to himself and the industry that he could not only handle the position, but thrive in it.

The fit in Houston seemed perfect. In Arizona, ownership had wavered in its commitment to the creativity that Hinch and Byrnes promoted. Here, Luhnow enjoyed the full support of Astros owner

Jim Crane. There was no question that he was going to be allowed to see his plan through.

The game itself had changed, too. It wasn't considered as unorthodox in 2014 as it had been in 2009 to involve a front office in game strategy. Analytics were becoming more pervasive than ever, and more than ever the manager was a collaborator, not a general.

It also helped to have a younger team, populated not with bitter veterans but eager, moldable talents.

In George Springer and Carlos Correa, Hinch could not have asked for a pair of more engaged and intelligent stars. José Altuve was quiet in the clubhouse—too reserved to be a leader—but he was not a problem for Hinch, either. Altuve was merely a serious person who went about his business.

Those members of the team's young core had already begun to arrive, and, in some cases, thrive, by the time Hinch joined them.

Springer debuted and hit 20 home runs in 78 games in 2014. Altuve won the batting title that year, hitting .341. Correa was ready the following June.

The pitching staff was also beginning to coalesce. In 2015, Hinch's first year, Dallas Keuchel took a major leap forward, winning twenty games and the A.L. Cy Young Award.

That season, the Astros took the significant step that Luhnow believed they were capable of, winning eighty-six games and finishing in second place in the American League West. That was good enough to earn a wild-card berth, which was the team's first postseason appearance since the 2005 Roger Clemens/Craig Biggio pennant winners.

Keuchel defeated the Yankees in the wild-card game. The Astros then fell in the division series to Kansas City, who would go on to win it all.

Despite the way the season ended, hope and excitement overshadowed disappointment. Luhnow's Astros had finally arrived.

The team started slowly in 2016, going 7-17 in April. That put them in a hole in the standings, but they quickly resumed their upward trajectory, posting a winning record in each of the next four months, including eighteen wins in June.

The Astros missed the playoffs that year (finishing with a record of 84-78) but felt poised to take another leap in 2017. Before doing so, they would need to fill an important leadership position.

At the end of the 2016 season, Trey Hillman, who had served as Hinch's bench coach for the past two seasons, took a job managing in the KBO League in South Korea.

Luhnow and Hinch quickly agreed on the best candidate to replace him, but they had to act fast. Alex Cora was ready to jump back into the game and was drawing significant interest.

Boston Red Sox executive Ben Cherington called it "Peter Gammons's breakfast club."

Often during the first decade of the 2000s, when the Sox had a night game at Fenway Park, a small group would gather in the home dugout at one-thirty or two in the afternoon to tell stories and talk baseball.

Gammons, the Hall of Fame baseball writer and broadcaster, would always be there; he was the rare reporter who attracted ballplayers rather than repelled them. His typical companions included second baseman Dustin Pedroia, catcher Kevin Cash, and third baseman Mike Lowell. They didn't gossip, but engaged in serious discussions about the game's finer points.

Cherington had named the group after Gammons, but the real leader—the guy always moderating—was infielder Alex Cora. In a group populated by passionate craftsmen, Cora's love for the game might have burned hottest, and his ability to lead was becoming clearer every year.

On August 27, 2008, the Red Sox acquired the veteran outfielder Mark Kotsay from the Atlanta Braves. That afternoon in the breakfast club, Pedroia asked about him.

"What's the story with this new guy we got?" the second baseman said.

Cora and Cash answered in unison, as if in a sitcom: "Greatest college player who ever lived!"

Kotsay had indeed been a standout for Cal State Fullerton, but was he the best ever? The group ate up the next however many minutes with a spirited debate on that point.

What Gammons and the breakfast club buddies saw in a moment like that were the complementary traits that defined Cora: He was highly sociable, but also highly studious.

The latter quality stemmed from an upbringing that emphasized education over all over pursuits. Cora attended the University of Miami, and his older brother, Joey, went to Vanderbilt. Both starred at their respective schools and became major league players, but the Cora family considered baseball an avenue to college, not the other way around.

Alex was born in 1975 in Caguas, Puerto Rico, and within a few years developed the brashness that would become part of his adult persona.

He reminded family members of his mother, Iris, who was more outspoken than her husband, José Manuel. By the time Alex was five or six years old, he was telling coaches that they should be batting him leadoff.

Joey took after their father, stoic but caring. José Manuel was tall and dark-eyed, his gray hair and deep voice lending authority to his presence. Both sons carried his name: Joey was José Manuel and Alex was José Alexander.

By the time Joey was in high school, it was clear that he would have a chance to play ball at a major university. José Manuel pushed him to pursue this, and though Joey landed at Vanderbilt, his reserved nature and lack of English-language skills made the transition challenging.

But it was also successful. By 1987 Joey had not only earned the education so important to his family but made his debut for the San Diego Padres.

At that time, he was carrying around a terrible secret that he kept from twelve-year-old Alex: José Manuel was dying of colon cancer.

Alex would sometimes accompany his father to doctors' appointments, but the two would talk baseball in front of them. He didn't know that anything serious was happening.

A few weeks before Alex's thirteenth birthday, his family brought him from a junior varsity volleyball game to the hospital, where his father had been admitted. Alex still didn't know why.

The family went home, and was awoken at 4 a.m., when a neighbor knocked on the door to tell them they had to return to the hospital.

When they got there, Alex was struck by the way that the doctor kept speaking about his father in the past tense. But still he didn't know what was happening. It was a trauma that revealed itself with excruciating slowness.

Finally, the doctor spelled it out: José Manuel Cora had died.

Alex walked into the room where his father lay. He just looked like he was sleeping. This did not seem real.

Unusual for his outgoing nature, Alex sunk into himself. For days he could not even cry. The strong man who had set his values and ruled his life was gone without warning. This took a long time to absorb.

Though absent during the baseball season, Joey stepped into the void, encouraging Alex with the tough love that José Manuel would have provided. When Joey was in college, he called home every Sunday. After turning pro, he started calling on Mondays.

Alex followed the path that Joey had set by committing to play at the University of Miami, which had a topnotch team.

But school proved more challenging than expected during Alex's early days there. South Florida felt foreign, and after six weeks he became desperately homesick. Acting on an impulse, Alex packed a bag and bought a one-way ticket to San Juan. He was done with college.

For some providential reason, Joey called home on the day that Alex returned—even though it was a Thursday, not his typical day to phone.

Alex picked up.

"What the fuck are you doing there?" Joey said.

Alex explained that he no longer wanted to play at Miami.

Joey responded that if Alex did not turn around and fly back immediately, he would leave his own team to come home and throw Alex on a plane himself. Alex was programmed to listen to Joey, so he returned to school.

His emotional nature would surface many more times during his college career, most memorably at the end of his final season.

In 1996, Miami was one out away from winning the College World Series, leading Louisiana State by one run with two out in the ninth inning.

Standing at his position at shortstop, Alex could hardly contain his excitement—to clinch, to celebrate, to call Joey and relive it all.

Then Louisiana State's Warren Morris stunned Miami with a game-winning two-run homer. As Morris rounded the bases and his teammates erupted from the dugout, Alex collapsed on the field, buried his face in the grass, and cried so hard that his back and shoulders shook.

This was a man as emotional about baseball as anyone could be. Alex Cora was in love with the game—and that day, he was reminded of how badly it could break his heart.

—

Peter Gammons first met Cora in the early 2000s, when he was in Vero Beach, Florida, working on a feature for ESPN on Dodgers pitcher Kevin Brown. While there, he chatted with the young infielder César Izturis, whom he considered a smart and engaging player.

Izturis asked Gammons if he knew Alex Cora. Gammons said that the two had never really talked in depth.

"He's the smartest guy on the team," Izturis said.

That was a striking comment, considering that the roster included not only Izturis but Shawn Green, a master of sign stealing and an all-around intellectual, and Dave Roberts, a future manager. But Izturis meant it.

Gammons began watching more closely, and saw that Cora knew where everyone in the game was at all times, and what everyone was supposed to be doing. His field awareness was as sharp as anyone's. He was also down-to-earth and likable, and struck up a lasting friendship with Gammons.

In seven years with the Dodgers, Cora posted a .246 batting average and played excellent infield defense. A free agent after the 2004 season, he signed with the Indians for 2005.

His time in Cleveland didn't go as planned. The Indians saw the twenty-nine-year-old Cora as transitioning into a phase of his career that was more about mentoring younger players than making regular contributions on the field.

This was difficult for an intense, prideful player to accept. Cora enjoyed teaching teammates, including his future managerial opponent Aaron Boone. He was already one of those players who could look at a pitcher's glove flare out a millimeter and know that a changeup was coming.

But he did not mesh well with Cleveland manager Eric Wedge and lasted just over three months before the Indians traded him to the Boston Red Sox.

That proved to be the perfect turn toward the second half of Cora's playing career. Red Sox manager Terry Francona valued his baseball

IQ and viewed his seriousness of purpose as an asset on a team that had won the World Series the year before while calling themselves "The Idiots."

Francona knew that for players like Manny Ramirez, Johnny Damon, and Kevin Millar, who grew their hair long and sipped whiskey before playoff games, the line between freedom and chaos was thin. The studious Cora was a perfect counterbalance.

During his years in Boston, this played out in significant ways that the public never glimpsed. Cora and Ramirez weren't particularly close socially, but Cora saw it as part of his role on the team to keep the mercurial slugger focused.

Deep down, Ramirez loved the game, too, but he was also highly distractible—whether that meant sneaking into the Green Monster mid-inning to relieve himself or popping up at a downtown bar when he was supposedly too sick to play.

During the 2007 postseason, when they were on the road, Cora and Lowell, along with strength and conditioning coach David Page, would rouse Ramirez every morning at ten—even after night games—and drag him to a local gym. The group worked out, chatted, and joked around, leaving Ramirez in the right mental and physical space to excel later that night on the field.

The Red Sox won the World Series that year. In three postseason rounds, Cora batted just once. Only Francona and his teammates understood just how essential he had been to Ramirez's production.

But Cora's greatest contribution in Boston involved one of the few players arguably even more important to the franchise than Ramirez: He became a friend and mentor to a young Pedroia.

Cora could have played it much differently. There was no avoiding the fact that Pedroia's emergence in late 2006 would cost Cora significant playing time, and probably ultimately his spot on the team. Plenty of insecure veterans freeze out the rookies who, through no fault of their own, will ultimately unseat them.

It was impossible for Cora to do this, because he found in Pedroia an instant baseball soul mate, a player just as obsessed with the details of the game as he was. Cora dedicated himself to doing everything he could to help Pedroia succeed as the Red Sox second baseman—in other words, to groom him to take Cora's job.

During Pedroia's first full season in 2007, he and Cora would meet to talk in the dugout nearly every afternoon at three-thirty, and then take grounders on the infield.

During games, Cora would time pitchers' delivery to home, which told him if and when to attempt a stolen base. He passed the information to Pedroia, who increased his stolen base total from 7 in 2007 to 20 in 2008—the year that he won the American League Most Valuable Player Award.

With Cora behind him, Pedroia's emergence was remarkable. By the time he turned twenty-four years old, he was a world champion and MVP.

Pedroia wasn't the only infielder who received help from Cora despite squeezing his roster spot. Prior to the 2007 season, the team signed free-agent shortstop Julio Lugo to a four-year, $36 million deal. Lugo had played most of his career in sleepy Tampa Bay, and his transition to big-market Boston was bumpy.

Cora offered counsel, doing what he could to help Lugo succeed at short. Between that and his work with Pedroia, he was virtually assuring himself of a seat on the bench going forward.

The industry took notice of this selflessness, and Cora began hearing his name discussed in baseball circles as a future manager or even GM.

Catching wind of this reputation, Mets general manager Omar Minaya recruited Cora to sign with New York after the 2008 season. The club needed more veteran leadership, having just blown large division leads to miss the playoffs in two consecutive seasons.

Minaya especially wanted Cora to help with his electric young shortstop José Reyes, hoping he could do for Reyes what he had just done for Pedroia.

Reyes was a tricky case—his physical gifts, especially his speed, were beyond compare, but he lacked the field awareness that made Cora an overachiever.

A reporter once told Reyes that his counterpart with the Phillies, Jimmy Rollins, looked in for location on every pitch, thought about the hitter's swing, and positioned himself accordingly. Did Reyes do the same?

"Bro," the amiable Reyes said, laughing. "There's like two hundred pitches in every game. I can't focus on every one of them."

It was Cora's job to work with that. He would always notice that Reyes was positioned incorrectly when the pitcher threw the ball, standing back on his heels rather than the balls of his feet.

"He won't get off his heels!" Cora once explained to Gammons, upon running into his old friend.

The two years that Cora spent with the Mets, 2009 and 2010, turned out to be difficult years for the team. After exhibiting so much promise with a run to the 2006 National League Championship Series, the Mets followed their two collapses with a ninety-two-loss season in 2009.

They started strong in 2010 but fell apart in July on a season-killing swing through the National League West. On July 20, the Mets fell meekly to the Arizona Diamondbacks, who were twenty-one games under .500 and in turmoil, having just fired A. J. Hinch and Josh Byrnes.

Afterward, the Mets clubhouse was stale and mournful, packed with players who knew they would have to endure meaningless games until the end of September. But the misery did not extend to one corner, where pitcher Mike Pelfrey stood at his locker, surrounded by roughly half a dozen reporters.

For several minutes, Pelfrey and the reporters talked loudly and laughed, oblivious to the vibe around them. Cora sat at his own locker, toweling off from his shower and dressing.

As the noise continued a few feet away, Cora cursed in Spanish to backup catcher Henry Blanco, whose locker was next to his. He cursed again, but louder.

That didn't quiet anyone, so Cora switched to English and turned up the volume.

"Little respect," he said.

He repeated it. "Show a little respect."

Now he stood, glared at Pelfrey, and headed out of the room.

"They're shoving it up our asses out there! Show a little respect."

Cora turned out of the main locker room area, and into a hallway that led out of the clubhouse. His neck was craned back, now staring at the suddenly hushed group in front of Pelfrey's locker.

When he turned to face forward, he was so worked up that he didn't realize he was headed directly into a wall. He smashed his nose against the partition and continued, storming out of sight.

If no one else was going to care that the Mets' season had died in July, Alex Cora was. Baseball was serious business to him.

The Mets released Cora later that summer, and he began the final stage of his playing career, bouncing around to a few teams while trying to hang on.

On his way out of New York, Minaya had tried to do Cora a favor by repeating several times in media interviews that he would be a manager or GM before long. The New York writers dutifully quoted him.

One day in 2011, when Cora was playing for the Washington Nationals, a Mets reporter stopped by his locker to say hello. Cora looked up with characteristic intensity.

"Can you guys stop writing that I'm gonna be a GM soon," he said. "I'm still trying to prove I can fucking play."

That turned out to be Cora's final season in the big leagues. He played ninety-one games for Washington, batting .224 with no home runs. The St. Louis Cardinals invited him to spring training the following year, but it was clear his skills had eroded with age, and the team released him before opening day.

It was a retirement that immediately suggested bigger things to come. Cora became the GM of Puerto Rico's Criollos de Caguas in the Puerto Rican winter league, and of Puerto Rico's squad in the World Baseball Classic. MLB executives and writers continued to mention him as a future leader in the game.

But rather than jump right into working for a team, Cora decided instead to take a job as an analyst for ESPN.

There he joined an old teammate, Aaron Boone, who had been with Cora on the Cleveland Indians back in 2005. Boone's own playing career had ended in 2009, and he immediately began working as a broadcaster.

He was glad to work again with Cora, whose baseball expertise and engaging personality he'd always enjoyed.

Boone was surprised at first when Cora explained to him why he was at ESPN: He wanted to push himself out of his comfort zone to sharpen his English-language skills, in preparation for the two news conferences a day that a big-league manager holds.

Boone had known Cora for many years and had always taken it for granted that his English was excellent. When Cora talked about the game or joked around, he did not give the impression of searching to express himself in a foreign tongue but was seemingly as comfortable as anyone else.

But Boone did remember the intense pressure he'd felt at first once the camera's red light switched on, and the effort it took to battle the nerves, calm his swarming thoughts, and express complex points on air with confidence and clarity. If you could master a studio show or broadcast booth, you could handle a news conference.

On days when Cora was preparing for the show *Baseball Tonight*, especially early on, he would text Boone with his topics and ideas, and ask for advice on how to put them together.

In return, he would watch Boone's *Sunday Night Baseball* games and feed him a stream of texts with helpful insight on what he saw—pitch tipping, manager strategy, and anything else that his sharp eye flagged. The nuggets always enriched Boone's commentary.

During his four years at ESPN, Cora developed a reputation among coworkers and crew as one of the most amiable ex-athletes on the staff. He learned the names of stage managers and makeup artists and generously shared insight and information with fellow on-air talent.

He also used his Twitter account to engage with viewers. Like his personality, Cora's online presence was sometimes affable, sometimes edgy and intense. But he was more accessible than the typical ex-player and broadcaster, and that only added to his profile.

By the end of the 2016 season, he signaled that he was ready to take the step for which he had long been planning. He would seek a coaching position with an eye on parlaying that into a manager job within a few years.

Several clubs lined up for interviews, but the Astros jumped out as a strong fit. Luhnow had already brought in several ex–media members to serve in his front office and had once tried unsuccessfully to recruit ESPN writer Keith Law.

Having played for the Red Sox during the era of GM Theo Epstein, Cora was conversant in analytics, and, at forty-one years old, young enough to know that data was not a threat, but a tool to help coaches make their players better.

Cora and Hinch had known each other around the game for years, and at that time they got along well. Cora was also friends with Astros coach Alex Cintrón, a fellow native Puerto Rican.

With Cora, the fit was mutual and obvious. On November 14, 2016, the Astros announced that he would be their new bench coach.

Though the team had only just begun to experiment with organized sign stealing—remember, it was in the fall of 2016 that the intern Derek Vigoa came up with the Codebreaker program—it didn't hurt that Cora held a reputation as one of the best in the business at the legal side of that.

Cintrón was good at it, too, which was part of his appeal to the front office when they hired him around the same time. Cintrón came in as the Spanish-language translator, coaching assistant, and advance scout for the 2017 season. He would eventually work his way up to first-base coach, and then hitting coach, and was the one who the Yankees accused of illegal whistling in 2019.

The Astros were assembling a support staff that knew how to pick sequences and tell you when a pitcher was tipping. And they would soon add a veteran player who was better than almost anyone at those same skills.

Chapter 12

THE SCHEME BEGINS

"**G**uys," Carlos Beltrán told his new Houston Astros team-mates in the spring of 2017, "your sequences have always been way too easy. I can pick all of them from second base."

To that, bench coach Alex Cora added, "You know what all winning teams do? They steal signs from second."

Both men were fresh additions to the Astros, and both were bringing a message similar to the one that outfielder Chris Young had trumpeted to the Boston Red Sox the year before: Other teams were better at getting the opposing team's signs, and our team needed to catch up.

That reality was a dangerous one for anyone working under Jeff Luhnow. Obsessed with innovation, the GM made his top baseball operations lieutenants feel that they were always behind, and that other teams were always at their heels. Beltrán's warning seemed to confirm the institutional paranoia.

For this and other reasons, the Astros' front office felt that Beltrán was the perfect addition. They had been looking for two years for a guy like him—and really, for him, because there was no one else in the game quite like Carlos Beltrán.

Ever since 2015, when the team's tanking phase finally started to shift into on-field success, A. J. Hinch and the front office knew that they needed at least one strong veteran leader to anchor the clubhouse.

Dallas Keuchel was smart and outspoken, but starting pitchers are typically too wrapped up in their own routines to lead an entire team.

Shortstop Carlos Correa and Alex Bregman, the rookie third baseman whom the Astros drafted with the compensatory pick earned by failing to sign Brady Aiken in 2014, were strong personalities with leadership potential, but they were only just emerging in 2015 and 2016.

In the winter of 2016–17, after nearly three years with the Yankees and a few months as a Texas Ranger, Beltrán was once again available for hire.

The fit was perfect for the Astros, but for Beltrán it was more complicated. After starring in Houston during the 2004 postseason, he had spurned the team and city to sign his $119 million deal with the Mets. Astros fans held on to that perceived slight, raining vicious boos on Beltrán for many years when his teams came to town.

That aside, the current version of the Astros did offer what Beltrán was looking for. Forty years old and entering his twentieth season in the major leagues, he was starving for a championship.

After that traumatic strikeout that ended the Mets' playoff run in 2006, he'd made it to the World Series just once, when his Cardinals lost to Boston in 2013. He was an all-time postseason performer, with 16 home runs and a batting average over .300 in 55 games. But he had never experienced baseball's greatest joy, and he was hungry for it.

Beltrán knew the game well enough to see that the Astros were primed to contend for a ring. And he loved their pitch about providing mentorship to the young players, his favorite aspect of playing on a team.

It also helped that the Astros were willing to overpay for a forty-year-old designated hitter whose bat had slowed since his prime. Their offer of a one-year contract for $16 million was well in excess of what their analysts had recommended based on the numbers alone. But here the intangibles were worth the splurge.

Houston agreed to terms with Beltrán in early December 2016, pairing him with the catcher Brian McCann, acquired from the Yankees a few weeks earlier. They now had the veteran presence to help elevate a dynamic young core from a playoff team to a championship-caliber one.

Beltrán arrived with big ideas about how to unify the Astros clubhouse. Always holding the memory of his isolation during the early years in Kansas City, he made sure to mentor white and Latin American players alike, drawing close not only to his fellow Puerto Rican Correa but to Bregman and others.

In 2017 nearly every major league clubhouse was still divided by race and ethnicity, a split that any visitor could see upon walking in the door and spotting Latin American players huddled in one corner, the few remaining African Americans in another, and the white players forming their own group. Beltrán wanted better for the Astros.

Beltrán's friendship with McCann was a perfect emblem of this outreach. In 2013, McCann had been involved in a high-profile incident that spawned reams of commentary about the game's cultural rift. Milwaukee Brewers star Carlos Gómez, who had come up with the Mets when Beltrán was there, paused to admire a home run he hit against Atlanta Braves pitcher Paul Maholm because Maholm had plunked him with a pitch earlier in the season. McCann, catching for Atlanta, stood in front of home plate when Gómez tried to cross, blocking it and screaming in his face.

McCann was a Georgia native who played most of his career for the Braves; Gómez hailed from the Dominican Republic and played in the expressive style that was more socially acceptable in Latin America than among white American athletes—flipping bats, yelling, dancing.

After this incident, it seemed that all of baseball retreated into one camp or another, McCann's or Gomez's, treating it as a proxy battle over acceptable on-field behavior going forward, and, on an even deeper level, a fight over race and culture.

Beltrán took a different approach: He was close with both men and worked to understand their divergent perspectives. Watching Gómez from afar on TV, he would text when he saw celebrations that he felt crossed the line into poor sportsmanship. Because of Beltrán's stature in the game, Gómez always listened. Later, playing with McCann in New York and Houston, Beltrán would assure the catcher that Gómez was a good guy.

When the Astros reported to spring training in West Palm Beach, Florida, in February 2017, Beltrán immediately got to work at what he loved, and what the Astros had asked of him, teaching younger players.

In doing this, he and his teammates also took their first steps toward the cheating hole into which they would eventually fall. It really did start innocently, and the untold story begins with the legitimate use of an exciting new toy.

In 2011 an inventor in California named Mike Matter began work on what became the Edgertronic camera, named after Harold "Doc" Edgerton, a mentor of his and an MIT professor for more than five decades. Edgerton was a pioneer of advanced photography, whose major contributions were the development of high-speed photography technology and electronic flashes on cameras. His friends at MIT called him "Papa Flash."

Matter developed the Edgertronic as a high-speed device that could capture one thousand frames per second. Four years later, an Astros group headed by manager of baseball operations Brandon Taubman, director of research and development Mike Fast, and player-development assistant Pete Putila was looking to learn what high-speed cameras could do for a baseball team. Cleveland pitcher

Trevor Bauer had already experimented with the Edgertronic, but Houston was the first MLB team to purchase one, paying $4,000.

For the next two years, the team used it to film bullpen sessions and capture arm angles and grips, helping pitchers tweak and improve their arsenals. This was an important innovation that would soon become widespread throughout the game, and an example of how the creative thinking for which Luhnow pushed could result in true brilliance.

During spring training of 2017, Beltrán helped the team expand its use of the Edgertronic to include hitters. Going into that season, the Astros had identified specific changes that they wanted to make with Springer's, Correa's, and Jake Marisnick's swings. In essence they asked those players to flatten the bat as they brought it through the zone, in order to launch the ball at a different point in the swing. Taubman and his group thought that the Edgertronic would be a useful tool in this.

This was the sort of thing that Beltrán loved to help with, and he got right to it, spending countless hours in the batting cage with these young teammates, along with first baseman Yuli Gurriel, who was also working on changes to his swing.

Beltrán had brought with him a favorite piece of equipment, a fastball machine that delivered pitches at a high level of speed and intensity. Before leaving to play for Puerto Rico for a few weeks in the World Baseball Classic, he introduced it to his teammates, and utilized the Edgertronic camera for feedback.

In doing this work, Beltrán was already earning his salary. Initially he was even more enthusiastic about the Edgertronic than hitting coach Dave Hudgens or José Altuve, the homegrown veteran. Hudgens's interpersonal style was very player-friendly and laid-back; he wasn't the type to force a new task or tool on anyone. Altuve was receptive to the tech for his own work but too introverted to take Springer, Correa, and the others under his wing.

Beltrán not only ate up the new toy, thrilled by its possibilities, but also used it as a teaching tool. Benefiting from Beltrán's unique ability to unite factions—not to mention the heaping portions of talent on the roster—the Astros broke camp hopeful that the 2017 season would be a special one.

On opening day, Keuchel shut down the Seattle Mariners and the Astros won 3–0. Afterward, Beltrán held court in the locker room and announced a new tradition, the awarding of championship belts after each win to the hitter and pitcher of the game.

The bad vibes of the 2014 season, when the Astros' own players complained to the press that Luhnow treated them as entries on a spreadsheet, were nothing more than a distant nightmare.

For a fleeting moment, the whole thing was clicking: Beltrán was the player mentor, Hinch was managing games by using both data and instinct, and Cora was back in the game and contributing his insights.

One day, a member of the front office saw Beltrán looking at Edgertronic video with Marisnick and felt oddly moved. Not long before, the Astros' front office had been baseball's high-tech outcasts, hated by their own players. Now the team had bought in.

Over the next few weeks, the Astros' legitimate and shadier pursuits began to mingle.

Decoding sign sequences and identifying pitch tippers was a natural part of Cora's skill set, and he, like Beltrán, was giddy at all the new tools available. He had last been in uniform in a big-league clubhouse when he played for the Washington Nationals in 2011, and that might as well have been a different century. It was a time before high-speed cameras or even replay-review rooms.

Walking into Minute Maid Park in 2017, he couldn't help but wonder what the great teams of his generation would have done with all the fancy tech. Imagine the powerful Cleveland Indians of the 1990s studying their swings with Edgertronic cameras and picking sequences off a monitor.

For a baseball nut like Cora, the possibilities were endless. Meanwhile, Beltrán continued to encourage his own pitchers and catchers to complicate their sequences, and his hitters to get better at picking signs.

He also continued to work with Correa, Springer, Gurriel, Marisnick, and others on their swings. By this time Hudgens, the hitting coach, had bought into the Edgertronic camera as a valuable tool, and much of the team was using the video room to look at swings slowed to one thousand frames per second.

They would also use the room to study opponents and sign sequences.

There Beltrán and Cora noted an inconvenience that was relatively unique to the Astros—and one that would become absolutely key to the scandal that soon developed.

Many teams had built their replay rooms behind the dugout, but the replay room at Minute Maid Park was much farther away. In order to get there to watch at-bats, a player had to walk down the dugout steps, up a separate set of stairs to the clubhouse, then down a hallway.

That not only made it harder to watch legal video during games, but it complicated the early version of the sign-stealing operation.

During the initial weeks of the season, Astros employees in the replay room used the Codebreaker idea to log sequences in an Excel spreadsheet and call the dugout with signs once they figured them out.

Typically it was Cora who would pick up the phone. This was not a cell phone but a landline that rang loudly. That almost ended the cheating right there.

Sitting on the bench, Cora would wince when he heard it. *Ring! Ring!*

People were looking. This wasn't exactly covert. There had to be a better way.

Cora tried using an Apple Watch, but also approached Tom Koch-

Weser, who was working in the video room, about getting a monitor behind the dugout. Koch-Weser took the request to Luhnow, who approached business and facilities personnel to check on the cost and viability of what they called a "video annex" before approving it.

The folks in baseball operations reacted to this request with excitement. It felt like a new day in the game, when analytical front offices, players, and coaches were all rowing in the same direction.

As far as most members of the front office knew at the time, this wasn't a tool to be used for cheating. The ostensible purpose for this monitor, the way that most team officials understood it, was for players to look at their at-bats after the fact, as recorded by the Edgertronic cameras.

But the Edgertronic explanation turned out to be a cover for sign stealing. It was possible on the new monitor and the mouse and keyboard in front of it to toggle between the Edgertronic feed and one that offered a regular live feed from a camera mounted in center field. One only needed to learn the IP address that would bring up the center-field feed, and then watch the catcher put down his signs.

Think of it this way: A player could use the monitor for a legitimate purpose, the one the front office assumed it was for—looking at his swing at one thousand frames per second. He could also switch to a regular camera mounted in center field in order to cheat.

With his patient, caring style, Beltrán taught teammates how to decode sequences. Players would arrive at the ballpark early, watch footage of that day's pitcher, and bond over the shared pursuit.

Bregman proved an especially quick study, while Altuve showed little interest. That was fine; if a player wanted to participate in sign stealing, he was welcome. If he didn't, Beltrán was cool with that, too.

The next step after players picked the signs from the monitor was to get them to the batter. If teammates made a noise that the hitter could hear, it wasn't necessary to have a runner on second base signal the hitter.

For several weeks, the Astros experimented with a series of different sounds, from clapping their hands to whistling to yelling.

It didn't take long to realize that there was an easy way to make a noise loud enough for the batter to hear under normal circumstances, as long as the crowd wasn't roaring too loudly. A plastic garbage can was sitting right there.

First the players tried drilling into the can with a massage gun. The next step, the one that would stall great careers and bring down a potential dynasty, arrived in the organic way that had defined the whole process since Beltrán and Cora had arrived that spring: It did not feel sinister or surprising, but flowed from a process already under way.

The players simply picked up a bat and banged on the trash can to tell batters what pitch was coming.

There was no dramatic reveal or clandestine group meeting the night before this began. One day, and they didn't even take note of exactly when, Hinch, Hudgens, and other coaches and players were in the dugout and heard the bang. No one reacted, and they went about their business running the game.

Major League Baseball's later investigation and report did not specify when the trash-can scheme commenced. In fact, that big event came at the beginning of a series against the Baltimore Orioles at Minute Maid Park the weekend of May 26–28. People directly involved are sure of it.

Here's how it worked: A player and/or video staffer would go to the monitor behind the dugout and switch the feed from the Edgertronic to the center-field camera. That camera provided a clear view of the catcher's hands, which made it easy to figure out his sign sequences.

Once those were decoded, the Astros would provide the infamous audio cue by banging on the garbage can. One or two bangs meant an off-speed pitch was coming. No bangs meant a fastball. In that way, whether they made a sound or not, the Astros had just about every pitch.

Beltrán, Cora, and the players had a strong belief that other teams were doing the same sort of thing, though that has never been proven. Several people involved in the scheme now concede that the Astros took sign stealing further than any opponent.

This was not looking in at the catcher from second base. This was not a complex series of gestures between a base runner and a batter—a touch of the jersey to show you had the pitch, a tap of the helmet to say you wanted it, a step to the right or a glance into the outfield to fulfill the request.

This was not studying the pitcher to see if his glove flared, his tongue rolled, or the skin of his palm showed.

This was not the hidden language of baseball, the game within the game. This was using cameras to cheat.

On Friday, May 26, the first night of the trash-can banging, Baltimore manager Buck Showalter knew that the Astros' swings were just too comfortable, their takes too confident.

Showalter was one of the savviest in the game at defending against sign stealing. While assessing the threat each night, he would look into the opposing dugout, then glance at each of the base coaches to see if anyone was moving in a suspicious way.

His seasoned eyes told them that the Astros had his signs. But he was unsettled that he couldn't spot how they were doing it, even as Houston swept the three-game series and outscored the Orioles 15–6.

When the Orioles returned home from the road trip, Showalter mentioned his suspicions to general manager Dan Duquette.

Duquette had had the same thought—watching the games, he just knew that something was up. Especially odd to him was the Sunday series finale, in which the Astros tagged young starter Alec Asher for six runs in two innings.

"Asher had good stuff," Duquette told his manager, who agreed. "They're doing something."

They ran through a series of guesses, including that the Orioles' eyes had not adjusted to the LED lighting in Minute Maid Park. The real answer, of course, eluded them. During that Sunday game alone, Astros players had banged on the trash can twenty-eight times. In the second inning, the one that did Asher in, Correa singled off a cutter that had been signaled with a bang and Springer homered in a five-pitch at-bat where he benefited from garbage-can bangs on four of the pitches.

Once, when the Astros returned from a series in Oakland in which they were swept, players complained to a member of the front office about the A's.

"Oakland was banging a trash can in their dugout," one player said. "They had our signs."

The front-office member came to believe that the players were projecting—there was absolutely no evidence, or even any credible allegations, regarding the A's and trash-can banging. But the Astros had convinced themselves that they weren't alone.

Because of this, many players were enthusiastic participants in the scheme, internalizing Beltrán's message that other teams were doing it. Ultimately, nearly all of the Astros hitters at least dabbled. This is proven not only by eyewitness accounts but by the work of Tony Adams, an Astros fan who later spent more than fifty hours watching video of every available at-bat of the Astros' season and logging the bangs.

Adams, a web developer and graphic designer by trade, created an app that allowed him to collect data from MLB's publicly available Statcast platform. He used spectrograms, which showed pictures representing the variance in sound caused by the banging.

Adams didn't have video on twenty of the games played at Minute Maid Park, so his data was incomplete. It also registered scattered bangs from before the May 26 Baltimore series, when the trash-can system was not yet in place. But Adams did not claim that his system was precise, and it did effectively illustrate larger trends.

According to Adams's research, which he posted on his website signstealingscandal.com, utility man Marwin González benefited the most of any Astros hitter, receiving 147 bangs on 807 pitches.

After González, the players aided most were Springer (140 bangs), Beltrán (138), Bregman (133), Gurriel (120), Correa (97), Marisnick (83), and Gattis (71).

It's important to note that the number of bangs did not provide a full accounting of the information that the batters had. Any player accepting the bangs was also accepting non-bangs—that is, when there was no sound, he knew to expect a fastball.

Farther down Adams's list was a trio of more complicated cases.

Altuve was the most resistant of the Astros stars. When the option to have a teammate bang the trash can first arose, he declined.

When Altuve was batting and there would be a bang, he would glare into the dugout.

"He doesn't want it," teammates would say frantically. On more than one occasion, Altuve returned to the dugout after his at-bat and yelled at the others to knock it off.

He was one of those players who felt that the additional information merely clouded his mind; he preferred to simply react to the pitch. McCann was also iffy on participating, as was right fielder Josh Reddick.

In the end, all three did receive bangs during their at-bats—McCann received 45 documented bangs that year, Altuve 24, Reddick 28—but very few times did those bangs match the general pattern that helped players know when a fastball or off-speed pitches were coming.

A closer look at specific plate appearances in which those players heard bangs provides further context.

Adams logged 233 of Altuve's at-bats, and 22 of them contained a bang. But nearly all of those at-bats included an off-speed pitch that didn't draw a bang. Sometimes a bang occurred on a fastball.

McCann's and Reddick's at-bats were similar. In data that Adams gathered for this book, McCann received the bangs in the correct pattern in just nine at-bats that season. For Reddick, it was three at-bats.

Some players, it turned out, wanted help in other ways. This explains some of the at-bats in which every changeup did not lead to a bang. There were times when the sound did not indicate that a changeup was coming but told the batter about location, like when the pitcher was going to throw inside. Other players only wanted the pitch in certain counts.

As the majority of players carried on, a quiet discomfort set in among a handful of Astros. The pitcher Mike Fiers told a few people on the team that he thought it was wrong. Others, like pitcher Collin McHugh, felt the same but chose not to make a big deal out of it.

As for manager A. J. Hinch, the situation was far more complicated. He was the leader of a team that included players who designed the scheme and players who disapproved of it. He did not personally think that sign stealing was a worthwhile pursuit.

Hinch's objections to the cheating began with small moments, before the trash-can scheme started and players were looking into the dugout for signs stolen in the replay room and related to Cora. He preferred that base runners focus on getting a better secondary lead, inching farther down the baseline to be in a better position to run.

"God," he would mutter to hitting coach Hudgens in the dugout, as base runners focused on stealing or receiving signs. "I wish they wouldn't do that."

But while watching the cheating develop and registering quiet disapproval, Hinch did not try to stop it. People who knew him well believed it was because he wanted to preserve the largely positive environment, and was conflict-averse to a fault.

Hinch would sometimes tell close friends that he considered leadership to be a matter not of what you preach, but what you tolerate. In this way he was failing by his own standard.

This was as loaded a situation as he could encounter. As the star recruit for a top program, Hinch had been at the top of the baseball mountain before even graduating high school. He went on to a playing career that fell below expectations, then a failed tenure managing in Arizona.

Now he was close to the top again, managing a team capable of winning it all and trying to hold its suddenly successful clubhouse culture together. He was simply not up to the task of taking a stand and disrupting the mojo, which could mean another fall down the mountain, even as he fretted about it.

Also in his subconscious were memories of what had happened in Arizona, the terrible arguments he'd had with veterans. Ever since, he had devoted his energy to developing as a leader, and part of that meant cultivating stronger relationships with established players. He was up against his own desire to be liked.

Compounding the situation for Hinch was Beltrán. Hinch was only three years older, and had once been a fringy catcher on a Kansas City team on which Beltrán was a bona-fide star. Their relative status within the same generation of players made it awkward, in theory at least, for Hinch to project authority.

But in reality Beltrán did not discriminate against or pressure lesser athletes. When utility man Tony Kemp arrived from the minor leagues in September, he was just twenty-five years old and had barely played in the big leagues.

Asked if he wanted to participate in the banging scheme, Kemp politely declined. He thought it was unethical. And that was it. No pressure from Beltrán or anyone else, and zero bangs during Kemp's thirty-nine plate appearances.

Prior to batting practice on July 17, George Springer carried three foam headstones out to center field. Soon after, Brian McCann appeared in a black robe.

The Astros were rolling, a full 32 games over .500 at 62-30. They held a 15.5-game lead over Seattle in the American League West, a 10.5-game lead over Boston for best in the A.L. Over in the National League, the Dodgers, at 64-29, represented a gathering threat to Houston's championship hopes.

On this day, the players were not worried about that. They were busy planning a funeral for Beltrán's glove.

Once among the game's elite center fielders, Beltrán had lost a step and been moved to right by his final year with the Mets in 2011. By 2017, he was almost exclusively a designated hitter, and an increasingly anemic one at that. On July 17 he was batting just .234, with a .291 on-base percentage.

When the Astros signed Beltrán, they knew his best days were behind him, but hadn't predicted quite so swift a decline. It was becoming clear that a great career was nearly over.

Beltrán was so beloved by teammates that even this provided an excuse for camaraderie. Hinch had not used him in the outfield since May, so McCann decided to hold a memorial service for Beltrán's glove.

Acting as the priest, McCann gave a brief and profane speech in the outfield. Beltrán filmed it with his phone and laughed.

Asked about it later that afternoon, Hinch grinned.

"I've not quite given up on [his] glove," the manager said, "even though they're going to bury it in the outfield today."

In the game that followed, Beltrán showed that he still had something left, launching a two-run homer in the sixth that tied the score.

Of course, even this light moment was tainted by secret cheating. The banging scheme was in effect that night—though in somewhat reduced form, because Seattle catcher Mike Zunino tipped pitches with sloppy mechanics, enabling the Astros to skip the complex sign-stealing system at times.

Beltrán batted in the second inning against Seattle's Ariel Miranda and struck out on five pitches. The first three were fastballs and did not draw a bang. The fourth was a splitter: Bang. Beltrán fouled it off. The fifth was a fastball. No bang.

In the fourth, Beltrán struck out on three pitches: fastball (no bang), slider (bang; fouled it off), fastball (no bang).

In the sixth, he homered on a 1-0 fastball from James Pazos that he knew was coming because, of course, there was no bang.

Also of note in that particular game, Springer, Correa, Gurriel, Bregman, Marisnick, González, and outfielder Nori Aoki all received bangs, while Altuve, Reddick, and McCann did not—further validating that trio's claims to reluctance, at least relative to their teammates.

Two weeks after that fun but tainted night, a darker vibe befell the Astros' clubhouse. July 31 was the deadline for teams to make trades without players having to pass through waivers. After that date it became much trickier to add impact talent.

The Astros were still rolling through the American League with an eye on the juggernaut Dodgers as potential World Series competitors.

Houston's need for pitching was clear. Behind Keuchel, the starting rotation was thin, and the bullpen needed help.

Luhnow and his staff got to work discussing trades with other clubs but were stubborn in their unwillingness to surrender top prospects. They did strike a tentative deal with Baltimore to add All-Star closer Zack Britton, but the Orioles nixed it due to health concerns about one of the players Houston planned to send their way.

When the deadline passed, Luhnow had added only veteran reliever Francisco Liriano, who was no longer an impact arm.

The Yankees, barreling toward a playoff matchup with Houston, added pitcher Sonny Gray. The Cubs had already traded for top starter José Quintana. At the last minute, the Dodgers snagged All-Star Yu Darvish from Texas.

Inside the Houston locker room, players felt angry, deflated, and unsupported. All of the old, bad feelings about Luhnow and his group began to resurface—We're working our butts off, the players thought, and they can't get us any help?

Keuchel gave voice to the group's sentiments. Asked by reporters that afternoon for his reaction to Luhnow's inactivity, the pitcher stood in front of his locker, jaw tight, voice even tighter.

"I mean, I'm not going to lie," Keuchel began. "Disappointment is a bit of an understatement. I feel like a bunch of teams really bolstered their roster for the long haul and for a huge playoff push. Us kind of staying pat was a huge disappointment."

Anger in the clubhouse was not the only source of internal strain during those summer months.

Starting earlier in the season, a group of unfamiliar faces was making a quiet presence known around the offices at Minute Maid Park. They first showed up at a pre-draft meeting of scouts, observing meetings of both large and small groups.

Who were these strangers? the scouts wondered.

Before long, a troubling bit of gossip went around. As one scout told another, "Those are consultants from McKinsey."

Some of the scouts knew what McKinsey was, and that it had a reputation for advising businesses to trim fat and cut jobs.

Astros scouts were already nervous about their standing. Those friendly enough with Luhnow to engage in honest conversations with him had known for years that their boss did not place a high value on what they did.

Luhnow's questioning of scouts went back to his days in St. Louis, when he pushed them to document their predictions and prove their accuracy. As technology improved and the Astros began to lean on new tools like the Edgertronic camera, the GM became even more skeptical that sending scouts on the road at significant expense was necessary.

In addition to the proprietary tech that the Astros had at their own facilities, most pro ballparks were equipped with a TrackMan camera, a high-tech device that gathered data that could be used to evaluate players with more precision than a scout's eye. A scout could grade a pitcher's curveball as a 70 on the 20–80 scale, but the Track-Man could tell you its exact spin rate.

But to see that as an argument for the obsolescence of scouts was to ignore their many other contributions. The best scouts showed up hours before games to watch batting practice and any other drills, gathering data that no machine could measure.

Scouts observed body language, interactions with teammates, attention to details, and many other intangible qualities that went toward what baseball people called "makeup," meaning the character of the player.

If the Astros were looking to trade for a prospect, was that prospect a good teammate? Did he listen to coaches?

Scouts also functioned as reporters, working their contacts for info they could pass back to the home office. Their days at the ballpark included talking to managers, broadcasters, writers, and one another. When their team was considering acquiring a player, the scouts would call around to ask about that player's makeup.

Luhnow was aware of all this; he simply didn't consider it as important as the scouts did.

"Your only job," an Astros scout remembered Luhnow once telling him, "is to get me scouting info on players that I can't get on TrackMan."

In the midst of the anxiety caused by the arrival of the McKinsey consultants, Astros executive Kevin Goldstein sent an internal email in August that further elevated stress among the rank and file: He asked scouts to use cameras to steal signs from the stands.

"One thing in specific we are looking for is picking up signs coming out of the dugout," Goldstein wrote. "What we are looking for is how much we can see, how we would log things, if we need cameras/

The New York Giants' Bobby Thomson crosses the plate after hitting the "Shot Heard 'Round the World" off Brooklyn Dodgers pitcher Ralph Branca to win the 1951 National League pennant. Branca's friend Jackie Robinson stands on the field to make sure that Thomson touches every base. Thomson was the beneficiary of a sign-stealing scheme. *(Getty Images)*

Former Mets manager Bobby Valentine was one of the game's most innovative characters. In 1997, he pioneered the use of team-owned cameras to decode opponents' signals. *(Rick Stewart/Allsport)*

Shawn Green (left) and Carlos Delgado (right) were among the best in their generation at watching games closely enough to legally pick up on pitch tipping and catcher signs. While with the Mets late in their careers, they mentored Carlos Beltrán in those skills. *(Photograph by Chris McGrath/Getty Images)*

Shortstop Carlos Correa was one of the Astros' brightest young stars. After the team was caught cheating, he became one of the staunchest defenders of its legacy. *(Photograph by Robert H. Levey)*

Astros manager A. J. Hinch (left) and general manager Jeff Luhnow (right) won a championship together in 2017. But both lost their jobs on the same day in 2020 when commissioner Rob Manfred released his report on the team's sign-stealing scheme. *(Photograph by Robert H. Levey)*

Carlos Correa, Alex Bregman, José Altuve, and A. J. Hinch (left to right) in spring training 2017—a year that would first come to represent their greatest triumph, and later their greatest shame. *(Photograph by Robert H. Levey)*

When the Houston Astros won the World Series in 2017, they provided a welcome distraction to a city still reeling from the devastation of Hurricane Harvey. Here, Carlos Correa (far left), owner Jim Crane (center, in necktie), and center fielder George Springer (right) are among those enjoying the team's championship parade. *(Photograph by Robert H. Levey)*

Brian Cashman, general manager of the New York Yankees since 1998, rebuilt his team with young stars in mid-to-late 2010s, only to run into the Astros in the postseason *(Photograph by Corey Sipkin)*

Clayton Kershaw was the best pitcher of his generation but struggled for years to win in the postseason. Here, he walks off the mound in defeat in the fifth inning of Game Five of the 2017 World Series in Houston. The Astros hung their sign-stealing monitor during World Series games, according to witnesses. *(Photograph by Rob Tringali/MLB via Getty Images)*

New York Yankees manager Aaron Boone, who took over a team with championship aspirations in 2018. *(Photograph by Corey Sipkin)*

Boone and Cashman (right) represented a new trend in baseball, where managers collaborated closely with analytics-driven front offices. *(Photograph by Corey Sipkin)*

Yankees right fielder Aaron Judge (left) was part of a young core that hoped to bring a new dynasty to the Bronx. But José Altuve (right) and the Astros twice defeated them in the American League Championship Series. When the Astros' cheating became public, Judge deleted a congratulatory social media post. *(Photograph by Robert H. Levey)*

Alex Cora, riding on a float in the Boston Red Sox victory parade in 2018, celebrates winning a World Series in his first year as an MLB manager. He was almost universally regarded as one of the game's most promising young managers. *(Photograph by Adam Glanzman/ Getty Images)*

After winning Game Six of the 2019 American League Championship Series with a walk-off home run against the Yankees' Aroldis Chapman, José Altuve clutches his jersey while crossing home plate. The gesture would later lead to intense speculation about whether he was cheating in ways that went far beyond the banging of a trash can. (*Photograph by Robert Levey/Getty Images*)

New York Mets general manager Brodie Van Wagenen (left) and chief operating officer Jeff Wilpon (right) introduce Carlos Beltrán as their new manager on November 4, 2019. Beltrán was thrilled to return to his former team and lead a group of young players. (*Photograph by Corey Sipkin*)

Beltrán is all smiles as he talks about how leading the Mets is a dream come true for him. He would be fired before ever managing a game. *(Photograph by Corey Sipkin)*

Major League Baseball commissioner Rob Manfred addresses the widespread outrage over the Astros scandal at a news conference in North Port, Florida, on February 16, 2020. *(Photograph by Mary DeCicco/MLB Photos via Getty Images)*

binoculars, etc. So go to games, see what you can (or can't) do and report back your findings."

The scouts who received this email didn't know what to do. Already worried about their job security, they were now being asked to behave in a way that would breach etiquette and make them pariahs in their brotherhood.

Scouts from all teams sat together in a section behind home plate; if one pulled out a camera and began shooting, everyone would see and judge harshly.

"This will be a stain on the organization, and it's a tough position to put us in," one scout told Goldstein.

Just days later, on August 18, the Astros fired eight pro scouts.

"This is not a cutback in scouting," the GM told the *Houston Chronicle* that day. "We are reconfiguring within and across the three scouting departments—international, domestic and pro."

This framing surely felt accurate to Luhnow, who was always trying to make the organization leaner and smarter. But to the people who lost their jobs, it sounded like hollow corporate-speak.

They knew that Luhnow did not see traditional scouting as an important aspect of a baseball operations department, and they didn't appreciate his cold touch. The McKinsey consultants came and went, and the Astros never indicated to scouts if their recommendations led to the firings.

After losing his job, one of the scouts called Luhnow, demanding an explanation for the disruption to his life and career. He was met with characteristic paranoia.

"What's this all about?" the scout said.

"Frankly," Luhnow said, in the scout's recollection, "I'm not going to tell you what this is all about, because I don't want you to tell another club what our thinking is."

The scout wondered why he had been axed when others with poorer reputations had kept their jobs.

"Put it this way," the scout remembered Luhnow saying. "Some people are on two-year deals. They will be in the same situation next year."

The scouts were not the only employees put off by the firings and the way they were handled. Hinch felt that Luhnow and his front office were undervaluing the contributions of scouts.

Once viewed in Arizona as a tool of the front office, an analytics geek from the future, Hinch now found himself in a dramatically different role in Houston. He was the one pounding his fist on the table, insisting that his team respect traditional concepts. Sometimes it felt that there was no one else to do it.

On his way out, one of the fired scouts heard from an irritated Hinch.

"These people don't realize that they're going to miss your insight," the manager said, his unease with the organization growing.

As the season wore on, another source of discomfort began to follow Hinch: an increasingly complicated relationship with the bench coach he had only recently sought to hire.

He and Cora were perhaps bound to regard each other with suspicion. Hinch was a Stanford graduate now lauded by the game's intelligentsia as the model of the contemporary manager. Cora was educated, too, and aware of the differences in how the sport and media that covered it treated white and nonwhite players and coaches.

The two disagreed on the sign-stealing scheme, but did not discuss it much. Instead it simmered and finally boiled over on August 31, though still in a way that avoided the core dispute.

Two weeks earlier, Hurricane Harvey, a Category 4 storm that killed more than a hundred people and ravaged parts of Texas and Louisiana, had flooded downtown Houston and rendered Minute Maid Park unplayable. The Astros were forced to move a home series against the Texas Rangers to Tropicana Field in St. Petersburg, Florida.

In the final game of that series, Hinch argued an interference call in the first inning and was ejected. That left Cora to manage for the rest of the day.

Cora immediately set to running the game his own way; he was the manager for the day, after all. But pitching coach Brent Strom seemed to have his own ideas, telling relievers to start throwing in the bullpen without checking with Cora. The energy in the dugout was oddly tense.

Adding to that, Astros Hall of Famer Craig Biggio, randomly visiting the team that day, stood at the bottom of the dugout steps, appearing to keep a close eye on the moves. He glared at Cora with his arms folded.

The Astros won the game. Later, an air-traffic-control holding pattern over Dallas extended their trip home, straining the group's already tense mood.

During the plane's final descent, Astros personnel saw the flooding out their windows. Their team's city, where many of their families lived, looked like an ocean. No one knew how they were going to navigate the streets and get home.

After the plane landed, the team boarded a bus to take them from the airport to the ballpark. Typically, on bus rides, Hinch sat in the front with Cora right behind him. That's the pecking order: manager, bench coach, staff, and players.

But on this ride, Biggio took the seat behind Hinch, forcing Cora back toward the middle of the bus: a sign of disrespect, whether or not it was intentional.

Once on the road, nearly everyone took out their phones to call their families and work out the logistics of reuniting. After about fifteen minutes, Cora popped in his headphones to listen to some music. When his headphone batteries died, he didn't stop the music, which now blared through the bus from his phone.

Astros television analyst Geoff Blum, a former major league player, stood and approached Cora.

"Hey, man," Blum said, "a couple of us are just trying to make a few phone calls. Can you please turn it down a little bit?"

"Okay, I'll turn it down for you," Cora said, in a tone that struck the people around him as aggressive.

Blum went back and sat down. Before long, Cora followed. He bent over Blum and began screaming.

"You think you know what you're fucking doing?" he yelled. "You and A.J. are trying to fuck me over. I know what you're doing."

Blum was friendly with Hinch but didn't understand what Cora was getting at.

"You're a pussy," Cora continued. "I hope the next time there's a hurricane in Puerto Rico you care as much about that as you care about this."

Blum, worried that a fight would cost him his job, tried to defuse the situation.

"Alex," he said, "let's talk about this when we get to the ballpark."

Hearing the commotion, Hinch stood and motioned for everyone to sit down and relax. Nothing more happened on the bus, but Cora's rage resurfaced as the team walked from the parking lot to the stadium entrance.

Hinch walked over to Blum and Cora, and Cora immediately forgot about Blum.

"You're just a pussy," he yelled at Hinch, advancing toward him. "You're just working for the man."

Cora and Hinch screamed at each other for several minutes, the players they were charged with leading looking on.

Beltrán was walking behind them, and finally stepped forward and played peacemaker.

After sleeping on it, Cora felt that he'd taken it too far on the bus. The next morning, roughly half the team visited the George R. Brown Convention Center in Houston, trying to cheer up people who had been displaced by the storm. While there, Cora apologized to both Blum and Hinch for directing language at them that he was not proud of, particularly the word "pussy."

But the manager and bench coach remained divided on the extent of the team's sign stealing, and the overall tension did not dissipate.

A day already made long by an argument between manager and bench coach was not over yet. Before Hinch went to bed, he would have a shiny new pitcher, courtesy of Luhnow.

When Hinch had returned home that night, he sat on his back patio with his wife, Erin, and debriefed about the intense time that they were living through. Much of their adopted city was underwater. He had just argued with his top coach in front of players. And not least in his thoughts was the fact that his team's final opportunity to add a pitcher was closing in—expiring at midnight that very night.

Baseball's convoluted rules actually allowed for two trade deadlines. The non-waiver deadline on July 31 was the main event, but teams had the month of August to acquire players who passed through waivers.

This is how it worked: In August teams placed many players on revocable trade waivers. If another team claims that player, they can have him as long as they take on the remainder of his salary. The claiming team can also work out a trade.

If none of the twenty-nine teams claims the player, the player has cleared waivers and can be traded. If the trade occurred before August 31, that player was eligible to play for his new team in the postseason.

Most of the highest-paid players cleared waivers, so it was no surprise on August 4 when erstwhile Detroit Tigers ace Justin Verlander made it through unclaimed.

Verlander's storied career in Detroit included a Rookie of the Year award, a Cy Young, and an MVP. But he was thirty-four years old, owed $65 million through 2019, and in apparent decline.

For several seasons his level of performance had sat significantly below his peak; with Detroit in 2017 he was 10-8, with a 3.84 ERA. These numbers were more than respectable, but hardly suggested he was still an ace who could lead a team to the World Series.

Still, when the Tigers decided they were ready to shed veterans and begin a rebuilding process, Verlander became the best available option to teams looking for pitching late in the season.

Both the Yankees and the Astros dabbled in talks with the Tigers GM Al Avila, but the Yankees withdrew because ownership wouldn't sign off on picking up the salary. Astros owner Jim Crane was willing to assume the financial risk if Luhnow could find an acceptable trade.

Avila and Luhnow were far enough apart on value on the morning of the deadline that the Tigers GM told Verlander that he was probably staying. But when Avila later traded star outfielder Justin Upton to the Angels, both he and Verlander came to believe that a move would be best for everyone.

Verlander saw himself as too far along in his career to suffer through a long rebuilding phase, and Avila didn't need a star pitcher on a last-place team. He and Luhnow re-engaged and set to hammering out details. An agreement drew closer.

Luhnow was visiting family in Los Angeles, keeping Hinch and his inner circle briefed via text. While he was at his nephew's Little League practice, his talks with Avila accelerated to the point where it was time to get final approval from Crane.

He secured that and raced back to his in-laws' house, where he was staying. When Avila called to close, Luhnow was in the shower. He stepped out, soaking, and agreed to terms. The Tigers would send Verlander and $16 million to Houston in return for three of the Astros' top eleven prospects.

The teams now had to review medical information on the players changing hands. This was no mere formality, as it had derailed the Zack Britton trade a month earlier.

Even more of an unknown was Verlander's willingness to become an Astro. Because he had played in the league for more than ten years and on the same team for more than five, he had what was called "10 and 5" rights, meaning he could veto any trade.

While wanting to play for a contending team, Verlander was wary of the Astros' reputation around the league as a cold, data-driven organization. One trendy concept that gave him extra pause was the theory, often put into practice by Houston, that starting pitchers should not be allowed to face the opposing lineup more than two times.

Sound data backed this strategy, as most pitchers saw a sharp decline in effectiveness after navigating the order twice. But Verlander was old-school and wanted the chance to finish his games.

He was on his way home from a dinner out with his fiancée, the model Kate Upton, when Avila called to tell him they had a deal. Verlander had to decide if he was going to accept it. He told Avila he was more likely to veto the trade.

But it wasn't a firm no, and as 11 p.m. approached—an hour from the deadline—the deal wasn't totally dead.

Crane called Verlander and tried to reassure him. Then he called Keuchel, the same veteran who had criticized the organization a month earlier for failing to acquire a pitcher.

Now it was Keuchel's turn to sell Verlander on the Astros.

With about ten minutes to go, the two connected. Keuchel made a quick sales pitch about the Astros being ready to win the World Series, and how the achievement would be extra special to a community in need of distraction from the devastation caused by Hurricane Harvey.

Verlander, stressed out about the life-altering decision he faced and looming deadline to make it, sputtered a tense thank you and ushered Keuchel off the phone. He needed to discuss it with Upton.

In the end, Verlander could not resist the temptation to chase a championship. He signed the paperwork at 11:59 p.m. and gave it to a Tigers employee whom the team had dispatched to his building.

Back in Houston, Hinch received a text from Luhnow with Verlander's phone number: He was free to reach out to his new ace, which he did.

It had been quite a day, beginning with his ejection at a "home game" played in Tampa Bay, and coming to include a view of the city's submersion in water and an argument with Cora. Now he had a brand-new All-Star on his team to help with the pursuit of a championship.

Exhausted as he was, after speaking with Verlander, Hinch didn't sleep for several more hours. These were complicated but exciting times.

Chapter 13

YEP, THE ASTROS USED THE TRASH CAN IN THE WORLD SERIES

As the summer rolled on and autumn drew closer, the Astros' deception deepened, and so did opponents' suspicions.

On August 1, Tampa Bay Rays pitcher Chris Archer won a game at Minute Maid Park but suspected that on at least a few occasions the Astros had his pitches. Later that night, Archer was back in his hotel room when an Astros player FaceTimed him.

"Dude, you've got good shit," the player said, as later reported by *The Athletic.* "You were just tipping."

This was a lie. Archer was not tipping his pitches. The Astros had banged the trash can thirty-nine times that night, and the Houston player was trying to cover his team's tracks by tossing a red herring at Archer.

Although rumors had begun to spread throughout the league about the Astros, opponents remained short on facts. Pitchers tended to know when hitters had the signs. So did managers, coaches, and savvy position players. But it's one thing to feel it and another to prove it.

Opposing teams would try to nail down what was happening. Oakland A's manager Bob Melvin once confronted Hinch and accused the Astros of using first-base coach Rich Dauer to steal signs. This gave Hinch, Cora, and the staff a good laugh: Dauer was a sixty-five-year-old lifer, a nice guy who wasn't in on any scheme.

Elsewhere in the American League West, the Texas Rangers told starting pitchers to cover their mouths with their hands or gloves when they walked in from pregame warmups in the bullpen. That's when the batterymates often discussed pitch selection and strategy, and at Minute Maid you never knew if someone was watching.

On September 15, when commissioner Rob Manfred completed his investigation into the Boston Red Sox's use of an Apple Watch to steal signs, he issued the memo promising harsher penalties going forward for electronic sign stealing.

That day, Tom Koch-Weser, the Astros replay official who was part of the Codebreaker plan, approached a higher-ranking member of the front office.

"We've got to stop Codebreaker," Koch-Weser said.

"Why?" his superior answered. "It's legal."

As far as this team official knew—and he was not nearly alone—there was nothing wrong with the Codebreaker program, because it had never been used for in-game sign stealing. He thought it was simply a tool for studying catchers' sign sequences before and after games.

Now Koch-Weser was telling him it violated Manfred's newly emphasized rules?

A moment far more tense came on September 21, with the Chicago White Sox in town. Sox pitcher Danny Farquhar noticed a banging—he later described it in the *Athletic* article that blew the lid off the scheme as the sound of a bat hitting a bat rack—immediately after his catcher would put down the sign for a changeup.

With Evan Gattis up in the eighth inning, Farquhar's catcher Kevan Smith signaled for a changeup. BANG. Gattis took the pitch for ball one.

Next, Smith called for a fastball. There was no bang. Gattis took a healthy cut and missed.

For the 1-1 pitch, Smith called for another changeup. This drew two bangs, and Gattis took it for a ball.

The 2-1 pitch was a fastball—no bang—and Gattis fouled it off.

Next came a changeup, which naturally had elicited a bang. Gattis smacked it down the third-base line, just foul.

The ballpark wasn't particularly loud that day, making the pattern of bangs audible. Farquhar called Smith out to the mound.

"They for sure have something," he said.

Smith said that he felt the same way, but didn't know what to do about it. They'd already changed their signs.

They decided to verbally plan out the next four pitches. Farquhar then struck out Gattis on a 2-2 off-speed pitch that didn't draw a bang, because Smith hadn't put down a sign.

Seeing that their scheme had been detected, Astros players hurried to remove the monitor from the wall.

The incident had a chilling effect. During that September 21 game, the Astros banged the trash can forty-one times. The next day they banged it once. In the team's two remaining regular-season home games, they banged the can a total of two times. But by October they were again regularly using the trash can—all the way through the end of the World Series.

This would remain a point of contention for years. The initial report from *The Athletic* had sources saying the system continued into the postseason, and another source insisting that it did not. Astros players would later issue vehement denials that they were cheating in October.

"I'm telling you, World Series games are too important to use easy signs," Correa told MLB Network reporter Ken Rosenthal later. "There are Morse codes out there. There are signs that nobody can get. There are so many variations you can use, and nobody can get that."

In February 2020, Manfred said that there was "conflicting evidence" on that point, though he considered the evidence of cheating more credible than the denials.

Specific data on the trash-can banging during the American League

Championship Series and World Series doesn't exist, but there is a reason for that.

Tony Adams, the Astros fan who spent countless hours reviewing video of the season and counting the bangs, said that the crowd noise in the playoffs was far in excess of anything he'd encountered in the regular season.

A review of sound files from crowd noise during the regular season and all postseason rounds reveals a dramatic change after the division series, lasting through the ALCS and World Series. In the ALCS, the cheering becomes much louder and is at the forefront of the mix.

This and other changes in the audio rendered the counting of specific bangs impossible.

As Adams explains: "The crowd noise level in the ALCS and World Series is much louder. . . . It's tough to hear anything in the lower range of the audio (where the banging sound is). It may have to do with different networks and their audio technicians setting up the mics differently. It's almost as if the audio has been clipped.

"I've listened to the ALCS and World Series several times and can hear faint sounds that could be banging, but I can't say they are with a level of confidence I'm comfortable with. The noises are so faint they don't even appear on the spectrograms. I've spent many hours working with the audio to see if I could isolate any banging sounds, but nothing worked."

Even without exact data to count the bangs, people with direct knowledge of the Astros' actions that year, including one person involved in the October sign stealing, say that the team did indeed use its trash-can system during the postseason. Correa was right to say that sign sequences become more complex in the postseason, and he is not alone in doubting whether the playoff cheating helped— but, at best, he dodged Rosenthal's question, perhaps because the truth was simple and damning.

That truth, per witnesses who participated, was that the Astros became more careful about concealing the monitor with the live feed after Danny Farquhar appeared to notice the banging incident in September, but they did not stop using it. Up to the end of the World Series, the team kept the monitor off the wall prior to games. With MLB officials, reporters, and others milling about, it seemed too risky to display—what if someone noticed and figured it out? But right as games were about to start, the Astros rehung the monitor. Then they removed it just as the games ended.

The cheating continued on the game's biggest stage, and the Farquhar incident proved a mere blip. Period.

As soon as Justin Verlander arrived in Houston, the Astros introduced him to the Edgertronic camera, hoping that it could become the key to a career resurgence for him.

To it they added the Rapsodo, another high-tech camera, which could measure the quality of pitches and help pitchers design new ones.

The results were immediate: The Edgertronic showed that Verlander's slider was leaving his hand too early, allowing hitters to pick it up. He moved his hand, and the slider became deceptive again.

The Rapsodo demonstrated that Verlander's two-seam fastball or sinker, a pitch in which movement is slightly more important than velocity, had become ineffective. Verlander stopped throwing it and emphasized the four-seamer, a pitch reliant on pure speed.

Verlander quickly became addicted to the technology, demanding to review nearly every pitch he threw with help from the Edgertronic and Rapsodo.

The adjustments restored him to his former status as a world-class ace. He made five starts for the Astros in the regular season, won all of them, and posted a 1.06 earned run average. The trade quickly proved to be a masterstroke by Luhnow and Crane.

With the rejuvenated Verlander atop their rotation, the Astros entered the postseason as strong contenders to advance to the World

Series. They won 20 games in September and finished with 101 wins, one shy of the Cleveland Indians, whose 25-win September gave them the best record in the American League.

An earnest desire to inspire the city after Hurricane Harvey had galvanized the team. Verlander felt a connection to his new home, too, and wanted to provide a distraction by leading a long postseason run. Hinch tapped him to start the playoff opener on October 5 at home against Boston.

Minute Maid Park was loud that day, as it always was during big games. Players and coaches disagree on how effective the cheating was with that level of crowd noise, but opponents note that efficacy does not change the moral equation.

And on the topic of efficacy, here are the home/road splits of several key Astros' batting averages during the 2017 postseason: Altuve, .472/.143; Correa, .371/.411; Bregman, .273/.154; McCann, .300/.037; Gattis, .300/.200. The Astros were 8-1 at home that postseason and 3-6 on the road.

Tony Adams's research uncovered just one bang during the first game. Boston ace Chris Sale worked quickly, making it harder to gather and convey the information in a hurry.

Batting second in the bottom of the first inning against Sale, Bregman took a fastball that touched the lower part of the strike zone, then fouled off another fastball. Next, he kept his bat on his shoulder for a changeup that went for ball one.

Sale then tried to get Bregman to chase a high fastball, a common strategy for a 1-2 count. The pitch sailed well north of the strike zone, and Bregman took it for ball two.

Bregman fouled off another fastball, then he crushed a slider to deep left field for a long home run. The ball clanged off the wall behind the seats, and put the Astros up 1–0.

Altuve followed by hitting a homer of his own, this one on an 0-2 fastball.

Sale, who had started the All-Star Game for the American League three months earlier, continued to struggle.

In the fourth, Marwin González—the player who received more documented trash-can bangs during the regular season than any other Astro—batted with two runners on base. He took a first-pitch changeup, fouled off a slider, then hit a fastball to right-center for a two-run double.

This was a talented team, their scoring not always the result of a camera and trash can. Altuve, the most reluctant and infrequent of the cheaters, hit three home runs in that game. Verlander allowed two runs in six innings, and the Astros cruised to an 8–2 win.

Game Two ended with an identical score. Correa and Springer homered, and Gattis and Altuve drove in runs. Keuchel pitched effectively, and the Astros took a 2–0 lead in the best-of-five series.

For Game Three, the teams moved to Fenway Park, where the Sox had recently been busted for electronic sign-stealing. Boston mauled Astros starter Brad Peacock and won 10–3. The next day, again in Boston, the Astros edged the Red Sox 5–4 and clinched the first round.

For the first time in twelve years, Houston was moving on to the League Championship Series. A matchup with the New York Yankees awaited, the pennant at stake.

The Yankees' window opened faster than even they expected. The 2016 season was when general manager Brian Cashman made the decision, virtually unprecedented for the franchise, to trade away veteran players for prospects.

It typically takes a few years for an organization to recover from a sell-off like that and win again at the major league level. Privately, the Yankees' front office believed that they were one or two seasons away from their next winning phase.

But 2017 turned out to be a surprise. From the beginning of spring training, the team performed better than expected. Pitcher Masahiro Tanaka was excellent, even contributing to a combined no-hitter with several other Yankees pitchers. Greg Bird hit eight home runs.

The Yankees finished an MLB-best 24-9-1 in the preseason. A team's spring-training record rarely means much, but the Yanks felt an extra crackle of excitement that February and March because of all the young talent in camp. For a ball club so often weighed down by overpaid veterans, this was a refreshing change.

Top infield prospect Gleyber Torres, acquired the previous summer from the Cubs, offered reason to hope. So did Bird, Gary Sánchez, Luis Severino—and, above all others, the towering right fielder Aaron Judge.

For a franchise that had lost its face when Derek Jeter retired in 2014, Judge seemed the perfect replacement. He had a big smile and a smooth manner. He was interested in becoming a team leader. And he hit majestic home runs that thrilled the home fans.

Judge had a national coming-out party in July, when he won the Home Run Derby the night before the All-Star Game. Despite a slump through much of the season's second half, he ended up setting a record by hitting fifty-two home runs in the regular season, the most ever for a rookie at that time.

Judge got hot again before the end, and the Yankees won 23 of their final 34 games and captured an American League wild-card spot. After beating Minnesota in the wild-card game, the team moved into an unlikely playoff run, their new era suddenly under way.

The Yanks edged Cleveland in the division series in five games and moved on to face the Astros in the ALCS.

As a division winner, the Astros held home-field advantage, so the series began with two games in Houston. The monitor was wired up, and the trash can in place.

The first game featured a premier pitching matchup, Keuchel versus Tanaka. Both were excellent, but Keuchel was sublime; he threw seven shutout innings and struck out ten.

The Astros' scoring came in the fourth inning, when Carlos Correa doubled in a run on a 2-1 slider, and Yuli Gurriel singled on an 0-1 slider to drive in another.

The eighth inning brought an ominous development, one that would soon blossom into a full-fledged problem and stretch Hinch to the limits of his instincts and creativity. Ken Giles, the Astros' closer, had been effective all season, but was faltering on the bigger stage. In the division series Giles had seemed shaky, allowing a run in each of his two appearances against the Red Sox. The Astros overcame it to win that round, but knew that their top reliever was not at his best.

Now, in the first game of the ALCS, Giles inherited a tense situation in the eighth: The speedy Brett Gardner stood on first, Judge was up, and the Astros clung to a 2–0 lead.

Giles threw a wild pitch, allowing Gardner to advance to scoring position, then got Judge to ground out. He followed by walking Sánchez, bringing up the potential go-ahead run in Didi Gregorius. Giles struck him out to end the threat, but still had to return for the ninth—and he did not look right.

In that inning, Bird homered to make it 2–1, then Giles struck out Jacoby Ellsbury to end the game. The Astros had drawn first blood, but did it with their hearts in their throats. This wasn't going to be an easy series.

Game Two was another thriller. Verlander found still another gear, twirling a complete game before a deafening home crowd.

In the fourth inning Correa poked a Severino fastball just over the right-field wall and out of Judge's grasp. Several minutes of tension followed.

Inside the Yankees' dugout, bench coach Rob Thomson pointed out that a young boy sitting in the front row had extended his glove toward the yellow line that marked a home run. When the ball caromed off the side of the boy's mitt, Judge's own glove was mere feet away.

Manager Joe Girardi asked the umpires to review the play to make sure that the boy hadn't reached over the line to touch the ball. If he had, it would be fan interference, Correa would be out, and the thrumming ballpark would shift from excitement to rage.

The umpires gathered to put on headsets and communicate with the replay center in New York.

Correa paced the dugout. Judge stood in right field, hands on his hips, chewing gum. The crowd's cheering sank to a lower register. Everyone waited.

Finally, the umps removed their headsets and signaled that the original call stood. The ball had indeed cleared the yellow line before the boy touched it, and the Astros led 1–0. Correa exhaled and clapped. Minutes later, Todd Frazier tied the game for the Yankees by hitting a ground-rule double to drive in Aaron Hicks.

In the bottom of the ninth inning, the game was still 1–1, with series momentum hanging in the balance. If the Astros could walk it off, they would head to New York with a nearly insurmountable lead of two games to none. If the Yankees pulled off a win, they would clinch a split on the road and return home in a strong position.

Every pitch by Yankees closer Aroldis Chapman carried these broader implications.

Chapman began by striking out Reddick on a slider low and away. That brought up Altuve, who flashed his elite bat speed in smacking a 100-mph first-pitch fastball into left-center for a single.

Correa followed. Chapman started him with two blazing fastballs outside, both of which Correa took for balls. The Yankees' closer, drawing deep breaths and sweating bullets, followed with a slider for a called strike one.

Inside the Astros dugout, Verlander drummed his fingers on the railing. He'd just finished nine innings of dominant work and hoped his team could deliver the win.

Chapman threw another slider and missed, then Correa fouled off a fastball. Full count.

The eleventh pitch of the inning was a low fastball, 99 mph. Correa drove it to right field, where it landed on the ground in front of the warning track.

As Judge scooped it up and prepared to throw it in, Altuve raced around the bases. He had not been running on the pitch but was fast enough to try to score from first.

Judge threw to Gregorius near second base just as Correa was sliding in. Gregorius spun and fired home.

The throw beat Altuve, but the ball bounced out of Sánchez's glove.

Altuve slid in safely, then popped up with his arms in the air. His teammates poured from the dugout. The Astros had won again.

The Yankees appeared cooked that night, their special season nearly over. But upon returning to New York for Game Three, they transformed into a different team. For three days they dominated the Astros, winning 8–1, 6–4, and 5–0. Judge homered in two of the games, and the Astros' bullpen issues surfaced again in the middle game.

In the eighth inning that night, Houston once again had the Yankees on the ropes. Trailing 4–2 in the eighth inning, New York was six outs away from falling behind 3–1 in the series.

Frazier led off the inning with a base hit off Astros reliever Joe Musgrove. Pinch hitter Chase Headley singled to left, sending Frazier to third and bringing the Bronx crowd to life.

Hinch popped out of the dugout, his right hand in the air to signal for the shaky Giles.

Brett Gardner was up next. He hit a grounder to the right side of the infield that was deep enough to score Frazier and make it 4–3.

Judge followed, and at the end of a tense at-bat, launched a 2-2 slider off the left-field wall, tying the game. Giles had blown it again.

By the time the teams flew back to Houston for Game Six, the

Yankees were up 3–2, a win away from the pennant. It seemed that for all the Astros' talent, their bullpen would keep them from the World Series.

Verlander started Game Six and saved the season by throwing seven shutout innings. Back in the friendly confines of Minute Maid Park, the Astros' offense scored seven runs against Severino and a procession of Yankee relievers.

Giles, under less pressure with a six-run cushion, pitched a scoreless ninth, and the teams moved on to a deciding Game Seven.

The Astros took an early lead in that win-or-go-home contest, 4–0 after five innings, but Hinch knew that it wasn't secure. His gut told him not to trust Giles or the soft underbelly of his middle relief corps. With the pennant on the line, he needed to improvise a new plan.

After starter Charlie Morton contributed five scoreless innings, Hinch summoned Lance McCullers Jr.—a starting pitcher—from the bullpen.

It's common to use a starter in relief during the postseason, but rarely to the extent that Hinch did on that day.

With an eye trained closely on McCullers, Hinch liked what he saw—the quality of his pitches, body language, everything—and sent him back out for the seventh. Then the eighth. Then, forgoing Giles, the ninth.

For more than a century, pitchers mixed fastballs and off-speed pitches, working hitters and keeping them guessing. But on this day the Astros' high-tech cameras were giving real-time feedback that told them McCullers's curveball was dominant, and that he should stick with it. Hinch's eyes, and those of pitching coach Brent Strom, agreed.

Fans watching at the ballpark and on TV saw the perfect marriage of analytics and gut instinct—and they were also, likely without realizing it, watching the emergence of A. J. Hinch as a modern manager in full, taking full command of his team and the game.

Listening to the technology, the Astros had McCullers finish the game by throwing a remarkable twenty-four straight curveballs. Listening to his instincts and trusting his gut, Hinch left him in to do it.

When Bird flew out to Springer with two outs in the ninth, the skipper saw his gutsy decision vindicated.

The man who had once failed to take charge of a team in Arizona, who spent the years after determined to prove he could do better, had just spun a managerial masterpiece. He was going to the World Series.

His counterpart, Girardi, lost his job a few days later. He had managed the Yankees for ten years and won the franchise's most recent World Series. Had the Astros not been cheating in this tight series, perhaps he would have won the pennant and been allowed to continue.

BEST. TEAM. EVER?

The cover of the *Sports Illustrated* issue that hit newsstands on August 28, 2017, set a high bar for a team that hadn't won the World Series in twenty-nine years. But these Dodgers were not only winning at a record clip, but doing it with the flair that marks a ball club as special.

Behind that bold headline, the *SI* cover featured a photo of Yasiel Puig, the mercurial slugger from Cuba, pouring a bucket of Gatorade over the head of third baseman Justin Turner after one of the team's many thrilling victories.

The pair represented much of what was memorable about these Dodgers. Puig defected from Cuba and signed with the Dodgers in 2012. By the following year he had become a controversial sensation, hitting and throwing the ball like a rocket, licking his bat, talking to himself, showing up late for games—whatever he did, it generated attention and made him a polarizing but captivating figure.

Turner was a stocky veteran with red hair down to his shoulders and a lumberjack beard. Once marginalized as a bench player with the Mets, he signed with the Dodgers in 2014 and emerged as a star and clubhouse leader.

Those two helped to form the core of a Dodgers team that entered the postseason as favorites to win the World Series. Manager Dave Roberts brought a light touch, collaborating with the new-age front office on game strategy while allowing the players to be themselves.

Perhaps no one wanted a chance at the World Series more than Clayton Kershaw, who was still among the best pitchers in baseball, but whose inevitable physical decline had begun. On July 23 he left a start with back tightness and didn't return until September 1.

Despite the five-week absence, Kershaw led the team in wins with 18, and posted a 2.31 earned run average.

The Dodgers finished the regular season with 104 wins, eleven games ahead of Arizona in the National League West. They proceeded to sweep the Diamondbacks in the division series and blow past the Cubs in the NLCS in five games.

On October 24, Kershaw started Game One of the World Series. This series presented an opportunity not only to finally win a ring, but to burnish a legacy before it was too late. He would have only so many opportunities to prove he wasn't an October choker.

Game One brought extreme weather—at 103 degrees at first pitch in Los Angeles, it was the hottest World Series game ever. Kershaw, lucky to draw the assignment at Dodger Stadium and not Minute Maid Park, where the Astros had their sign-stealing setup, came out blazing.

From the first inning, the Astros knew they were in trouble. Kershaw was using his backdoor slider to own the inner part of the plate, and was pitching with a presence that had often eluded him during his checkered postseason career.

The Dodgers' Chris Taylor homered off Keuchel's first pitch of the game. Bregman tied it with a solo homer in the fourth, and Turner hit a two-run blast in the sixth to make it 3–1, Dodgers.

Kershaw twirled seven dominant innings, striking out eleven, and closer Kenley Jansen earned the save. Kershaw drew one game closer to redemption.

The next game was a wild one, a 7–6 Houston win in eleven innings. The teams set a record for most combined home runs in a World Series game with eight, including five in extra innings, which also set a new mark (in his 2020 interview with Ken Rosenthal on MLB Network, Correa would insist that the Astros did not have the Dodgers' signs that night, adding—tellingly—"We were on the road").

Springer's two-run homer in the eleventh ultimately decided it.

For Game Three the teams moved to Houston, and the Astros devoured Dodgers pitcher Yu Darvish. The trash can was in place, as was Beltrán's legal skill of picking up on pitch tipping. He noticed—and of course shared with teammates—that when Darvish prepared to throw a fastball, he rotated the ball in his glove in search of the proper grip. He didn't do this for off-speed pitches.

The Astros knocked Darvish out of the game after one and two-thirds innings—the shortest outing of the pitcher's distinguished career.

In his 2020 interview with Rosenthal, which was intended to show that the Astros did not benefit from cheating in the postseason, Correa would note that the scoring plays in that game were not a result of changeups crushed out of the ballpark, but weaker hits and poor fielding: "Marwin hits a (single) with men on first and second. That's (two) runs. Brian McCann hits a single with a man on second. Again, multiple signs. That's (three) runs. (Alex Bregman added a sacrifice fly later that inning.) Evan Gattis, with Reddick at first, hits a chopper to the pitcher, (Tony) Watson. He throws it away. Reddick scores from first. Those are the five runs we scored that day."

The problem with that logic? It wasn't always the hit that made a sign-stealing process effective; it could also be the takes earlier in the at-bat that enabled it to progress to a chopper or a throwing error.

In the plays that Correa referenced, González took a first-pitch slider before hitting his single on a fourth-pitch slider. McCann worked a seven-pitch at-bat. Gattis's chopper came on the third pitch, right after he took a changeup.

There was no way to know exactly how sign stealing affected these at-bats, but to reference only the pitch that produced contact is an incomplete accounting.

Correa also noted that the Dodgers changed their sign sequences for the series, making it much more difficult to decode them. That is true. But again, the trash can and monitor were there, as were Astros players making the same ethical calculation about using them as they did during the regular season.

The second inning of that game brought another example of the Astros' hubris, when Yuli Gurriel hit a 2-1 fastball deep to left field for a home run off Darvish. As Gurriel returned to the bench and sat, he used his fingers to pull the skin around his eyes up, an apparent reference to Darvish's Japanese heritage.

In case there was any doubt about his intentions, Gurriel then mouthed the term *chinito,* which in his native Cuba translated to "little Chinese boy."

As Gurriel's actions quickly made their way around social media and became an instant controversy, high-ranking members of Houston's baseball operations department privately downplayed the incident, believing that it was not a big deal. This was gross miscalculation, as the public backlash against Gurriel grew during the game.

Luhnow had to take over the crisis management from his underlings. Gurriel spoke to the media after the game and apologized to Darvish. He drew a suspension that would take effect the following April.

It was Darvish himself who bailed out the Astros later that night, when he posted a gracious tweet forgiving Gurriel.

"No one is perfect," the pitcher wrote. "But I believe we should put our effort into learning rather than accuse him."

He was perhaps one of the only Dodgers in a conciliatory mood that week. Others on the team suspected methods of potential cheating that went beyond sign stealing.

Before every game, an employee of the home team is assigned to "rub up" or "mud up" the game balls, massaging a dark substance into the baseball in order to make it less slick and easier for a pitcher to grip.

Often at Minute Maid Park that was the job of clubhouse manager Carl Schneider, who did it in the umpires' room with varying degrees of supervision—umps didn't tend to watch this closely.

The balls then went to a batboy, who, of course, was an employee of the home team. His job was to give those balls to the umpire throughout the game.

Shortly after the series moved back to Houston, the Dodgers felt that Astros pitchers were rejecting baseballs more frequently than is typical, tossing them back to the umpire and requesting new ones.

Then an L.A. pitcher approached his front office with an observation: The balls that the Astros were using were mudded up differently. They were visibly darker.

"These game balls are suspicious," the pitcher said.

A similar issue had arisen in 2010, when the San Francisco Giants accused the Colorado Rockies of misusing the humidor that stored baseballs at Coors Field. The humidor was there to help deaden the baseballs in the Rocky Mountain altitude, where they tended to fly out of the park for cheap home runs.

The Giants believed that the Rockies were using the humidor balls only for their pitchers and were giving opposing pitchers untreated balls. MLB instituted a new policy that the umps had to personally watch as the balls were removed from the humidor and placed in a ball bag. The bag had to remain in the umpires' sight throughout the game.

This time, the Dodgers thought that the Astros had balls mudded up more heavily for their pitchers, and that the batboy would deliver those to the ump during innings when the Dodgers were batting. When a Houston pitcher accidentally got a ball intended for the opposing pitcher, he would toss it back.

It was unclear if this actually helped the Astros pitchers. According to Dr. Alan Nathan, professor emeritus of physics at the University of Illinois, whose work on the physics of baseball had proved useful to the league and front offices, the over-mudding of a ball is unlikely to have a significant impact.

Says Nathan:

"I can speculate that a heavier application of mud *might* make the ball a tiny bit heavier which would reduce exit velocities [off the bat], all other things the same. But I am skeptical that there is much effect."

In 2017 MLB did not offer much guidance on how a baseball was supposed to be mudded up, so it was difficult to punish a team for it. In 2018 the league created and distributed posters showing the acceptable level of darkness for a game ball. Teams were directed to hang them in clubhouses.

Meanwhile, A. J. Hinch's bullpen tortured him again in Game Four, when Giles allowed three runs in the ninth. Musgrove followed by giving up two runs of his own, and once again the Astros' pen did not seem capable of closing out a World Series.

That comeback set up the Dodgers with a chance to take a lead of three games to two the following night—and with Kershaw on the mound.

As if delivered on a platter, it was the chance Kershaw had been waiting for to prove he could prevail in the biggest moment. After the masterpiece in Game One, winning this one would end all talk of Kershaw as a choker.

It did not play out that way. In Game Five, played in Houston, Kershaw allowed four runs in the fourth inning and two in the fifth, and yet again walked off the field dejected.

An epic slugfest followed, with the teams combining for three game-tying home runs. After five hours and seventeen minutes—

the second-longest World Series game in history—Bregman won it with an RBI single in the bottom of the tenth. The final score was an exhausting 13–12.

It was a heavyweight fight for the ages, but the storyline could have been much simpler. Kershaw could have dominated and sent the Dodgers home to L.A. one win away from a championship. Instead, his legacy suffered a massive setback.

The explanation for Kershaw's ineffectiveness that night is complex. Inside the Astros' dugout, players and coaches immediately noted that he wasn't pitching inside the way he had been in Game One at Dodger Stadium.

They speculated that perhaps the cozier dimensions at Minute Maid Park had made him afraid to go inside, because if he missed over the plate he would risk allowing a cheap home run, especially to left field. For whatever reason, he just didn't have the backdoor slider working, the pitch that had been so effective for him in the first game of the Series.

But another fact—a remarkable one—also rendered this failure not only unique, but suspicious. Kershaw threw a total of 51 off-speed pitches that night—curveballs and sliders—and the Astros swung at just one of them: 51 off-speed pitches, 50 takes. This simply does not happen to a pitcher, not to mention one whose curveball was among the best in his generation. The Dodgers had a hard time believing that it would have happened at all had the Astros not been cheating.

The Dodgers also believed that Kershaw was receiving slicker baseballs than Keuchel and the Astros relievers who followed.

In the clubhouse afterward, Kershaw seemed to suspect that his chance to author a better career narrative had just passed. He stood in the center of the room, taking the obligatory questions from a thick mass of reporters, his voice quiet, his eyes down, his answers offering only one or two words at a time.

When the Series returned to Los Angeles for Game Six, yet another set of cheating allegations arose. Before the game, umpires warned both sets of base coaches to remain in the boxes that marked their position.

The Dodgers, like the Oakland A's in the regular season, believed that the Astros were using their base coaches to either peek in at the catcher for signs or look to the dugout for stolen signs to relay to the batter.

The Astros responded by accusing the Dodgers of the same. They said that the L.A. base coaches, George Lombard and Chris Woodward, were wandering too far out of their boxes. The umps told everyone to knock it off.

The Dodgers went on to win Game Six, pushing the Series to its limit. But Game Seven brought another managerial masterpiece from Hinch.

McCullers started but allowed three early runs. There is no margin for error in a Game Seven, so Hinch went to his wobbly bullpen.

Brad Peacock, Francisco Liriano, and Chris Devenski got him to the sixth inning, and his plan was to ride Devenski an inning longer. But a bit of managerial chess by Dave Roberts forced him to make a quick adjustment.

In the sixth, Roberts elected to intentionally walk both González and Gattis, bringing up Devenski and forcing Hinch to pinch-hit.

To replace Devenski in the bottom of the inning, Hinch called for Charlie Morton, a starting pitcher operating on just three days' rest instead of the standard four.

Because of this, Hinch wanted to use Morton for a maximum of three innings. But that would take him only through the eighth—and he didn't want Ken Giles anywhere near the ninth inning in Game Seven of the World Series.

Watching Morton as closely as he had McCullers in Game Seven of the ALCS against the Yankees, Hinch determined after the eighth that the pitcher could go one more frame.

And so Morton was still on the mound with two outs in the ninth when Corey Seager grounded to Altuve, who threw to Gurriel at first and leapt into the air.

The Astros had won the World Series for the first time in franchise history. Hinch had emerged as the model of a contemporary manager, and Cora was poised to join him, already drawing interest from teams with a vacancy to fill.

In the final game of his twenty-year playing career, Beltrán was a champion at last. The team's young core, from Bregman to Correa to Gurriel to Springer, who was named World Series MVP, promised years of excellence.

The city, ravaged by floods less than two months prior, had a team to rally around. The Astros were fun, smart, and almost certainly at the beginning of a dynasty. What could go wrong?

Two weeks after the World Series, in a conference room at the Waldorf-Astoria in Orlando, MLB executive vice president Chris Marinak addressed the game's highest-ranking baseball-operations execs at the annual general managers' meetings.

Marinak was there to discuss pace of play, about which the league was increasingly concerned. In the 2017 regular season, the average game lasted three hours and five minutes, or fourteen minutes longer than at the beginning of the decade.

The postseason had been even worse. In the World Series, six of seven games exceeded 3:05, with Game Five coming in at 5:17.

This was a significant drag on the entertainment value of the product. Even the most compelling playoff games stretched into the wee hours, and regular-season games sometimes felt as if they had ground to a halt.

Baltimore Orioles GM Dan Duquette spoke up about the impact that sign stealing had on pace of play. As a GM who had been victimized that May in Houston—though he still didn't know exactly how—Duquette was acutely aware of how defending against sign stealing could slow the game.

Once a team had a runner on second base, especially when it was a fishy team like the Astros, the opposing pitcher and catcher had to work overtime to complicate their sign sequences. That resulted in mound visits that halted the game's action.

Duquette suggested that baseball look into high-tech ways for pitchers and catchers to communicate with the dugout, from wearable tech to earpieces. The only way to keep signs from being stolen, he said, was for the catcher to stop using his fingers to signal for pitches. If this happened, sign stealing would go away and games would move faster.

That concept proved a few years ahead of its time, but baseball did move to put new procedures in place.

Over the course of that off-season, Marinak and other MLB officials would work on a plan to address pace of play. Commissioner Rob Manfred was initially enthusiastic about installing a pitch clock in ballparks but found in discussions with the union that players were largely opposed to that.

It turned out that many players agreed with Duquette in believing that sign stealing was one of the most significant causes of the game's slowed pace.

As MLB and the Players Association negotiated solutions, Manfred tabled his pitch-clock idea—as much as he liked it, he didn't consider it worth a labor war—and focused instead on mound visits.

The league decided to limit mound visits for the first time, settling on six per team per game. In addition, MLB announced that it would introduce the ability to record all phone calls from the dugout to the replay room, bullpen, dugout, and press box.

The commissioner's office also issued a three-page memo addressed to all club presidents, general managers, and assistant general managers that reiterated the new standards made clear in Manfred's September 15 announcement of the Red Sox Apple Watch punishments.

"Electronic equipment, including game feeds in the Club replay room and/or video room, may never be used during a game for the purpose of stealing the opposing team's signs," the memo read.

The 2017 season was in the books and the Astros were champions. It would take another two full seasons for the world of electronic sign stealing to come crashing down. Those years would bring no shortage of drama and outrage.

Chapter 14

THE ASTROS' FRONT OFFICE STARTS TO COME APART

On May 8, 2018, Toronto police arrested Blue Jays closer Roberto Osuna after an incident in which Osuna allegedly beat up the mother of his three-year-old child.

The woman fled to Mexico and refused to return, so Osuna ducked charges. Major League Baseball immediately placed the pitcher on administrative leave, and later hammered him with a seventy-five-game suspension, reflecting its belief the incident was a severe one.

Meanwhile, the defending-champion Astros still had a bullpen problem, and it was getting worse.

Closer Ken Giles's increasing wobbliness had nearly cost the team a World Series before Hinch papered over it with brilliant manipulation of his pitching staff. But now Giles's issue was not only one of performance—there was a personal conflict, too.

On July 11, Giles entered in the ninth inning of a game against Oakland and allowed three hits before recording an out. Hinch came to get him.

"Aw, fuck you, man," Giles said as he left the mound.

This wasn't the A. J. Hinch of 2009, who allowed himself to be emasculated in a dugout confrontation after removing pitcher Doug Davis. He was a stronger leader now, and wasn't going to allow this to pass.

The Astros sent Giles to the minor leagues, and knew they had to get rid of him altogether.

As the front office gathered to discuss strategy for the July 31 trade deadline, Osuna's name came up as a possibility, but no one in the front office worried too much that Jeff Luhnow would pursue him.

When the Cincinnati Reds put All-Star closer Aroldis Chapman on the trade market in the winter after the 2015 season, the Astros had passed. They simply didn't want to get involved with a player accused in an ugly domestic-violence incident.

Chapman had allegedly choked his girlfriend the previous October while arguing at their Florida home. He then smashed a car window, took a handgun from the car, and fired eight rounds. Major League Baseball would later suspend him for thirty games.

The Yankees traded for Chapman, and Luhnow swung a deal with the Phillies to acquire Giles instead.

Then, during the 2016 season, the Astros released a minor league outfielder, Danry Vásquez, after video surfaced of Vásquez punching a woman three times in a ballpark stairwell.

Because of these prior actions, nearly all of Luhnow's top lieutenants were stunned when, in July 2018, the GM indicated he was open to pursuing Osuna.

The front office did the standard behind-the-scenes diligence on Osuna and did not like what it learned. Few details about the alleged incident had surfaced publicly, but the staff's digging led them to believe that the accusations against Osuna were particularly horrific, and that MLB's seventy-five-game ban had actually been too lenient.

They also heard negative feedback about Osuna as a teammate. All told, their sources made clear that this was not a guy a team would want as a part of its culture. But Luhnow was taking a long look at Osuna, despite what the Astros had learned about him. His staff spent days hoping it wouldn't happen.

The Astros were already a great team—defending champions with a chance to repeat—and most in the front office didn't see the need to make the moral compromise, let alone bring a tsunami of negative public relations on themselves.

When, on July 27, Luhnow acquired reliever Ryan Pressly from Minnesota, other team officials felt deep relief. Maybe they wouldn't go for Osuna after all.

As the trade deadline approached, Luhnow gathered in his war room at Minute Maid Park a group of five top front-office officials: Brandon Taubman, Kevin Goldstein, Mike Fast, Will Sharp, and Matt Hogan.

While discussing a possible trade for Osuna, the group expressed a general opinion that, based on what it knew about the alleged incident, Major League Baseball had not issued a stiff enough punishment.

Then Luhnow went around the room for each individual to weigh in. Taubman stood and advised Luhnow not to do it (this would make the later incident that ended Taubman's Astros career more shocking and complex than nearly anyone realized).

Goldstein also stood from his chair and delivered an impassioned speech about how acquiring Osuna would be a bad idea, the wrong thing to do.

"I don't want your moral opinion," Luhnow snapped. "I want your baseball opinion."

That line would haunt the group long past the day that Luhnow delivered it.

"This is my baseball opinion," Goldstein said. "I don't think he'll fit in."

The general sentiment in the room remained strongly opposed to trading for Osuna. Given Luhnow's demand for a baseball argument, the group adopted Goldstein's approach and tried to shift the discussion to Osuna's potential negative impact on the clubhouse.

When Vásquez had been caught on tape hitting his girlfriend, Justin Verlander and Lance McCullers Jr. had tweeted harsh criticism about it. Verlander had written, "I hope the rest of your life without baseball is horrible." How would an Osuna acquisition resonate with these players?

Luhnow was still having none of it. He stopped talking to his advisers.

On the day of the trade deadline, the front office gathered in a conference room at the ballpark. Initially, Luhnow was not there.

Then he walked in the room and said that he had just traded Giles to Toronto for Osuna. One of the team officials in the room remembers feeling like he had been punched in the gut.

Now the organization was going to have to defend the move. Right after making it, Luhnow departed for a vacation in Mexico, leaving Taubman to explain it internally to the many Astros employees who were upset.

In the news release that announced the deal, Luhnow was quoted as saying, "The due diligence by our front office was unprecedented."

Pressed on this in a subsequent conference call with reporters, he said that he spoke with Osuna and unnamed Astros players.

Then, asked how the team's stated "zero tolerance" policy regarding domestic violence could possibly square with a trade for Osuna, Luhnow held his ground.

"Quite frankly, I believe you can have a zero tolerance policy and also have an opportunity to give people second chances when they have made mistakes in the past in other organizations," he said. "That's kind of how we put those things together."

The press was unforgiving.

AS ASTROS WELCOME ROBERTO OSUNA, THEY WAVE GOODBYE TO THEIR INTEGRITY, read the headline in *USA Today*. Added *Yahoo! Sports:* IN TRADING FOR ROBERTO OSUNA, THE HOUSTON ASTROS SHOW THEY HAVE NO CONSCIENCE.

In the clubhouse, Verlander made clear that he was not thrilled. Saying that Luhnow had not consulted with him, he added, "It's a tough situation. . . . Obviously, I've said some pretty inflammatory things about stuff like this in the past. I stand by those words."

What Luhnow said in private struck friends as more solid than the explanations he offered in public. Major League Baseball had suspended Osuna for seventy-five games. After that, the pitcher was eligible to play. If the punishment was too light, wasn't that an issue with baseball's policy—not an Astros issue?

Still, the decision left Luhnow's front office in the awkward position of having to support a player whose acquisition violated their personal sense of right and wrong.

Coworkers thought that it especially affected Taubman. As the person largely responsible for helping the players understand and work with analytics, Taubman had to sit with Osuna after the trade and go over the team's TrackMan data and other information.

After that, the two were collaborators, both invested in Osuna's success. Taubman was also loyal to his front-office group—meaning that he simultaneously agreed with and resented much of the media criticism lobbed at the Astros after the trade. It was easy to see how this could become emotionally complicated.

Taubman was a thirty-two-year-old Long Island native whose ferocious interest in fantasy baseball led him out of a career in banking and into the Astros' front office. His career was on the fast track; within a few months of the Osuna trade, Luhnow promoted him to assistant GM.

With that ascension came mixed feelings about the new closer. The trade left scars that would pop up in dramatic fashion later on for Taubman, but it began to tear apart one of baseball's smartest front offices almost immediately.

Before the regular season was even over, Mike Fast informed Luhnow that he was leaving. To colleagues, he had sunk into himself and not been the same since the Osuna trade.

This was a significant loss. Fast, a former semiconductor engineer and writer for *Baseball Prospectus,* had been among Luhnow's first hires with the Astros. He brought groundbreaking research on how catchers framed pitches, and a reputation as a person of character. By

2016 he was in charge of the Astros' analytics department, as important a role as any with that club.

Immediately in demand around the league, Fast took a job with the Atlanta Braves almost as soon as the postseason ended. Though he never said publicly why he left the Astros, friends would firmly believe that the Osuna trade was the final straw.

The Astros were slowly coming apart.

Chapter 15

MASS PARANOIA

E arly in the 2018 season, a person working for the Astros detailed to another club an inside tip involving a massage gun and the wall behind the dugout.

According to that person, an Astros player would stand behind the wall that separated the clubhouse from the dugout. Equipped with the gun, which functioned like a power drill, he would drill into the wall to signal when a particular pitch was coming.

An Astro sitting on the dugout side would feel the vibration and signal to the batter verbally or to the base runner with a hand signal.

That Astros source told the other team that the drilling scheme came in handy when Minute Maid Park was too loud to hear the trash can, or when the Astros were feeling paranoid about being caught. Not as many coaches and pitchers knew about it as the banging, because it was not as loud or obvious.

A high-ranking official for the club that received that information instructed members of the team's traveling party to arrive extra early for a game at Minute Maid Park.

"Pretend to get lost," the executive said, "and see what you can find."

A small group from that visiting team arrived in the middle of the afternoon before a 7 p.m. game and wandered around the park, playing dumb.

They found their way to the bathroom behind the Astros' dugout. In the wall was a particular spot where the concrete had eroded, exactly as it would be by a drill. This was not irrefutable proof that a drilling scheme had occurred, but it was consistent with what the source had said. The erosion was only in one spot.

After finding the damage in the wall, the group wandered out to center field, where the Astros had an additional video room.

As they approached, a security guard stepped in front of them and said, "Sorry, guys, but I can't let you in here."

These were but two of many experiences that left opposing clubs more suspicious than ever about the now-defending-champion Astros. As the spring and summer of 2018 progressed, paranoia spread through the game, and new incidents continued to add to it.

In the summer of 2018, the Seattle Mariners arrived at Minute Maid Park for a three-game series and found several GoPro cameras hidden around their dugout. This was most certainly not normal. Mariners personnel covered the cameras with towels.

A handful of teams began sharing information about the Astros with one another, resolved to bust Houston and create a fair playing field in the American League again.

Many times, teams called Major League Baseball with these complaints. Often, league officials like Peter Woodfork and Chris Young would chase them down and find a lack of proof.

In roughly ten instances between 2017 and 2019, the league's investigators looked into sign-stealing complaints.

Until the investigations that led to penalties against the Astros and the Red Sox in 2020, the DOI interviewed people but did not request emails and other communications or documents. It took Astros pitcher Mike Fiers (who had disagreed, in 2017, with the ethics of the Astros' sign-stealing operation) speaking on the record to compel that to change.

When teams became frustrated with what they perceived to be a lack of action, MLB countered that it didn't have subpoena power to compel the Astros to come clean. Teams would accuse and the Astros would deny—over and over again.

For the 2018 season, the Astros did end one important aspect of their cheating: They were no longer banging on the trash can.

The cessation of this method was as subtle and organic as its start. There was never a meeting or a specific moment when the players decided to discontinue it. No one even recalls a conversation about the issue.

When the Astros reported to 2018 spring training after a winter packed with World Series celebrations, the trash can was simply not top of mind.

For one thing, Carlos Beltrán had retired and Alex Cora had taken a job as manager of the Boston Red Sox. Those two were hardly the only forces behind sign stealing in 2017, but their absence did leave the team without two veterans who had led the charge and who were skilled at it.

There were always Astros players who thought the trash-can scheme was unethical, even if they tainted themselves by going along with it. Many of the pitchers disapproved, as did a few hitters. Hinch had never liked it. It had come to weigh on the group as a source of guilt and stress.

The extra monitor was no longer in place, either. After 2017, the Astros moved their replay review room closer to the dugout, rendering the video "annex" unnecessary.

The video-room code breaking—explicitly illegal after Manfred's September 2017 memo because it stole signs in real time—did continue. Other verbals to communicate stolen signs to the batter continued, too.

MLB's later investigation into the Astros would not nail down conclusively if illegal in-game code breaking stopped. In the report, Manfred wrote, "The investigation revealed no violations of the policy by the Astros in the 2019 season or 2019 Postseason." Privately, MLB felt that its failure to uncover violations in 2019 did not mean that those violations hadn't occurred—on that point, the investigation was simply inconclusive.

Eyewitnesses now concede that at least into 2018, Astros personnel continued to decode sequences in the video room and communicate the information to players in-game. This was a clear violation of MLB's rules, the exact offense that ultimately got the 2018 Red Sox in trouble.

With Cora as manager, the 2018 Sox were using their replay room to decode sequences and get them to base runners in real time. This would later result in an MLB investigation that cleared Cora of wrongdoing but resulted in the suspension of Boston's replay coordinator and the surrender of a draft pick. Cora did not bring the trash-can scheme to Boston; much like the remaining Astros, he just quietly decided to move on from it.

The Dodgers had an entire R&D department in what had once been the visitors' clubhouse, after a new clubhouse was built during a stadium renovation. They and the Milwaukee Brewers would both become subjects of mutual electronic-sign-stealing complaints before long.

But despite accusations against other teams, rivals watching closely believed that the Astros were in a league of their own when it came to cheating. As one opposing general manager remarked to a reporter, "A lot of us are operating in shades of gray. The Astros are black and white."

For their part, the Astros players and front office not only resented this scrutiny but remained convinced that other teams were just as bad. The institutional paranoia continued to run rampant in Houston.

Resentment bubbled to the surface in early May in a Twitter spat between a few Astros players and Cleveland pitcher Trevor Bauer. Bauer replied to a tweet about the elite spin rate of several Astros pitchers with a thinly veiled accusation.

"If only there was just a really quick way to increase spin rate," Bauer tweeted. "Like what if you could trade for a player know-

ing that you could bump his spin rate a couple hundred rpm over-
night . . . imagine the steals you could get on the trade market! If
only that existed . . ."

The Astros believed that Bauer was referring to the application of
clear substances to a pitcher's fingers, often in a mix containing Bull-
Frog sunscreen and other materials that created tack. This was similar
to pine tar in that it was technically illegal but socially acceptable as
long as it was done subtly.

Astros pitchers often used a clear mix on their fingers but wondered why Bauer was making a big deal of it. Didn't every team do
this? If Bauer didn't, the Astros grumbled privately, he surely had
teammates who did. These frustrations tumbled into public when
several Houston players responded to Bauer's tweet.

Wrote Astros starting pitcher, Lance McCullers Jr.: "Jealousy isn't
a good look on you my man. You have great stuff and have worked
hard for it, like the rest of us, no need for this. I will ask though
because my spin rate and spin axis on my 4 seem [*sic*] is a$$."

Pitcher Collin McHugh added, "If only there was this thing where
people who had been around baseball a long time taught people who
hadn't been around as long. Imagine the possiblity [*sic*] for improve-
ment yr over yr! We could call it coaching!"

Alex Bregman piped in with a taunt of his own.

"Relax Tyler . . . ," he tweeted, intentionally calling Bauer by the
wrong name. "Those World Series balls spin a little different . . ."

It was not unprecedented, this kind of public sparring between
ballplayers, but it wasn't common, either. As members of the same
union, opposing players usually had more to unite than divide them.
Most tended to view one another as allies, and the media and front
offices as their common enemies.

But the Astros had a way of triggering other teams. The Bauer
dustup was nothing compared to what would come later.

—

During the weekend of May 28, 2018, when the Astros came to Yankee Stadium for a three-game series, Brandon Taubman decided to launch a counterespionage mission. Taubman, the senior director of baseball operations at the time, strongly suspected that the Yankees were engaged in their own high-tech sign-stealing effort.

Walking to the center-field area of Yankee Stadium during a game, Taubman crossed over in the black "batter's eye" area, where opponents are not allowed to venture.

There he saw a Yankees intern standing in the camera well, operating a camera.

"Excuse me," Taubman said to the intern. He proceeded to accuse him of sign stealing.

The Yankees had an explanation. The team had received approval to purchase its own high-speed camera. Because they weren't sure if MLB would allow continued use of the camera, they didn't mount it right away, but assigned the intern to operate it manually.

After Taubman approached, the intern texted his superiors to notify them. Taubman shot video of the intern filming the pitcher; in that video, it's also clear that the high-speed camera captures the catcher's hands.

Yankees assistant general manager Jean Afterman called the league offices, where she spoke to Peter Woodfork, MLB's senior vice president of operations.

Afterman told Woodfork what had happened and reiterated that the league had told the Yankees that they could use the camera. Brian Cashman told Luhnow the same.

Bryan Seeley's DOI at MLB looked into the incident. The Yankees' intern turned over his phone, and the team gave Seeley's group access to internal texts and emails. Taubman gave MLB the video that he shot of the incident. The DOI interviewed the intern, who denied that his camerawork had anything to do with sign stealing.

The DOI report concluded after scrubbing the intern's phone that he had not been texting but writing down pitches in a notes feature on his phone, because the screen was freezing and he was concerned that all pitches weren't being reported.

Taubman and the Astros had found it suspicious that the high-speed camera was shooting the catcher. But the DOI report, according to a person with direct knowledge of it, says that the intern was "zooming in on [catcher's] glove because the pitcher's release point was in the same sight."

MLB cleared the Yankees, but the Astros remained deeply skeptical that New York was playing on the level. Both teams filed away the resentment and suspicion that had now been simmering for more than a year.

Meanwhile, a former Astros pitcher had gotten to work warning others about his old team.

In the off-season, starter Mike Fiers, who had never been onboard with the Astros' scheme, had signed with Detroit. In August, the Tigers traded him to Oakland. Fiers told members of both of these teams exactly what the Astros were doing.

In August, Oakland filed a complaint with MLB after noticing that the Astros were clapping in their dugout—clearly, the A's thought, to convey stolen signs. This was one of the instances when Manfred dispatched his Department of Investigations, but the DOI was unable to compel anyone on the Astros to admit wrongdoing.

Because of Fiers, the trash can was now an open secret around the league, and every incident in which a team alleged sign stealing pushed it closer to broader exposure. In fact, the A's 2018 complaint to MLB included details of the Astros' use of the monitor behind the dugout. But when MLB's investigators went looking for it, it was gone—removed, of course, after the 2017 season. The team had eluded detection.

The 2018 postseason brought many such moments and would ultimately see the trash-can scheme revealed to the public. The age of espionage was now in high gear.

—

During the third game of the American League Division Series between Cleveland and Houston, the Indians noticed a man in a gray checkered blazer and black pants standing in the camera well on the field level. The man pointed what appeared to be a cell phone directly into their dugout.

An Indians employee snapped a photo and told security to remove the mystery man, whose name was Kyle McLaughlin. McLaughlin was not listed anywhere as an Astros employee, but his Instagram account contained photos of him posing with Jim Crane.

It turned out he was a business student at the University of Florida who also worked at the Floridian National Golf Club in Palm City, Florida. There he had met Crane, and the Astros owner took a liking to him and tried to get him experience in baseball operations.

During the Indians game, an Astros front-office official thought Cleveland might be stealing signs. The official sent McLaughlin down to the dugout level to take pictures, but he didn't find any evidence of cheating.

Cleveland lost that game, ending their season. Their front office warned the Boston Red Sox, the Astros' opponent in the next round, about McLaughlin.

With Alex Cora as their manager, the Sox had enjoyed the winningest regular season in franchise history, capturing 108 victories and beating the Yankees by eight games in the American League East. They then went on to play New York and freshman skipper Aaron Boone in the first round.

Boone and Cora had been teammates in Cleveland and colleagues at ESPN, and were now facing each other as successful rookie managers.

—

Boston began the postseason with a problem almost identical to the one that had faced A. J. Hinch and the Astros the year before: a powerful offense, strong starting pitching, and a weak bullpen, despite the presence of All-Star closer Craig Kimbrel. If Cora was going to guide the team to the World Series, he was going to have to be careful and creative.

As the playoffs began, Kimbrel wasn't as shaky as Ken Giles had been for Houston the year before, but he wasn't dominant, either.

The Red Sox took an early lead in Game One in Boston, scoring three in the first against Yankees starter J. A. Happ, and led 5–3 in the ninth. Kimbrel entered and allowed a home run to Aaron Judge, escaping with a 5–4 win but allowing the Yanks to steal a bit of momentum.

That carried over to the next night, when Judge and Gary Sánchez homered early off Boston starter David Price, who was out of the game in the second inning. The series moved to New York tied, 1–1.

Back at Yankee Stadium, the Red Sox devoured the Yankees in Game Three, winning 16–1 and pulling to within one win of advancing.

In that game and the next one, Cora outmanaged Boone and established himself alongside Hinch as one of the game's great young managers.

To be a first-year manager and navigate the speed and intensity of a playoff game would be difficult for anyone. Boone, who won raves during that regular season and was widely viewed as a promising leader, struggled.

In the fourth inning of Game Three, starter Luis Severino was laboring against the bottom third of the Red Sox lineup. It was clear he wasn't long for the game, but Boone wanted to get him through the ninth spot in the order, and then summon Lance Lynn from the pen. The idea was that Lynn would be the best choice to induce a double play, and that his stuff would play well against the top of the Red Sox lineup.

But Severino allowed two singles and a walk, while Boone froze until it was too late. The subsequent 16–1 drubbing left the Yankees and their manager in a bad place. In Game Four, Boone made a similar mistake, leaving a struggling CC Sabathia in for too long in the third inning.

On the other side, Cora showed no such growing pains. He was both intense and relaxed, making changes to his lineup when needed and generally going to his bullpen at the right times. In Game One, for example, he had summoned scheduled Game Three starter Rick Porcello for a surprise appearance in short relief; Porcello got two huge outs in the eighth inning. Nothing about Cora's performance suggested inexperience. Leaning on a dugout step, chewing sunflower seeds, he looked like he'd been doing it for years.

In the bottom of the ninth inning of Game Four, Kimbrel gave Cora a profound scare.

With the Red Sox leading 4–1 and three outs from clinching the series, the closer began by issuing a leadoff walk to Judge. His face dripping with sweat and his chest visibly rising and falling under his jersey, Kimbrel soon loaded the bases. He then hit a batter to force in a run.

The bases were still loaded when Sánchez launched a ball deep to left. The entire ballpark seemed to inhale, waiting to see if it would be a game-winning grand slam. It was just short, and went for a sacrifice fly.

Gleyber Torres then grounded out in a play close enough to require confirmation by video review.

The Red Sox had survived the rally and vanquished their rivals, moving past the Yankees and into the ALCS—though Cora now had a Kimbrel problem in addition to his pre-existing issues with middle relief. And he would have to take down the Astros to win the pennant.

Since the Indians had reached out to the Red Sox to warn them about Kyle McLaughlin, Boston was prepared. Sure enough, when the ALCS began in Boston on October 13, McLaughlin was next to the Red Sox dugout, armed with a camera and using his phone to send texts.

The Red Sox had security remove McLaughlin in the third inning. When MLB officials met with Astros officials about the incident, the Astros claimed that McLaughlin was looking to catch opponents in the act of illegal sign stealing. The discussion became nasty, with Astros officials defiantly accusing the league of failing to monitor sign stealing, thus necessitating McLaughlin's assignment.

This wasn't the first moment of tension that year between Hinch's Astros and Cora's Red Sox. Warming up in the bullpen to face Boston during a regular-season start, Justin Verlander covered the TV camera in the bullpen. Cora resented the implication and complained to MLB about it.

It was a postseason of rampant sign-stealing allegations, and it didn't stop with the Astros, Indians, and Red Sox.

Over in the National League, the Dodgers and Milwaukee Brewers—whose general manager was former Luhnow assistant David Stearns—lobbed suspicions back and forth during a tense NLCS that Los Angeles won in seven games.

MLB officials investigated complaints about the Dodgers by unscrewing long lenses in the camera wells to look for hidden high-speed cameras. This complaint didn't even make sense to the league, but it tried to follow up on every tip. League officials also hunted down Dodger fan YouTubers in the stands who were holding their phones at angles that made opponents wary. None of this led to hard evidence of cheating.

The Dodgers said that they welcomed the scrutiny because they had nothing to hide. For their part, they believed that a Brewers coach was watching a live feed of the game in the tunnel. L.A. registered this complaint with MLB, which sent an official to look for it. "Not found," the official reported back, according to a confidential DOI report on which the author of this book was briefed.

The public knew nothing about these behind-the-scenes spying allegations. As far as fans knew, the Dodgers and Brewers were simply playing compelling ballgames.

On October 16, the world learned of the Astros' trash-can scheme. By then, Mike Fiers had told enough people in baseball about it to make it widely known. Plenty of other people had firsthand knowledge, too.

In a report for *Yahoo! Sports,* columnist Jeff Passan was the first to break the story of the trash-can scheme. Though not as explosive as the later *Athletic* report because it did not feature a player on the record, Passan's story revealed the scandal to the world. It read in part:

"Two major league players said they have witnessed the Astros hitting a trash can in the dugout in recent years and believe it is a way to relay signals to hitters. The Los Angeles Dodgers also believed the Astros were stealing signs during the World Series last season, according to two sources."

Word was out now. The only thing left was for a player to put his name to it. Before the ALCS, MLB's chief baseball officer Joe Torre met with Hinch, Cora, Luhnow, and Boston president of baseball operations Dave Dombrowski for a standard review of postseason commercial breaks, rules, and other details. But Torre also added a warning against engaging in sign stealing. If a team cheated, Torre said, it was likely to get out in public eventually.

The actual series between the Astros and Red Sox did not live up to its potential as a clash between American League powerhouses managed by Hinch and Cora.

The Red Sox were in the midst of a special postseason, and, despite a continually shaky Kimbrel, marched past the Astros in five games. The Astros would not repeat as champions, and it was Cora's turn to face the Dodgers in the World Series.

The 2017 Series had done much to crush Clayton's Kershaw's playoff reputation, so it was almost expected when the Red Sox jumped on him in the first inning of Game One, scoring two runs to take an early lead.

Kershaw would lose that night, and again in the deciding Game Five. This was not the epic that the Astros and Dodgers had produced the year before—rather, it was the most successful team in the 118-year history of the Red Sox rolling over yet another opponent.

It ended with a Hinch-like touch from Cora. After sweating through a month of Kimbrel's narrow escapes, he took no chances with the championship on the line.

Leading 5–1 in the ninth inning, he called for Sale, his ace. Sale struck out the side, finishing with a breaking ball that fooled a flailing Manny Machado.

Moments later, Cora stood on a stage in the middle of the field, his eyes red, his demeanor more stoic than the players who surrounded him.

Only a decade earlier, he'd been the last player on the Red Sox roster, mentoring Dustin Pedroia and keeping Manny Ramírez in line. Now he was their leader—and a champion, at that. It was almost overwhelming.

When Fox host Kevin Burkhardt teed up Cora for his first postvictory comments on national television, Cora was still summoning his composure.

"What a season," he said, exhaling.

A few minutes later, during a broadcast interview on the field, he finally allowed himself a broad smile.

That came when his daughter, Camila, fifteen years old and as emotionally engaged in the game as he had been (she started crying before Sale recorded the final out), wrapped him in a hug and said, "He's the best ever. I love him."

The future was bright, maybe even limitless.

Chapter 16

THE FINAL STAND

The 2019 season brought more complaints about the Astros cheating, and more on-field success in Houston. Hinch's team won 107 games and rolled into the playoffs, but tensions simmered about sign stealing.

Throughout the summer, a handful of teams—the Rays, Yankees, and Indians among them—continued to share intel with one another about what they believed was still going on at Minute Maid Park.

The Yankees' suspicions, already strong, were further encouraged in April 2019, when they traded for former Astros outfielder Cameron Maybin. Maybin warned them about Minute Maid Park.

"When you go in there," he said, "you've got to make sure your shit is totally buttoned up."

Teams had yet another suspicion that the 2019 Astros were up to something with their batboys. They observed that when the batboy jogged to second base to collect batting gloves from the base runner he appeared to spend an abnormal amount of time talking. This would be an easy way to transmit information on sign sequences from the video room to the field.

By the time the American League Division Series arrived, the situation had become so heated that the Astros' opponent, the Tampa Bay Rays, expressed to MLB a list of specific concerns. Among them:

1. During the season, several teams had noticed that the Astros' two aces, Justin Verlander and Gerrit Cole, were tossing baseballs back to the umpire with a greater frequency than was normal. This mirrored the Dodgers' concerns back in the 2017 World Series. The Rays asked MLB to be extra vigilant that Verlander and Cole were not receiving balls that had been mudded up differently.

2. Since early in the season, unproven rumors had circulated among teams that Houston was using some kind of wearable technology like Band-Aids or buzzers that would vibrate before certain pitches. The Rays asked MLB to look out for vibrating Band-Aids on Astros players.

3. The Rays suspected that the Astros had signals in their scoreboard that told the batters what pitch was coming.

4. The Rays thought the Astros were using hidden cameras in center field.

5. The Rays suspected that the Astros had a secret video room for sign stealing.

MLB officials looked into the allegations and said it found no proof of any of them. The second item was especially interesting in that it foreshadowed accusations against the Astros about Band-Aids and buzzers that would inspire significant chatter a few months later.

Most current big leaguers were probably unfamiliar with the history of buzzers, which had been part of sign-stealing stories for more than a hundred years, stretching back at least to the story from 1900, when Pearce Chiles of the Phillies stood on top of a buzzer under the third-base coach's box. When a team was known for sign stealing, these allegations sometimes arose. Now a club was asking MLB to watch for it with the Astros.

While MLB had been unable to nail the Astros on any of the other teams' accusations, it had been working for more than a year to tighten up regulations and procedures that made electronic sign stealing significantly more difficult to pull off.

At the annual general managers' meetings in November 2018, Commissioner Manfred and MLB made electronic sign stealing a point of heavy emphasis, telling team executives that the league would hold them personally accountable for violations.

In spring training of 2019, MLB specifically warned every club about audio cues like whistling at batters. That was part of an even tighter set of rules designed to combat sign stealing that went into place before the regular season.

The new rules included imposing an eight-second delay on clubhouse TVs, other than in the replay room. A team's video-replay coordinator could still watch a live feed but would be monitored and prohibited from communicating with any team personnel about signs. No TVs would be permitted in the tunnels or hallways.

Additionally, the league began conducting random sign-stealing audits during the 2019 regular season, in which it would inspect helmets, sliding gloves, dugouts, trainers' equipment, and storage boxes.

In practice, some of the people assigned to monitor replay rooms were more effective than others. Once, at Fenway Park, an opposing team spotted the Red Sox monitor sitting on the steps to the dugout, watching the game. Other monitors could be seen fiddling with their phones, appearing less than vigilant.

But there were also many stories of tightened surveillance. During the 2019 regular season, one team's replay coordinator opened the workplace communication app Slack on his computer and sent an innocent message to a coworker in the front office.

The monitor wrote him up, and the coordinator's superior told him he had to stop Slacking during games.

The Yankees erected a screen behind their replay coordinator to make clear that players weren't allowed to look over his shoulder. On one occasion a player forgot and popped into the room to peek at his at-bat, and the monitor reprimanded him.

As for the eight-second delay, MLB mandated that all televisions in the clubhouse—not just in the replay room—be delayed so players wouldn't have time to watch on TV and relay signs to the dugout before the pitch. It was clear that the myriad suspicions and complaints had caught MLB's attention and it was cracking down.

During the 2019 regular season, one team got a call from the MLB offices to scold them that their television delay was closer to six seconds than eight. The Astros' trash-can scheme had been common knowledge since at least September 2018, when *Yahoo! Sports* first reported on its existence. Teams also now had to account for every camera in their stadium, and explain what it was used for, how it was wired, and where its feed could be viewed.

It wasn't just the commissioner's office making sign stealing more difficult. By 2019 opponents were defending against the Astros and other fishy teams by devising sequences more complex than ever.

Prior to that season, the Yankees implemented a new anti-cheating defense system. They gave each pitcher a laminated card, roughly the size of a playing card, that could fit in the fold behind the brim of his cap. On that card was a series of different sign sequences, typically four or five for a starting pitcher and three or four for a reliever. The catcher had a corresponding card on his wristband (this was legal and league-approved). When either the pitcher or catcher suspected that an opponent had their signs, he would hold a finger in the air to change sequences: one for the first sequence on the card, two for the second, and so on.

This was a long way from the spring of 2017, when Carlos Beltrán could stand at second base and determine which of a small handful of sequences the catcher was using. Now it was significantly more complicated.

Despite all that, paranoia was rampant, and teams still found plenty to be suspicious about in Houston—and Houston was not alone. On May 27, the Mets' defending National League Cy Young Award winner, Jacob deGrom, labored through five innings at Dodger

Stadium. It was an uncharacteristic performance for one of the best pitchers in baseball, and something felt off about it. DeGrom, the coaching staff, and the front office agreed: The Dodgers seemed to be on every pitch, their swings and takes way too confident.

The day after the game, deGrom, general manager Brodie Van Wagenen, and bullpen coach Chuck Hernandez personally searched the stadium for proof of sign stealing. Anyone who happened to be at Dodger Stadium early that afternoon would have been treated to the sight of a world-class ace and his GM poking around in center field in search of a hidden camera. They found nothing.

But if the Dodgers and their massive R&D department on the field level occasionally made opponents nervous, the Astros were living fully in the heads of the rest of the league.

The Rays lost the 2019 division series to Houston in five games. In the deciding contest, Tampa Bay pitcher Tyler Glasnow allowed an uncharacteristic four runs in the first inning. He later realized that he was tipping his pitches and did not believe that it was a result of illegal sign stealing. He simply had a tell in his motion.

Still, before Game One of the Astros' next series, the ALCS against the Yankees, an MLB official approached a member of the Yankees' front office and posited that the Rays had been so distracted by sign-stealing paranoia that they hadn't been able to play as well as usual. They had been knocked off their game.

The Astros were rolling along, needing just eight wins for another championship. But there were severe storm clouds on the horizon. In just a month's time, the organization as they knew it would effectively cease to exist.

Before that first game of the ALCS, the Yankees' front office demanded that Major League Baseball lead them on a deep inspection of Minute Maid Park.

As the Astros shagged fly balls during batting practice on the field, a small group of officials walked the concourse, looked closely at the scoreboard, and examined every scouting camera.

The Yankees' representative on the tour, assistant GM Jean Afterman, made a show of taking notes and pointing to things; there was an element of gamesmanship there, but the Yanks also wanted the Astros to know that they were on to them.

It appeared to work. The Astros in the outfield looked up nervously at the inspection. Closer to the dugout, A. J. Hinch, Alex Cintrón, and the coaching staff seethed at the spectacle. Hinch believed that the 2019 Astros were playing on the level, and he resented any implication otherwise.

The bad blood spilled over into the game and spurred on the outsize reactions to Cintrón's whistling from the dugout in the first inning to signal Tanaka's pitches. In the first inning, after the Yankees thought Astros hitting coach Cintrón whistled and Boone complained, Cintrón stuck his middle finger out at the Yankees manager. That was when Yankees third-base coach Phil Nevin, a close friend of Boone's, told third baseman Bregman, "Tell your third-base coach I'm going to kick his fucking ass."

The Astros had been caught cheating again, two years after the trash-can scheme. It was a different violation, but a violation nonetheless. As Astros sources now admit, Yankees catcher Gary Sánchez was tipping the fastball that night by rising higher in his crouch. The whistling conveyed the sign to the hitter.

While audio cues had been a part of baseball for many years, MLB had made a point in 2019 that they were banned. Top league officials, including Joe Torre, Chris Young, and Peter Woodfork, had personally communicated this to managers, including Boone, during spring training in 2019.

Despite all of the distraction, Tanaka won Game One anyway. In Game Two, Carlos Correa hit a walk-off homer in the eleventh inning to even the series at 1–1.

With bad feelings between the clubs still percolating, Gerrit Cole beat Luis Severino in Game Three back at Yankee Stadium.

It rained the next day, forcing a postponement of Game Four. In the afternoon of the forced off day, the website for the New York sports network SNY published a report about the whistling incident.

Major League Baseball launched a quick investigation. They reviewed the video, then told a few reporters that they had found nothing conclusive to indicate cheating by whistling. The Astros, of course, knew they were guilty and had dodged any disciplinary action.

As Hinch read the SNY story, he was filled with old, complicated feelings. It wasn't pleasant. For two years, he had wrestled with guilt about abdicating his leadership with the trash-can scheme, and now it seemed that those skeletons would never stop chasing him.

"They are NASA," one anonymous coach was quoted as saying, referring to the team's ability to use advanced technology, in this case to spy and cheat.

Hinch bristled at this line. The trash can was in the distant past, and Hinch believed that opponents' continued suspicions were left over from old schemes. For example, the hole in the dugout wall from the massage gun/drill was discovered in 2018, but had been drilled in 2017.

He was still hot when the teams reconvened the following afternoon. After stalking into the interview room, he sat at the table and took a question on the whistling story.

"Man, I'm glad you asked that question," Hinch said, his voice loud and firm. "And I thought it would come up today. We talked about this the other day, and in reality, it's a joke, but Major League Baseball does a lot to ensure the fairness of the game.

"There's people everywhere, if you go through the dugouts and the clubhouses and the hallways, there's like so many people around that are doing this. Then when I get contacted about some questions about whistling, it made me laugh because it's ridiculous. Had I known that it would take something like that to set off the Yankees or any other team, we would have practiced it in spring training, because apparently it works even when it doesn't happen.

"To me, I understand the gamesmanship, I understand kind of creating a narrative for yourself or wondering how things are going. Now the game in question, we got three hits and no runs. Nobody heard it. You guys have audio, video, people in places and there's no evidence of anything."

Hinch then looked at the camera and took the unusual step of addressing that night's opponent—rather than the press—directly. On top of everything else that bothered him, the Yankees had disrespected Hinch when Nevin yelled at Bregman and Cintrón—a player and coach, not the manager.

"To the Yankees," he said. "There's nothing bad going on. The problem that I have is when other people take shots at us outside this competition. When you guys ask me this question, my face, my name is by my quotes.

"My opinions, my reactions are all for you guys to tweet out and put on the broadcast, but when we have people that are unnamed or you guys have sources that are giving you information, I suggest they put their name by it if they're so passionate about it to comment about my team or my players.

"There's nothing going on other than the competition on the field. The fact that I had to field questions about it before a really, really, cool game at Yankee Stadium is unfortunate, but we can put it to rest. That will be the last question I answer about pitch tipping or pitch stealing."

Hinch had to have known that the phrase "To the Yankees—there's nothing bad going on" wasn't strictly accurate, unless the only definition of "bad" involved a monitor and a trash can. He also knew that questions about the whistling weren't "ridiculous." His team had broken the rules by doing just that.

But in delivering the extended rant, Hinch was doing his job—defending his players and reflecting the Astros' internal anger about the Yankees' accusations. No one in the public knew about the inspection of Minute Maid Park before Game One or how it had stuck in the Astros' craw.

Hinch was also struggling with the realization that his team would be forever tainted by the perception of cheating. He regarded their success as the result of talent and hard work, and he was coming to terms with the fact that opponents would never get over 2017. This gnawed at him.

The Astros won the game easily that night on the strength of Springer and Correa home runs and took a 3–1 lead in the series.

A few minutes after the game ended, Boone left his office for the short walk down a hallway in the basement of the stadium to the press conference room. He answered questions from reporters, stood, walked out a side door, and returned to the hallway.

Hinch was about ten feet behind him, walking toward the door to hold his own news conference.

"Boonie!" he yelled, breaking into a jog to catch up.

Boone stopped and turned to Hinch.

Hinch cupped a hand over his mouth and whispered in Boone's ear. Boone leaned in to hear.

"Hey," Hinch said. "I wasn't referring to you personally."

Hinch wanted Boone to know that when he'd referred to "the Yankees"—not to mention when Cintrón had given Boone the finger—he hadn't wanted Boone to feel insulted. Boone said he understood, patted Hinch on the shoulder, and continued on to his office.

As the Yankees and Astros battled both on the field and off, Carlos Beltrán was having an intense October of his own. He was simultaneously working his first postseason as a member of a front office and interviewing to become the next manager of the New York Mets.

Following the Astros' championship in 2017, Beltrán had retired. He then took a year to decompress and travel with his family.

In the winter of 2018–19, Brian Cashman offered Beltrán a position with the Yankees. Cashman had interviewed Beltrán in 2017 for the managerial job that ultimately went to Boone, and while he thought that Beltrán wasn't nearly ready for that role, he was impressed by his baseball acumen and dedication to helping younger players.

Dipping his toe back into the game, Beltrán accepted a job as a special adviser to Cashman. The role was a light lift, and Beltrán could come and go as he pleased.

He would often stand on the field before home games, watching batting practice, joking, laughing, and offering advice to players. He would then hang out in the clubhouse for the early innings before heading back to his Manhattan home.

Respected by his employers and happy in his job, Beltrán had shed all traces of his former surliness and sensitivity and come into his own.

In April, when new acquisition James Paxton lost to the Astros, Beltrán watched and discovered that he was tipping his most important off-speed pitch, the knuckle curve. After working with Beltrán, Paxton cleaned up the tell and would go on to lean on that knuckle curve during a dominant stretch later in the season.

In June, Beltrán traveled with the team to London, where the Yankees were scheduled for a series against the Red Sox intended to promote baseball in the United Kingdom.

After the Yanks beat the Sox twice, Alex Cora used part of his postgame news conference to compliment Beltrán.

"Their attention to detail is phenomenal," Cora said. "I was joking with somebody that their biggest free-agent acquisition is Carlos Beltrán. I know how he works. He's helped them a lot. They're very into details, and we have to clean our details.

"It was eye-opening, the last two days, from top to bottom. I'm not saying devices, all that stuff. It's just stuff that the game will dictate. And we'll scream at people, and it's right there. Throughout the evening, I was looking, and I saw it. And right now they're a lot better than us."

Shortly after finishing, Cora hopped off the elevated podium and pulled aside the reporter whose question had led to that answer, Ken Davidoff of the *New York Post*. He wanted Davidoff to know that he wasn't accusing Beltrán of helping the Yankees cheat.

Indeed, Cora only meant that Beltrán was spotting pitch tipping and other legitimate tells, and his Red Sox had to clean that up. That did not assuage the Yankees, who were immediately annoyed.

As Cora was giving the news conference, the Yankees were in a separate part of the stadium, boarding the team bus. Phil Nevin heard about the comments and told Cashman. A wave of anger rose through the bus, as staffers felt that their hard work was being invalidated, explained away by an allegation of something untoward.

In fact, Beltrán had frustratingly little to say about electronic sign stealing. Any time Cashman or another Yankees colleague asked him what the Astros were up to, Beltrán would dodge, usually with a chuckle or a wry smile. Privately, he felt that one team's secrets should remain with that team, and it wasn't his place to discuss the Astros with anyone else.

The Yankees accepted this as a matter of Beltrán's principles, but couldn't help but feel that it would be nice for their employee to clue them in.

In early October, the Mets fired manager Mickey Callaway. Shortly after, Beltrán had lunch at Manhattan's Antonucci Cafe with two of his former general managers, Omar Minaya and Allard Baird.

The Antonucci Cafe was an Italian restaurant on East Eighty-first Street with a small dining room and tables on the sidewalk. It was quiet and relatively hidden if you ate inside. Minaya had long used it for under-the-radar meetings.

He and Baird were now both high-ranking members of the Mets' front office under Brodie Van Wagenen and wanted to catch up with their old friend.

Nearly a quarter-century earlier, Baird had scouted Beltrán in Puerto Rico for the Kansas City Royals. In 2005, Minaya had offered him a $119 million contract to sign with the Mets. Later, as an official with the Players Association, he had helped Beltrán push through his passion project, the rule requiring teams to hire interpreters for Spanish-speaking players.

The three had an easy chemistry derived from decades of shared history. Baird and Minaya both knew Beltrán as a thoughtful person, but a quiet one.

Because of that, they were surprised when Beltrán would not stop talking about his ideas regarding baseball, leadership, clubhouse culture, analytics, and other concepts. Baird, in particular, had known Beltrán as a deeply shy teenager, embarrassed by his lack of command of the English language. Now he was a forty-two-year-old man in full, confident and garrulous.

Particularly striking was a point that Beltrán made about communicating analytics to players, who could be resistant to new concepts.

"I like to call it information, not analytics," Beltrán said, explaining that the simple shift in terminology made athletes more receptive.

Dazzled by the conversation, Baird and Minaya recommended to Van Wagenen that he consider Beltrán for the managerial job.

Once the possibility arose, Beltrán quickly realized that he wanted it, and he made peace with his old grudges against Mets chief operating officer Jeff Wilpon, which stemmed from their dispute over Beltrán's decision to undergo knee surgery in 2009.

During the 2019 ALCS, he interviewed with Van Wagenen, and the two hit it off. He then returned to his job with the Yankees as a member of the postseason traveling party.

With characteristic earnestness, Beltrán asked everyone he could think of about the makeup of the current Mets club. What kind of manager did they need—strict or loose? Who were the clubhouse leaders?

His colleagues in the Yankees' front office lightly mocked him for his sudden desire to be a Met again. In the team's box during one of the playoff games, fellow special adviser Nick Swisher was joking loudly with a few people, typical of his famously outgoing personality.

"Hey, Beltrán," another member of the front office shouted. "The Mets called. You get to be manager but you have to make this jackass your bench coach."

Everyone laughed.

Facing elimination in Game Five in New York, the Yankees beat the Astros on a strong performance by James Paxton. That sent the series back to Houston with the Astros up three games to two.

As they typically did for road playoff games, top Yankees officials gathered just before Game Six in a suite at the ballpark. Early in the game, a lower-level team employee noticed a suspicious pattern of blinking lights in the outfield—he thought it looked like the flashlight on the back of an iPhone—and alerted the front office.

The Yankees felt that for about two innings, every time their pitchers changed sign sequences, the lights would go dark for a few pitches. A few pitchers later, there would be a rapid series of blinks, as if to indicate that the signs had been decoded again. Then the dance would start over. The Yankees would change signs, and the lights would again stop for a few pitches before resuming their blinking.

Assistant GM Jean Afterman asked the scouts in the box what they made of it. The scouts noticed a pattern—for example, two flashes for a fastball and no flash for a breaking ball. Not everyone was convinced that there was enough of a sample size to allege cheating.

Afterman called MLB vice president Chris Young, who was on site, and asked him to look into it. Young walked to the outfield area to investigate and reported back that he did not find anyone cheating. The blinking stopped.

MLB explained to the Yankees that the lights had probably been the flickering of television sets in a pub section on the center-field concourse. Yankee Stadium operations personnel later weighed in that the type of TVs used there and at Minute Maid Park didn't flicker.

Plus, the scouts had spotted a pattern of blinks that corresponded to the Yankees' pitches. Ultimately, all the Yankees could do was register the complaint and move on. Astros people pointedly wondered why the Yanks hadn't taken video of the lights, if they found them so suspicious.

A heartbreaking night for the Yankees followed. With both pitching staffs exhausted, New York started reliever Chad Green, and Houston tabbed reliever Brad Peacock.

In the first inning, Yuli Gurriel tagged Green for a three-run homer, but the Yankees did not fold, scoring one in the second and one in the fourth. Houston added an insurance run in the sixth, and took a 4–2 lead into the top of the ninth, three outs away from clinching their second pennant in three years.

With one on and one out in the inning, Yankees first baseman DJ LeMahieu stepped in to bat against Roberto Osuna. LeMahieu was an elite contact hitter who had signed with the Yankees the previous winter. He'd won a batting title with Colorado in 2016, and hit .327 in his first year in New York.

Now he delivered an at-bat for the ages. LeMahieu fouled off a total of five pitches, four of them fastballs that came in at 97 mph or above. He took Osuna's ninth pitch, a 2-2 fastball, to force the count full.

On the tenth pitch, Osuna left a cutter over the plate and LeMahieu drove it to right field.

Springer leapt to stop it from going over the wall, and nearly caught it—but the ball eluded his grasp. LeMahieu had tied the game with a two-run homer, one of the most dramatic that the Yankees franchise had seen in years.

Aroldis Chapman took the mound for the Yankees in the bottom of the ninth. He got two outs and then walked Springer. That at-bat ended with two fastballs out of the strike zone, and it brought up José Altuve.

The Yankees closer started Altuve with two fastballs. Neither was a strike, and he appeared to have lost his feel for the heater. It was no surprise when he followed with a slider, which Altuve took for strike one. With Jake Marisnick on deck—a lifetime .227 hitter to Altuve's .315—Chapman wasn't going to throw any more fastballs and let the superior hitter beat him.

Predictably, his next pitch was a slider, too, high and away. Altuve took a confident swing and drove it over the left-field wall. Chapman stood on the mound, his mouth curling upward into a mysterious grin.

Minute Maid Park nearly exploded. As the old New York Giants announcer Russ Hodges might have said, "The Astros win the pennant! The Astros win the pennant!"

The scene outside the ballpark was hardly less raucous. Fans created an impromptu parade, honking horns and shouting the names of their favorite players.

This was a team for the ages, one that the city was thrilled to buy into. Downtown Houston was one big party that night.

The Yankees' clubhouse was silent save for assorted sniffles and the sound of Aaron Boone thumping his hands on the backs of his players as he went around the room hugging each of them.

The Yankees had endured a series of devastating injuries that year, to sluggers Aaron Judge and Giancarlo Stanton, third baseman Miguel Andújar, and center fielder Aaron Hicks. They had kept winning through all of it, which had imparted in them a belief that the year was a special one, destined to end in a championship.

LeMahieu's homer had only lent credence to that feeling. To lose on the Altuve blast just minutes later was almost too much to process. The team had believed in themselves and been wrong. Boone would continue to grieve for weeks.

Over in the Astros' clubhouse, the scene was markedly different. As teams always do after clinching a postseason series, the Astros jumped around, blasted loud music, and sprayed Champagne and beer on one another.

Shortly after midnight, the party began to wind down. Several players were celebrating on the field, and the scene in the locker room had become more muted. Near the door stood three female reporters: Hannah Keyser of *Yahoo! Sports,* Stephanie Apstein of *Sports Illustrated,* and a reporter who asked not to be named in this book and who had been critical of the Astros' decision in 2018 to trade for Osuna.

Keyser saw a man nearby shouting something, possibly at her group. He looked like a front-office type, but she did not recognize him. He was well under six feet, thin, and bearded.

Keyser then heard "Fucking Osuna!" but didn't know why. The man seemed to be yelling at her group, but he was looking in a different direction. The whole thing felt awkward and aggressive.

Apstein picked up the entire sentence.

"Thank God we got Osuna!" the man yelled half a dozen times. "I'm so fucking glad we got Osuna."

The man was Brandon Taubman, Luhnow's assistant GM. He had been drinking and surprised even himself with the proclamation.

For more than a year, friends in the front office had watched Taubman struggle with the position that his boss had put him in. He had been in the group that opposed the Osuna acquisition. He even told a colleague about calling every woman in his family after the trade to tell them how he felt about it. But once Luhnow made the move, it was Taubman's job to work one-one-one with the player.

Taubman was torn. As a member of the Astros' front office, he often resented harsh media criticism of the team. But in the case of Osuna, he agreed with some of it.

This was a lot to process—and then he got drunk and allowed it to come tumbling from his mouth in the least graceful way imaginable. For a long time afterward, he would struggle with not only regret and shame, but a lack of understanding of his own behavior.

It was the sight of the reporter who had criticized the Osuna trade that set Taubman off. It wasn't her gender that triggered him. She was wearing a purple domestic-violence-awareness bracelet, but that wasn't it, either. It was the memory of negative coverage that Taubman both resented and on some level agreed with—it was that complicated mix of emotions that set him off.

Apstein was a respected reporter for *SI* who had written well-regarded profiles of Brodie Van Wagenen and the late pitcher Roy Halladay, among other pieces. She knew that she had witnessed a newsworthy event, a high-ranking member of the front office harassing a group of women in the locker room.

The next day she contacted Astros spokesman Gene Dias and offered Taubman the chance to explain himself. As the day went on and she did not receive an answer, Apstein had to tell Dias that *SI* needed either a comment or a no-comment. Dias texted that the Astros declined to comment.

On October 21, the night before the World Series was set to open in Houston, *SI* published a story headlined ASTROS STAFFER'S OUTBURST AT FEMALE REPORTERS ILLUSTRATES MLB'S FORGIVE-AND-FORGET ATTITUDE TOWARD DOMESTIC VIOLENCE.

The story quoted Taubman screaming about Osuna. His initial response was to deny it. The Astros issued a blistering statement, which Luhnow saw before it was released:

"The story posted by *Sports Illustrated* is misleading and completely irresponsible. An Astros player was being asked questions about a difficult outing. Our executive was supporting the player during a difficult time. His comments had everything to do about the game situation that just occurred and nothing else—they were also not directed toward any specific reporters. We are extremely disappointed in Sports Illustrated's attempt to fabricate a story where one does not exist."

Apstein was out at dinner when the Astros released their statement, and she was not immediately aware of it. Only when a few people approached to ask if she was okay did she realize what had happened: The team was trying to attack her credibility, which for a journalist meant attempting to tear down her very career.

The Astros had once again stumbled into a scandal of their own making. After several witnesses, including Keyser, publicly backed Apstein's account, public pressure built on the team to rethink its approach.

Major League Baseball dispatched its top investigators, Bryan Seeley and Moira Weinberg, to Houston, where they interviewed eyewitnesses. Taubman's account crumbled under scrutiny.

On Thursday, October 24, the Astros traveled to Washington, trailing the Nationals two games to none in the World Series. By then, the Astros knew they were going to have to fire Taubman. On the team plane, Luhnow's bosses on the ownership level told him that he would have to give a news conference in Washington. He would be the one to take the PR hit for the team.

The Astros issued another statement, beginning this one with "We were wrong," and going on to "sincerely apologize to Stephanie Apstein, *Sports Illustrated* and to all individuals who witnessed this incident or were offended by the inappropriate conduct."

Luhnow's news conference did not go well. After looking directly at Apstein when he entered the room, he was asked if he had personally reached out to her. He said that he had been busy dealing with the Taubman situation and hadn't had time.

The GM added that it had been "devastating" to learn the details of the incident.

"I wouldn't wish it on anyone in this room," he said of his own experience. "Just like I wouldn't wish it on anyone in this room to sit up here and answer these questions either."

The next morning—the day of Game Three of the World Series—Luhnow finally called Apstein. She was still sleeping, so he left a voice mail. When she woke and returned the call, he didn't pick up, so she left a message of her own.

Later in the afternoon, while players and media were on the field preparing for the game, Luhnow texted to ask Apstein to meet him in the Astros dugout.

When the two sat down a few minutes later, Apstein asked that the Astros issue a retraction of their initial statement, the one that had attacked her credibility.

Luhnow seemed reluctant.

"But we apologized in our statement," he said, referring to the second one.

"You apologized for his behavior," Apstein countered, concerned that anything but a full retraction could have a chilling effect on future coverage of the Astros by sending a signal that the team would personally discredit reporters.

"This was a different offense committed to me. If you had called me a liar in private, you could apologize in private. When you hurt someone in public you have to make them whole in public. What if the next person is a twenty-one-year-old intern?"

When Luhnow continued to resist, Apstein pressed.

"You tried to ruin my career over a thing you know is true," she said. "What if I had been twenty-three and this had been my first job and no one believed me?"

By the end of the conversation, Luhnow seemed more amenable, but didn't commit to a retraction. Perhaps, Apstein thought, he needed Crane's approval for that.

As they spoke, a swarm of media—typically Apstein's colleagues and competitors, now reporting on her—gathered outside the dugout.

"When I walk out there, they're going to ask me what I talked about," she said.

"I know," Luhnow said.

"I'm going to say that you apologized, that I asked for a retraction and you wouldn't commit to giving one."

Luhnow nodded.

The next day, Crane sent Apstein a letter personally apologizing and retracting the statement. She shared it on Twitter.

The Astros won that night and were tied 2–2 in what was becoming a thrilling World Series. But it seemed like no one was talking about their excellence. Between whistling and harassment, the Astros' culture was overshadowing their achievements.

Washington Nationals general manager Mike Rizzo, along with many of his scouts, had received a flood of warnings from all over the league after they won the National League pennant and Houston beat the Yankees, all of which shared a common theme: Watch out for the Astros.

This was hardly a shock, because word had been out about Houston, to one extent or another, for two years. Now momentum was building toward a crash, following the extensive—and at times emotional—complaints from the Astros' opponents in each of the first two playoff rounds, the Rays and the Yankees.

Preparing for the Series, the Nationals worked their contacts around the league. Manager Dave Martinez reached out to relief pitcher Tony Sipp, who had played for the Astros from 2014 to 2018, and who had briefly been a National in 2019.

Martinez didn't reach Sipp, but ace Max Scherzer did. *The Washington Post* later reported that Scherzer asked if the Nationals needed to worry about protecting their signs even with no runners on base. Sipp said that yes, they should worry.

Nationals infielder Brian Dozier heard from his former Dodgers teammates, many of whom were still chapped about their suspicions that Houston had cheated them out of a championship in 2017. Martinez also spoke to Alex Cora, whose Red Sox had missed the playoffs that year and knew a thing or two about the Astros, both from the inside and from two years now as an opponent.

Taking all this in, Washington got to work on a sign-stealing defense system of their own. Four days before the World Series began, the team's pitchers held a meeting with their catchers. The group devised five sets of sign sequences, and had them printed on index cards that they could store in the back pocket of their pants.

Nats catchers Kurt Suzuki and Yan Gomes outfitted wristbands with their own cards, as Yankees catchers had done at the beginning of the season. During the Series, they would tap their gloves or masks to switch to a different sequence.

The Astros lost all of their home games in that series. So did the Nationals. When Nats reliever Daniel Hudson struck out Michael Brantley to end Game Seven and clinch the championship for Washington, an entire era ended. Jeff Luhnow's Astros, after years of tanking and rebuilding, innovation and cynicism, were effectively finished.

The players didn't know this yet, but they did mourn the loss with particular intensity. The silence in the Astros' clubhouse was thick, save for a few sniffles. Carlos Correa sought out the reporter whom Brandon Taubman had targeted and told her that he was sorry she'd had to go through that in their clubhouse.

Pitcher Collin McHugh, who had been with the team since the tanking years and was now a free agent, sat at his locker and sobbed.

On November 1, the Mets hired Carlos Beltrán as their next manager.

The decision was both risky and inspired. He was the best position player in the history of the franchise, known for his deep knowledge of and respect for the game. But he had never coached or managed on any level.

Still, Beltrán's strong desire to do the job had impressed the team and its fans. He had made more than $220 million in his career—exponentially more than anyone who had ever managed—and in 2019 had a cushy, show-up-when-you-want gig as a special assistant to the Yankees.

He had turned down the chance to interview for managerial openings with the Chicago Cubs and the San Diego Padres, saying that he only wanted to be a Met.

In a news conference four days later at Citi Field, Mets GM Brodie Van Wagenen—the same Van Wagenen who, by coincidence, was A. J. Hinch's best friend and college roommate—praised Beltrán as "trustworthy," and added:

"Carlos is committed to beating his opponent. Why do I say that and why do I make that a point? Everybody wants to win, there's no doubt about that. Most coaches show up every day with the belief that they can try to get the best out of their players. Carlos has those two attributes.

"But he also takes it a step further. Carlos wants to beat his opponent. He looks at the little things. He looks for tips. He looks for any sort of weaknesses that he can exploit in his game planning. He did it as a player and we know that's going to be a key part of his success as a manager."

In doing his diligence before the hire, Van Wagenen did not find that Beltrán's habit of looking for tips had implicated him in a cheating scheme. The Astros had recommended Beltrán. The Yankees and Major League Baseball had, too. Everyone who had worked with him seemed to love him and want him to succeed.

It's not that those organizations were hiding the truth about Beltrán, at least not intentionally. They simply had no idea that a scandal would soon blow up, and that Beltrán would end up so central to its narrative.

After Van Wagenen introduced his manager, Beltrán stepped to the lectern. For a moment, his deep-seated shyness resurfaced. He spoke softly, nearly trembling with nerves.

He switched briefly to Spanish in order to address youth in Latin America, and then he began to cry. After apologizing for becoming emotional, he translated his message into English.

"Fight for your dreams," Beltrán said. "If I was able to have a good career and be in the position I am today, there is no doubt that anyone out there can do it."

Chapter 17

IT ALL FALLS APART

On the afternoon of Thursday, November 12, 2019, Jeff Luhnow was in a breakout session with other general managers and assistant GMs, when his phone pinged with the update that would cost him his empire.

Luhnow, along with the rest of the industry, was staying at a sprawling Omni resort in Scottsdale, Arizona, the site of the annual general managers' meetings, where agents, teams, and reporters gathered for sessions about rules, the state of the game, and preliminary discussions on trades and free-agent signings.

On the third and penultimate day of the meetings, reporters Ken Rosenthal and Evan Drellich of *The Athletic* published a story that featured former pitcher Mike Fiers speaking on the record about the Astros trash-can scheme. This was the first time that a player had publicly admitted to it.

"That's not playing the game the right way," Fiers told the website. "They were advanced and willing to go above and beyond to win."

Although *Yahoo! Sports* had published details of the trash-can banging a full thirteen months earlier, that account was reliant on anonymous sources. Fiers's quotes—and the detailed accounting of the trash-can feature of the Astros' cheating—now made it more tangible, and impossible to ignore.

The story also detailed the September 21, 2017, incident when Chicago White Sox pitcher Danny Farquhar heard the banging.

Suddenly, nearly every GM in baseball became engrossed in his phone. Luhnow read the story, stood, and quietly excused himself from the room.

After Brodie Van Wagenen read it, he reached out to Carlos Beltrán. His new manager's phone rang several times before sending Van Wagenen to voice mail.

At the hotel bar that evening it seemed there was no other subject. Executives from other teams cursed the Astros and rooted for harsh punishments.

A follow-up report the next day in *The Athletic* named Beltrán, along with Alex Cora, as central figures in the 2017 cheating conspiracy. Van Wagenen still had not heard back from his new manager, but that did not alarm him. Beltrán and his wife, Jessica, were on vacation in Iceland, celebrating their anniversary.

Still, the GM wanted to make sure that he had the chance to touch base with Beltrán and ask him about the Astros before the press did. He stepped up his outreach, sending word through intermediaries that Beltrán needed to call the Mets before anyone in the media.

After Van Wagenen checked out at the front desk and pulled his roller bag toward the curb, more than a dozen reporters and a cameraman swarmed him.

Van Wagenen prided himself on appearing composed in public at all times—hair perfectly styled, suits tailored, smile pasted on. But this morning, waiting to hear back from Beltrán, his voice couldn't help but betray a measure of agitation.

"Anything that happened, happened with another organization, with Houston," he told the reporters. "I have no idea if anything did or did not, but at this point, I don't see any reason why this is a Mets situation."

Frustrated, Van Wagenen loaded his bag into the trunk of a waiting SUV and settled into the backseat for a ride to the Phoenix airport.

Scrolling through his phone during the ride, he was stunned to see a tweet from a *New York Post* reporter that contained a fresh quote from Beltrán downplaying his involvement in the Astros scandal.

Van Wagenen had still not heard from his manager—but the media had? For the first time, the GM sensed that he might have a real issue containing this mess.

In the first twenty-four hours after the report in *The Athletic,* top officials at Major League Baseball tried to figure out how to conduct an investigation in a way that did not require cooperation from Astros players.

The only way to compel players to open up was to offer immunity from punishment, and that was not Rob Manfred's preference. One idea floated was to speak to Cora and opposing players, and try to piece it together that way.

By day two, the league resigned itself to the fact that there was no way to learn the truth without speaking openly with the Astros who had participated in or witnessed the cheating. They agreed with the Players Association to offer immunity in exchange for the truth, and began their investigation in earnest.

Meanwhile, a uniquely twenty-first-century element of the scandal helped prove Fiers's and Farquhar's claims to the public in real time. In his new apartment in Harlem, a Yankees fan and Internet entrepreneur named Jimmy O'Brien—better known online as Jomboy—was combing through game videos for evidence.

O'Brien had rocketed to fame among baseball players and fans earlier that year by narrating breakdowns of entertaining MLB moments like fights and ejections, many of which went viral. His clip of an Aaron Boone ejection in July garnered nearly three million views.

O'Brien was in the process of turning this skill into a successful business when *The Athletic* dropped its report on the Astros. With a Verizon technician still in his new pad installing cable and Internet, O'Brien set to work finding evidence.

That night he posted a two-minute, twenty-second video titled *Astros Using Cameras to Steal Signs, a Breakdown.* In it, Evan Gattis batted against Farquhar.

Not only did the video corroborate the pitcher's claims in the article, but it laid bare for all to see a scheme that was easy to understand. You could hear the bangs, and see how they corresponded to off-speed pitches.

In just a few days, the video had more than 4.3 million views on Twitter. In two weeks it accumulated 2 million YouTube views. Baseball execs and players sent it back and forth, along with O'Brien's subsequent findings, often punctuating their text messages with outrage.

O'Brien's work made the trash-can element of the Astros' sign stealing the most memorable, because there was tangible evidence of it. With no corresponding video of lights flashing or massage guns drilling or coaches whistling, those techniques would forever remain less prominent in the public imagination.

As the investigation continued, Bryan Seeley, Moira Weinberg, and their team accumulated a level of detail that impressed witnesses; one interviewee was surprised when investigators asked if he had ever seen Josh Reddick drill a massage gun into a garbage can.

Luhnow denied knowing about the cheating. Hinch told MLB that he was so agitated by it that he twice smashed the monitor behind the dugout.

Interviewees gave fairly consistent accounts of what went on in and behind the dugout. Beltrán emphasized his belief that many clubs were doing the same. Cora came clean about his role. Players said that the front office had not shared with them MLB's repeated memos since September 15, 2017, about electronic sign stealing.

In their interviews, Astros players consistently shared that José

Altuve had been one of the last players onboard with the trash-can banging. He didn't want the pitches, his teammates said, and would sometimes become angry when teammates gave them during his at-bats.

That finding provided a striking contrast to a rumor that MLB was looking into, which had the potential to be explosive: that Altuve had been wearing some kind of vibrating buzzer under his jersey when he'd homered against Chapman to win the 2019 ALCS.

The evidence was all circumstantial. After Altuve rounded third base, his teammates waited for him at home. As he approached, Altuve wagged his index finger and clutched his shirt. His message was clear: Don't rip it off.

Rosenthal, who was also the sideline reporter for the Fox Network, asked moments later why he didn't want to be disrobed—a common way to celebrate a walk-off homer.

"I don't know—I'm too shy," Altuve said. "Last time they did that I got in trouble with my wife."

This wasn't the only allegation of wearable tech that Seeley and his team looked into. The Rays had asked the league to be vigilant about vibrating Band-Aids before the 2019 division series. And Game Four of the World Series brought a suspicious moment involving Astros catcher Robinson Chirinos. When Chirinos swung and missed at a pitch in the first inning, a small piece of—tape? A Band-Aid?—fell off the head of his bat. Chirinos picked it up off the ground and put it in his back pocket.

This became one of the many moments that Jomboy analyzed in viral videos. But multiple witnesses independently told MLB a less interesting story.

Chirinos, who was deeply religious and had never expressed a willingness to cheat, had homered in Game Three. MLB had put a sticker on his bat to authenticate it as the one used to hit a World Series home run. It was that MLB sticker, not a vibrating Band-Aid or anything else illegal, that had fallen off the bat.

When one Astros player went in for his interview, the investigators clearly had a full picture of the trash can, massage gun, Codebreaker, texting the dugout, clapping, and whistling. They laid it all out for the player and asked if he could corroborate.

The next line of questioning seemed far less secure.

"Do you know anything about wearable tech?" the investigators asked. The player got the sense they were fishing.

"I one hundred percent don't know anything about that," the player said, after confessing that he had participated in the trash-can scheme.

Other interviews proceeded in a similar way. No one—not Hinch, not the front office, not players—had anything to add about wearable devices. MLB had decided to ask about it in the interviews not because it had evidence, but because a reporter had asked a league official about it early in the process. The official then notified the DOI.

When it came time for Altuve's interview, he adamantly denied using a buzzer. Investigators circled back to other players and staff, and everyone told the same story as Altuve.

MLB was left with no tangible evidence that this had happened. They were also unable to confirm that the Astros had cheated in the 2019 season or postseason.

Of course, they were well aware of the complaints that teams had registered all year and into the playoffs—but their position was that they had looked into them and found no conclusive proof. It was one thing to suspect and another to verify.

Astros players and Hinch continued to insist, even in private conversations with friends and family, that they knew nothing about wearable tech. The only way that a few Astros could have used buzzers or Band-Aids, teammates believed, was if they went rogue and pulled it off with help from their own people sitting in the stands.

—

When Van Wagenen did reach Beltrán later that day, the GM emphasized the importance of telling MLB's investigators the truth. The Mets had heard from the commissioner's office that the league did not intend to discipline players unless the players lied.

Beltrán was a player in 2017, and therefore would not be punished. He met with the Players Association for advice, but the union did not provide him with an attorney, as they did with players who were still active. This struck several friends of his as unfair.

Back in New York, Beltrán laid out the whole scheme. Soon after, Van Wagenen and Mets chief operating officer Jeff Wilpon heard from the commissioner's office. The Mets, MLB officials told them, did not have to worry about a suspension for their new manager.

The team moved forward with its off-season, assuming that it would remain untouched by the scandal.

Beltrán next flew to San Diego to attend his first winter meetings as a manager, where he faced a crush of media.

Seated at a table in a crowded hotel ballroom, he repeatedly deflected. This was not the happy reception he'd had in mind when he accepted the position six weeks earlier.

"Carlos," a reporter asked, "what's your level of concern that there could be a suspension for the whole Houston situation?"

Beltrán squirmed in his chair.

"Honestly, on Houston's situation, I don't have any comment for the respect of the process that has been happening," he said. "So I'm here to talk Mets baseball."

"So you expect to begin the season managing the team?" came the follow-up.

"I'm sorry?" Beltrán said, squinting and tilting his head at his questioner. All through his playing career, those were his tells when the press made him uncomfortable.

"You expect to begin the season managing, right?"

"I'm looking forward to managing this ball club," Beltrán said.

Another reporter chimed in. "If there is a suspension, would it be a setback if you couldn't start until May or June?"

"You know what," Beltrán said. "I'm not going to comment on that because, like I said, the whole investigation is in the process by MLB baseball. So anything related to suspension, the Astros, I don't have any comment on those."

"Have you spoken with MLB as part of their investigation?"

"I wouldn't talk about it."

And so it went.

Privately, Beltrán seethed. He was catching a bad vibe all over the meetings. Friends whispered behind his back that they worried he would not end up managing the Mets. A nasty rumor was going around—untrue—that Beltrán had lied in his interview with MLB.

Why is everyone trying to make me out to be the only bad guy here? he wondered. *We were just trying to use the replay room like every team does. The Astros didn't tell us it was illegal.*

On that last count, he had a point. The memo that commissioner Rob Manfred sent to teams on September 15, 2017, drawing a line on electronic sign stealing and promising harsh punishment for team officials who continue to pursue it, went to front offices—not locker rooms.

General managers, assistant GMs, and coaches were supposed to read it, but the players were not typically privy to that type of communication from the commissioner's office. Beltrán could not have been expected to know about an update to the rules during the 2017 season unless the Astros' front office told him about it. They had not.

He and his new Mets bosses remained confident that the investigation would not derail their plans for him to manage.

Through November and December of 2019 and into the New Year, Seeley, Weinberg, and their group remained hard at work on the investigation. They would ultimately interview sixty-eight people and review tens of thousands of electronic communications.

In January, Manfred sent Luhnow a letter alerting the GM that the league had "more than sufficient evidence to support a conclusion that you knew—and overwhelming evidence that you should have known—that the Astros maintained a sign-stealing program that violated MLB's rules."

Specifically, MLB had uncovered a pair of emails that Luhnow received about the Codebreaker program. The emails were from Tom Koch-Weser, who worked in the replay room and had helped to implement Codebreaker. In them, Koch-Weser referred to "the system" and "our dark arts, sign-stealing department."

As *The Wall Street Journal* would later report, Koch-Weser sent the first email on May 24, 2017. It contained the subject heading "The System," a term that Koch-Weser claimed included sign stealing.

The next day, Luhnow responded with "these are great, thanks," and "how much of this stuff do you think [Hinch] is aware of?"

Luhnow told investigators that he hadn't read to the bottom of the five-page email.

On August 26, 2017, Koch-Weser sent another email. He wrote: "The system: our dark arts, sign-stealing department has been less productive in the second half as the league has become aware of our reputation and now most clubs change their signs a dozen times per game."

Two weeks later, Luhnow answered the email, saying that Koch-Weser's information was "very helpful."

In response to Manfred's letter, the GM presented more than 170 pages of documents that attempted to refute the assertion that he'd known Codebreaker was used for in-game sign stealing. It became a he said/he said dispute between Koch-Weser and Luhnow, and MLB could not conclusively resolve it.

Other Astros officials considered it impossible that Luhnow would be ignorant of Codebreaker's existence—but technically plausible that he wouldn't know it was used illegally for in-game sign stealing. At any rate, he had fostered the endless demand for innovation that left employees scrambling for new schemes, legal or otherwise.

Close to the end of the investigation, Luhnow brought up the 2018 incident at Yankee Stadium when Brandon Taubman filmed the intern testing a high-speed camera as evidence that the Astros weren't alone in cheating. MLB had already investigated and cleared the Yankees, but went through the process again for the sake of thoroughness. Again, Seeley and his team found the Yanks innocent.

On January 6, 2020, as MLB was finalizing its report, Manfred summoned four people to New York for individual meetings with him: Jim Crane, Hinch, Luhnow, and Koch-Weser. The purpose of these final interviews was to confirm all information and make sure every detail was solid before the commissioner issued his findings.

On January 13, the report was ready to be published. The league alerted its television arm, the MLB Network, which initiated preparations in its Secaucus, New Jersey, studios. Rosenthal was on the set, as was veteran baseball writer Tom Verducci, iconic announcer Bob Costas, and former pitcher and national broadcaster Ron Darling. The league was bringing out its big guns for a major announcement.

At 2 p.m., the network went on the air with news of Manfred's report. Media members received it in their email in-boxes (rival GMs did not and had to ask members of the media to forward it).

Manfred suspended Hinch and Luhnow for one year and made clear he would suspend Cora after completing a second, far less serious investigation into the 2018 Red Sox. Cora's name was all over the report, which documented his electronic communication with the replay room.

MLB fined the Astros $5 million—the maximum amount allowable—and stripped them of four high draft picks.

The commissioner also suspended Brandon Taubman for a year, not for sign stealing but for his actions toward the reporter after the Astros clinched the ALCS. In the report, Manfred went out of his way to criticize the culture under Luhnow, and note that it enabled cheating:

"But while no one can dispute that Luhnow's baseball operations department is an industry leader in its analytics, it is very clear to me that the culture of the baseball operations department, manifesting itself in the way its employees are treated, its relations with other Clubs, and its relations with the media and external stakeholders, has been very problematic. At least in my view, the baseball operations department's insular culture—one that valued and rewarded results over other considerations, combined with a staff of individuals who often lacked direction or sufficient oversight, led, at least in part, to the Brandon Taubman incident, the Club's admittedly inappropriate and inaccurate response to that incident, and finally, to an environment that allowed the conduct described in this report to have occurred."

True to the promise that he deemed necessary to gather information, Manfred did not discipline any players. But that didn't prevent him from issuing what amounted to de-facto punishment of Beltrán.

When Van Wagenen got his eyes on the report, he found himself shocked by a single clause—three words that thrust the Mets back into the center of a scandal in which they did not participate, but that would alter the course of their franchise nonetheless.

In the second paragraph of the section labeled "Fact Findings," the commissioner wrote, "Approximately two months into the 2017 season, a group of players, including Carlos Beltrán, discussed that the team could improve on decoding opposing teams' signs and communicating those signs to the batter."

No, Beltrán had not been disciplined. But Manfred had chosen to make him the only player on the 2017 Astros to be singled out in the report.

Van Wagenen read it again.

. . . a group of players, including Carlos Beltrán . . .

This was a problem. Forever afterward, Beltrán and many of his friends would wonder why his name was the only one included among 2017 Astros players. Was it his precedent-setting refusal to rehab in Florida in 2000, which resulted in owners spending more money to upgrade their facilities? His decision to force the translator issue?

Van Wagenen closed the email and called Jeff Wilpon.

"Can we get a meeting with the commissioner's office as soon as possible?" he asked.

Meanwhile, at Minute Maid Park in Houston, Jim Crane called his manager and general manager, fired them, and convened a news conference. MLB Network carried it nationally.

Crane sat at a table, pulled the microphone closer to him, and, after a fifty-four-second windup, startled the industry with thirteen newsy words: "Today I have made the decision to dismiss A. J. Hinch and Jeff Luhnow."

The story became instantly—and exponentially—more consequential and newsworthy. Suddenly one of baseball's most successful managers was out of the game. A top general manager, too.

An entire Astros era—which began when Crane hired Luhnow in December 2011 at the Hilton Anatole hotel in Dallas, continued through several years of highly controversial tanking, peaked with a championship, and still seemed poised to become a dynasty, an era that elevated the Astros to beloved figures in a community ravaged by a hurricane and flooding, offering fans so many exciting distractions—was over. *Poof.*

At Fenway Park in Boston, Alex Cora was watching Crane on TV. It was already a busy day for the Red Sox, who had flown in dozens of scouts, players, and other personnel the night before for organizational meetings. Celtics coach Brad Stevens was at Fenway speaking to a group of young players as part of the team's rookie development program.

Like the Mets, the Red Sox had known that their manager was part of MLB's Astros investigation, but did not expect him to be so heavily implicated in the report.

When Crane fired his manager and GM, Cora knew instantly that he had a major problem. Until the Red Sox made a decision on his future, he would be the sole media focus of the entire organization.

He texted team president Sam Kennedy and chief baseball officer Chaim Bloom, requesting a meeting in Bloom's office.

The thirty-six-year-old Bloom, a wunderkind who had just taken the job in October after a successful run with the Tampa Bay Rays, was in the batting cage watching players from the rookie development program.

Reading the report and immediate fallout on Twitter, he knew it was bad—bad enough that the full ownership group should convene. He, Cora, and Kennedy agreed to wait until the next day, when principal owner John Henry and chairman Tom Werner could attend.

The Sox leadership group had immediate concerns about Cora's ability to continue in the job. But their initial inclination was to wait for MLB to release its report on their team, and then determine Cora's future.

Almost immediately after he entered their offices just after 1 p.m. on Tuesday, Cora made clear that he shared their concerns—and felt them even more urgently.

"We've got to work this out," he told his bosses, before they had the chance to do the same. "There's no way we can do this."

Cora went on to explain his position: Everyone in the room expected him to be suspended for a full season. When he returned from that suspension, he would face another round of scrutiny about the scandal. He didn't want to drag the organization through years of this.

The ownership group felt great affection for Cora, who had done so much for the Red Sox as player and manager and had always been affable and generous with the time he spent with the community.

Bloom regarded Cora as an excellent manager and had been excited to work with him. Even the communications and PR wing of the organization loved Cora, who got along well with the tough local press corps.

It could no longer work. After a few more breakout meetings, the parties all agreed. Despite winning a championship in his first season on the job, despite his rare ability to both relate to players and integrate analytics into game-planning, Cora—one of the sport's most promising young managers—had to go.

The air hung heavy with regret. Cora hugged everyone before leaving.

When the news release went out just before 8 p.m., it sent yet another shock around baseball. Rivals had assumed that the Red Sox would wait to decide on Cora.

Now everyone's attention turned to the Mets.

On Wednesday morning, Beltrán was still in uniform and on the back fields of the team's spring-training complex in Port St. Lucie, Florida. But as he worked with coaches and prepared for the arrival of players, his resolve began to waver.

Beltrán was deeply shy by nature, an introvert uncomfortable when attention was on him. He wanted fans and media to focus on his players, not their manager. And this firestorm revolving around him did not appear ready to subside.

Terry Collins approached. Collins was a seventy-year-old, salt-of-the-earth former Mets manager and close friend of Beltrán's. Now working as a special adviser to the team, he tooled around the complex and shared his expertise with players and staff.

In earlier years, some managers had mistaken Beltrán's taciturn nature for a lack of passion, but Collins had always recognized him for what he was: someone in love with the game and a potential leader of men. As such, Collins had helped Beltrán begin to emerge from his shell.

"Hey, you okay?" Collins asked.

He could tell that the answer was no. Beltrán had learned over time to be outgoing and even garrulous when in a good mood, but now he had retreated into himself again. His shoulders drooped, his voice was soft, and the smile he had worn since snagging his dream job had turned to a scowl.

"I'm fine," Beltrán said. "But you know what? I want to get the team ready to play. I don't want every day to have to start with me answering questions about this shit."

Collins hoped that Beltrán could keep his job, but felt the wind blowing in the other direction.

Around that same time, Beltrán's bosses were in New York gathering information. Wilpon had called the commissioner's office on Monday asking for a meeting, but the league, inundated with the Astros' fallout, couldn't get the sit-down on the calendar until Wednesday morning.

When the appointed time arrived, Wilpon and Van Wagenen sat down at MLB's offices on Sixth Avenue in Manhattan and set about learning why Manfred had chosen to make Beltrán the lone player named in his report.

As they quizzed league officials about the investigation, the Mets' owner and GM heard their fears realized: Their manager had been deeply involved in the cheating, and in fact was a leader of it.

MLB had many details and testimonials to prove this. Had Beltrán been a coach and not a player in 2017, his punishment would likely have been severe.

Wilpon and Van Wagenen left the meeting and went straight to the airport, where they boarded a plane bound for Florida. They had to sit down with Beltrán and decide if they could trust him.

As he mulled the decision, Van Wagenen worried about the judgment Beltrán showed in speaking to a reporter while the scandal was breaking, and in his ability to lead the clubhouse in the aftermath of the scandal.

His star pitcher, Jacob deGrom, and his closer, Edwin Díaz, had both suspected that they'd been victims of electronic sign stealing the year before. DeGrom, in particular, had been angry about it. The Mets' front office still remembered the day in May when, after a bad start at Dodger Stadium, deGrom and Van Wagenen had personally scoured the ballpark for hidden cameras. They couldn't prove that the Dodgers were cheating but knew that they resented the concept of electronic sign stealing.

Now Beltrán was going to manage deGrom? Or pitcher Marcus Stroman, who was already tweeting criticism of Cora to his sizable following? The path forward seemed like a minefield.

Upon arriving in Port St. Lucie on Wednesday afternoon, Wilpon and Van Wagenen summoned Beltrán to a meeting at the team's office. They wanted to look him in the eye and hear his side.

The group, joined by assistant GM Allard Baird, met for nearly four hours. At first, the vibe didn't reassure anyone.

Beltrán was quiet and seemed evasive, back in his shell.

The Mets officials in the room needed to feel a sense of connection with Beltrán, and for an hour or two, they weren't getting it. They pressed him on how difficult it would be to continue as the leader, and didn't sense that Beltrán agreed, or necessarily understood the scope of the problem.

Finally, Beltrán warmed up and conceded that some of what he'd done in Houston was wrong. Like Cora, he told his bosses that it would be hard to move forward and not be a distraction from the team and its players. But he wasn't nearly as resolved as Cora about leaving.

Beltrán went home. Van Wagenen, Wilpon, and Baird continued to talk, tossing back and forth the pros and cons of dismissing or retaining Beltrán.

They loved the version of Beltrán who had resurfaced midway through the meeting, but couldn't be sure that the less-engaging guy, the one who had first walked into the room, wouldn't emerge again with the team or the media. And they hadn't been satisfied that they were safe from further details emerging about Beltrán and the Astros' cheating.

As midnight drew closer, the group was not near a decision.

"All right," Wilpon said. "Why don't we sleep on this and reconvene in the morning."

He drove home, then tossed and turned until rising to work out five hours later.

While the front office met that night, Collins called Beltrán at home.

"Are you okay?" he asked again.

"Yeah."

Beltrán was friendly but short with his answers.

"There's a rumor going around that you resigned. Is that true?"

"Nope," Beltrán said.

Collins, worried for his buddy and upset on his behalf, went to bed fearing the worst.

Early Thursday morning, Van Wagenen called Collins.

"Can you come over to the complex?" the GM asked.

He wanted to consult as many people as he could before making such a significant decision. He'd already been to the commissioner's office and spoken with his longtime friend (and now former Astros manager) A. J. Hinch, Yankees general manager Brian Cashman, and many others.

"Do you think this can end?" Van Wagenen asked when Collins arrived. "Do you think there is anything he can say to make this better?"

He and Wilpon, clearly still agonizing over what to do, grilled Collins on how keeping Beltrán might play out publicly.

"If you're the manager here, how would you answer these questions?" Van Wagenen asked.

Collins said that he would begin a news conference by apologizing to the *New York Post* reporter to whom Beltrán had downplayed the scandal.

"Just tell him, 'I'm sorry, I just should have said no comment,'" Collins told his bosses. "Then say, 'The report is out, I'm sorry it happened.' And then move on."

Collins left, suspecting that his case for retaining Beltrán had not landed. On his way out, he saw Baird and asked what he thought was going to happen.

"All I can tell you, Terry," Baird said, "is that there's nothing to worry about—yet."

At 9:30 a.m., the team officials met again with Beltrán. This time it was quick. After all the agonizing and lost sleep, no one could see a smooth way forward. The Mets felt they had to move on.

Beltrán wanted to prove that he could be a good manager and was more than just a talented athlete—he was a smart baseball man. But he was beginning to agree with the team officials who worried that the scandal would be a distraction, both in the media and in the clubhouse.

With his shoulders still sagging and his smile nowhere to be found, Beltrán agreed to leave a job he was never able to start. It was clear to him that he didn't have much of a choice anyway, as the Mets seemed ready to move on.

Everyone in the room stood, shook hands, and parted in order to finalize details and compose their respective public statements.

Beltrán went home to Jessica in disbelief. He still wanted to manage the team.

Van Wagenen and Wilpon organized a conference call with the media to explain themselves and began to discuss how to approach the nearly unprecedented challenge of launching a manager search with less than a month to go before spring training.

Wilpon had to scurry off to an ill-timed obligation, the renaming of a street in Port St. Lucie after Mets icon Mike Piazza. Baseball marched on without Beltrán.

As for Collins, who had been in baseball for nearly fifty years and loved Beltrán more than nearly anyone he'd met in the game?

He went home that evening, had a few drinks, and picked up the phone when a friend called. In a rage that built as he spoke, Collins vented about how the sport had screwed over his good friend.

Chapter 18

"FUCK YOU."

Carlos Beltrán picked up the phone, which he hadn't been doing much in recent weeks. He had been ignoring calls and texts from good friends, from reporters, from allies in the Players Association. He felt hurt that his longtime friends Allard Baird and Omar Minaya had not backed him more forcefully with the Mets.

But when he saw Brian Cashman's name on his caller ID, he answered.

"Most important," Cashman began, "how are you and your family holding up?"

Beltrán said that he was doing fine, but the few others who had spoken with him lately would not have believed it. His voice sometimes cracked as he confided how hard it had been to go from starting an exciting new job to huddling with his wife and children at home in Manhattan.

After a moment of small talk, Beltrán answered the question that Cashman had called with.

"I didn't tell anyone at the Yankees anything [about Houston's cheating]," he said.

They were talking about a new report that had dropped that evening, February 11, 2020, from *The Athletic* about Beltrán's role in the Astros' cheating. The piece called Beltrán "the Godfather," a term that the *New York Post* used for its back page the next morning. When Alex Cora, lying low in Puerto Rico, saw it on the newsstand, he felt like throwing up. His friend was being demonized.

The *Athletic* report also contained a sentence that sent the Yankees into a mini-frenzy: "But Beltrán, according to one team source, divulged particulars of the Astros' scheme to certain low-level Yankees officials, providing confirmation the team was justified in ramping up its efforts to combat sign stealing."

That line surprised Cashman, who had spent the off-season auditing his own organization to make sure that he knew everything the Yankees had done.

During the years when the outfielder Chris Young, Alex Rodriguez, and Beltrán played for the team—prior to Rob Manfred's September 2017 memo drawing a new line on electronic sign stealing—the Yankees had used the replay room to decode sequences and pass them verbally to the dugout.

But Cashman was sure of a few things: His players had never gone nearly as far as the Astros or Red Sox. The Yankees hadn't violated the rules that Manfred put in place with his 2017 memo. And Beltrán had never let on while in the Yankees' front office what Houston was up to.

Cashman and Beltrán said goodbye and hung up. By then, Major League Baseball was in the midst of an extraordinary spring training, one of the strangest and liveliest in its history.

If Rob Manfred had hoped that his report on the Astros would put a close to the story that had dominated the off-season, the opposite happened. The game was consumed by talk about the scandal.

MLB players are union brothers, a bond that often supersedes that of the team for which they play. Opponents share agents and private trainers and work out together during off-seasons. For these reasons and more, it is rare for one ballplayer to speak out strongly against another. There is more to connect than divide them.

Almost immediately after Manfred issued his report on January 13, it became clear that the Astros' opponents would not be observing this unwritten rule, not this time. They were angry enough to lash out.

It began months earlier, quietly but pointedly. Back in November, when Aaron Judge first read about Mike Fiers's comments in *The Athletic,* he reconsidered a social-media post written in 2017 after he finished second to José Altuve as the American League Most Valuable Player.

"M-V-P! Nobody more deserving than you!!" he had written. "Congrats on an unforgettable 2017!! @josealtuve27."

Now Judge decided to go back and take down the post. He didn't publicize the gesture, but fans eventually noticed. It was a hint of what was to come throughout the league.

On January 16, when the Mets fired Beltrán to finish the clean sweep of all three managers who lost their jobs that week, it unleashed a wave of online anger and conspiracy theories.

That afternoon, a Twitter user claiming to be Beltrán's niece started writing about the Astros and buzzers.

"I'm told to stay quiet but I refuse sorry Tio," the post read. "Jose Altuve and Bregman wore devices that buzzed on inside right shoulder from hallway video guy. Let's get it all out now."

The tweet did not hold up to scrutiny. In 2017, Beltrán's only year in Houston, the video room wasn't in the hallway behind the dugout but down a set of stairs and through the clubhouse.

The account added another tweet that seemed confused about when Beltrán was an Astro: "I have pictures from locker I will keep for rainy day. Altuve didn't want shirt torn off if I remember maybe I misspoke but Chapman gave up in game."

Yankees fan Jimmy O'Brien shared these tweets on his Jomboy Twitter account and said that the buzzer allegations matched what he'd heard from five different people. O'Brien's work on the trash-can-banging videos had earned him many followers, so his message was amplified.

O'Brien wasn't the only person who had heard the accusation about Altuve and the buzzer. A few reporters had been chasing it for months, well before Manfred released his report. Just like MLB's DOI, the media had been unable to verify the rumors.

Now it was out anyway. Beltrán's "niece" went on to accuse Yankees infielder Gleyber Torres of wearing a buzzer on his leg, and said that the Yankees "use two video guys hide one in bullpen with live feed."

Jessica Beltrán immediately told ESPN reporter Marly Rivera that this account did not belong to Carlos's niece or any other family member. Internet sleuths later discovered that the username, @SO_blessed1, appeared to be a burner belonging to the Twitter user Incarcerated Bob, who had long been spreading false information.

Once a rumor caught fire online, it couldn't be contained. And the Astros hadn't earned anyone's trust, no matter how unverified a particular allegation was.

Another series of photos circulated showing Josh Reddick in a postgame celebration, with a piece of golden confetti stuck to his chest. An unsubstantiated theory arose that the confetti was an electronic cheating device.

Cody Bellinger, a member of the 2017 Dodgers team that lost to Houston in the World Series—and a quiet, measured person—was angry enough about the buzzer allegation to weigh in on Twitter.

"For the sake of the game I Hope this isn't true," he wrote. "If true, there needs to be major consequences to the players. That Completely ruins the integrity of the game!!!"

Altuve issued a statement through his agent, Scott Boras, saying he had "never worn an electronic device in my performance as a major league player."

When opponents began reporting to spring training in February, many of them made clear that they did not believe Altuve, who had been a widely respected colleague until then. At the Yankees' facility in Tampa, players and staff alike picked apart every frame of the 2019 ALCS-winning homer as if it were the Zapruder film.

The moment that still raised the most suspicion came as Altuve was about to cross the plate. The film was scrutinized frame by frame. With teammates preparing to swarm Altuve, he wagged an index finger, clutched the lapels on both sides of his jersey, and crossed his arms over his chest.

The Yankees and other opponents wondered why Altuve changed into a T-shirt before his interview with Rosenthal. But as raw footage of the celebration later revealed, he had actually remained on the field celebrating for a considerable amount of time before changing.

The buzzer allegation came to dominate the discussion in the wake of MLB's report to such an extent that MLB Network's Tom Verducci asked Hinch about it on February 7 during Hinch's first post-firing interview.

"We got investigated for three months," Hinch said. "The commissioner's office did as thorough an investigation as anyone could imagine was possible. I know you mentioned the emails and the texts and the messages. And I believe it. And I believe in the findings."

This struck many in the game as a non-answer, and Hinch later tried to clarify by issuing a statement that read in part, "After my interview with Tom Verducci last week, there has been a significant reaction to my answer to the 'buzzer' question. To be clear, I have never seen any such device used in baseball. I am not aware of any such device existing or being utilized with the Astros, the players, or any other team."

The buzzer allegation had actually thrown Hinch. He confided to his remaining inner circle that he didn't believe it to be true. But there was so much talk about it that he began to question himself, asking a confidant, "Wait, is this true?" Ultimately he knew that if any individuals had worn a buzzer, it was kept secret from the rest of the team.

The next morning, when Yankees catcher Gary Sánchez arrived in Tampa and spoke to reporters, he made clear that he found the behavior suspicious.

Sánchez was soft-spoken, and almost never quotable. He gave interviews to English-speaking media through an interpreter and rarely offered insight into his true feelings about any topic.

For that reason, reporters were pleasantly surprised when Yankees interpreter Marlon Abreu passed along Sánchez's response to the question about Altuve and buzzers.

"I can tell you, if I hit a homer, and I get my team to the World Series, they can rip off my pants," Sánchez said. "Everything. Take everything off. If I get my team to the World Series hitting a homer or a walk-off or something like that, take everything off."

A broad smile spread across Sánchez's face. Reporters laughed: So this was how it was going to be in Yankees camp this year.

At his daily media briefing after the team's workout that day, Aaron Boone delivered another surprise.

"Are you fully convinced that the Astros were not using any devices in last year's ALCS?" asked Ken Davidoff of the *New York Post*.

"Um . . . no," Boone said. "That's certainly one of those great unknowns."

The answer showed just how extraordinary the situation had become. The commissioner's investigation had found no evidence that Altuve and the Astros used buzzers—and now the manager of the league's highest-profile franchise was publicly doubting that conclusion. This was the sort of comment typically reserved for private conversations.

Boone went on to say that he felt "mad, frustrated, disappointed." He added that he had not spoken to his friend Hinch and didn't yet want to.

"I'm not ready to go there," he said.

Perhaps lost in the surprise about Boone's raw comments was an important detail: He had not been the Yankees' manager in 2017, the year of the trash-can scheme—the only cheating that the Astros admitted to. By saying he was angry, Boone was strongly telegraphing his beliefs about what went on in 2018 and 2019.

The next morning, the Yankees kept talking. Aroldis Chapman reported to camp and said that he found Altuve's behavior "suspicious." Chapman did clarify that his post-home-run smile, which many had interpreted as a tell that he knew Altuve had stolen his sign, was merely a reaction to Altuve hammering a slider after taking one—a smirk that said, "You got me."

Around the time that Chapman spoke, the Astros convened at their complex in West Palm Beach for a news conference. Bregman and Altuve read brief, generic remarks, then sulked for the remainder of the event.

Jim Crane said, "Our opinion is that this didn't impact the game. We had a good team. We won the World Series. We'll leave it at that."

Less than a minute later, Crane said, "I didn't say it didn't impact the game."

And so it went. The news conference was a PR disaster.

The Yankees remained incredulous.

"I think that's quite a stretch," Boone said in the early afternoon, when asked about Crane saying that the Astros' cheating had not impacted the game.

"On what level did it impact things? I guess we'll never know and that's for people to draw their own conclusions on. I think clearly when we're talking about some of the things that went on, those things had an effect on games."

Asked if he believed the Astros' continued protestations—reiterated in West Palm that morning—that they had not engaged in electronic sign stealing during the 2019 postseason, Boone continued his streak of blunt comments.

"Not really," he said. "It at least feels like there's a lot of coincidental things and a lot of smoke."

Publicly, Boone left it at that. Privately, the "coincidental things" and "smoke" to which he was referring were the whistling in Game One of the ALCS and the lights on the outfield concourse in Game Six.

With the Yankees having made their feelings abundantly clear, focus shifted west to the Dodgers' reaction. Bellinger, who had already weighed in with the angry tweet in January, became the league's latest low-key star to break character.

Standing tall in front of his locker in Glendale, turning his hat backward and propping it high on his head, Bellinger spoke in a measured tone—but the disgust was evident in his pinched face and flat voice.

Asked first about the Astros' "apology" news conference the day before, he said, "I thought the apologies were whatever. I thought Jim Crane's was weak. I thought Manfred's punishment was weak, giving them immunity. I mean, these guys were cheating for three years. I think what people don't realize is that Altuve stole an MVP from Judge in '17."

Asked a few minutes later if he really believed that the Astros had cheated in 2018 and 2019, Bellinger said, "One hundred percent," and noted all the talk around the league throughout those two years, along with the sense that the Astros were a different team at home.

Those were significant shots, and they landed hard back in West Palm. The next day, Carlos Correa conveyed an angry response through MLB Network in an interview with Ken Rosenthal.

"The problem I have is when players go out there and they don't know the facts," Correa said. "They're not informed on the situation and they just go out there and go on camera and just talk. With me, that doesn't seem right. It doesn't seem right at all.

"So when [Bellinger] talks about that we cheated for three years, he either doesn't know how to read, is really bad at reading comprehension, or is just not informed at all. The commissioner's report clearly says that all those activities were conducted in 2017. Two thousand eighteen, nothing happened. Two thousand nineteen, nothing happened. It was just talented players playing the game of baseball with passion and winning ballgames."

Rosenthal pressed Correa on the fact that the report had actually said that Houston's electronic sign stealing continued into the 2018 season.

"Yeah," Correa answered. "But it said about the Codebreaker but not about the trash can or any of that. That stuff, it came from the top on the Codebreaker, but we don't know about that stuff down there. So when I look at those comments, they're not true. Two thousand eighteen, we played clean. Two thousand nineteen, we got to a World Series playing clean baseball all around."

Unpacking that paragraph goes a long way to understanding the entire era of Astros cheating. Inside the clubhouse, Correa and many other players clung to a deeply felt belief that they had cheated only in 2017 (of course, given that they won the World Series that year, the offense alone was more than enough to anger opponents and fans). That's because they stopped banging the garbage can after that season.

But by the rules of baseball made clear in Manfred's announcement on September 15, 2017, and in subsequent memos from the league, the Astros did continue to cheat during the two subsequent seasons.

Even tossing aside for a moment all the wilder incidents and allegations from 2018 and 2019—the Mariners discovering GoPro cameras in the dugout; the opponents who found a hole in the wall when an Astros mole told them about drilling; the batboys' conversations with base runners; the Rays and Yankees complaining in the playoffs about over-mudded balls, possible Band-Aids and buzzers, and flashing lights in the outfield—a basic fact remains: Astros people admit to in-game video code breaking after 2017 and to whistling in 2019. And MLB considers those cheating.

Rosenthal also asked Correa about the Altuve buzzer allegation.

"Earlier in the year, he hit a walk-off at Minute Maid Park; I ripped off his shirt with Tony Kemp," Correa said. "There are pictures of that. There are videos of that. You can go look at it. I ripped off his shirt, and his wife told my wife, 'Why is Carlos ripping Altuve's shirt? I don't like that.'

"So when he's running from third base to home plate, I'm the guy up front. The first one waiting for him. He's like, 'Don't take my shirt off.' The second reason—he doesn't want me to talk about this, but I'm going to say it—is because he's got an unfinished tattoo on his collarbone that honestly looked terrible. It was a bad tattoo, and he didn't want nobody to see it. He didn't want to show it at all."

The next morning, after the Astros clubhouse opened to the media, Altuve walked to his locker with a towel over his chest. He then turned to the reporters, dropped the towel, and revealed a tattoo on his left clavicle. It said MELANIE, his daughter's name, and was accompanied by a pink heart.

If it seemed like the plot couldn't possibly bring any more bizarre or dramatic twists, the fireworks weren't nearly over. On the same day that Bellinger spoke in Glendale, Reds pitcher Trevor Bauer sounded off to *Athletic* beat reporter C. Trent Rosecrans and a few other members of the Cincinnati media.

Bauer, who in 2018 had become the subject of derisive tweets from Bregman, Collin McHugh, and Lance McCullers Jr. when he accurately suggested that Astros pitchers were using illegal substances to grip the baseball, said, "For two years, three years, they mocked me for bringing up the fact that they could possibly be cheating."

He spoke for nearly half an hour. In his answer to the first question, a response that lasted nearly ten minutes and spanned approximately fifteen hundred words, Bauer gave voice to the issue at the core of why the Astros had rattled fans and players so deeply.

"It pisses me off because all we want to do—everyone comes here to win, but we agree to play by a set of rules and we want to play fairly and compete and see are we better than you or not?" he said.

"So we all assume that's what's going on. When it's not, it's, 'Hold on a second, why is it that I have to abide by the rules? That guy has to abide by the rules. That team has to abide by the rules, but you guys think you are better than everyone and you don't have to abide by the rules.' Fuck you."

The entire spring was turning into a giant "fuck you" to the Astros, and Manfred found himself increasingly swept up in others' resentment, too.

On February 16, the commissioner made two attempts at damage control: an interview on ESPN that aired in the morning, and a previously scheduled appearance at a spring-training media day in North Port, Florida.

The ESPN spot backfired and generated more anger. When asked if he considered stripping the Astros of their title, Manfred answered, "The idea of an asterisk or asking for a piece of metal back seems like a futile act. People will always know something was different about the 2017 season, and whether we made that decision right or wrong, we undertook a thorough investigation, and had the intestinal fortitude to share the results of the investigation, even when those results were not very pretty."

Manfred and his inner circle had seriously discussed vacating Houston's 2017 championship before releasing his report but decided against setting the precedent.

But in referring to the World Series trophy as a "piece of metal," Manfred offered a serving of red meat to the players who already questioned his feel for this situation and for the sport overall.

The Dodgers' Justin Turner weighed in with a particularly biting comment, saying, "For him to devalue it the way he did just tells me how out of touch he is with the players in this game. At this point the only thing devaluing that trophy is that it says 'commissioner' on it."

These were not good times for the sport. At the news conference that afternoon in North Port, Manfred sneered at Jared Diamond, the *Wall Street Journal* reporter who had first written about Codebreaker.

"You know, congratulations," the commissioner said at the lectern, his voice oozing with sarcasm. "You got a private letter that, you know, I sent to a club official. Nice reporting on your part."

The next two days brought additional shots from prominent Yankees who were typically the furthest thing from outspoken.

Gleyber Torres, a shy twenty-three-year-old from Venezuela, felt strongly enough about the subject to speak at length about it in his second language. Standing nearly alone—save for the group of reporters—in a quiet locker room after the team's morning workout, Torres spoke softly and appeared to deliberate over every word choice. He was not popping off but delivering a premeditated critique.

Asked if he believed that the Astros were cheating in 2018 and 2019, Torres became the latest player to effectively call Carlos Correa and his teammates liars.

"For sure," Torres said firmly—perhaps more firmly than he'd ever said anything in public.

"If you cheated in 2017 and you won, why don't [you] do [it] the next year, and the next year, too? I'll use an example: If I play video games with you and we face the TV and I see your controller and I know what is coming and I hit really well and I win, if you tell me we play again, I'll do the same thing because I win. So [the Astros] did in '17 for sure, they did in '18 and they do in '19. It's really easy."

Torres went on to draw an analogy between what he believed was the Astros' continued cheating and his experience playing the video game *MLB: The Show* with teammate Luis Severino.

"When I face Severino, I saw the controller and I did really well and he didn't know, and the next one I did the same thing and I win," he said. The line drew a laugh, but Torres was serious about his accusations.

The next day, Judge walked into a media room at the Yankees' complex and sat at a table. In front of him were rows of plastic chairs occupied by reporters, and many television cameras.

Asked if he thought the Astros should be stripped of their 2017 title, Judge inhaled, paused, and seemed to be turning his wheels.

Did he want to join Bellinger, Bauer, Torres, and the others in creating a headline? Yes, he did. He felt that strongly about it.

"Yeah," Judge said. "I just don't think it holds any value. You cheated. You didn't earn it. That's how I feel. It wasn't earned."

Nine pitchers lost their jobs immediately after facing the Astros in 2017. One, Mike Bolsinger, did not pitch again after losing in Houston on August 4. He later filed a lawsuit against the Astros.

Given the human toll of the cheating, Judge resented that Astros like Correa had remained defiant in saying that their championship was not tainted. He voiced the view prevalent in every camp that spring that the players still weren't contrite enough.

"If I have a bad game and I mess up, I'm going to stand in front of the mic and say, 'Hey, I'm sorry I messed up, I did this and that, it's on me,'" Judge said. "Not to really hear that from some of the players is what bothers the baseball community. People lost jobs, people lost money, people lost a lot of things important to them."

None of the players who spoke out had concrete evidence of the Astros cheating in 2018 and 2019. What they did have was something else powerful: a broken faith in their own game. They were now doubting the results of the sport to which they had devoted their lives.

That afternoon, Manfred held his annual briefing for baseball reporters in Arizona. His demeanor was entirely different than it had been the previous week in Florida—while he had then projected energy and even defiance when speaking to Jared Diamond of the *Journal,* he now seemed downtrodden, exhausted, embattled.

Manfred apologized for referring to the World Series trophy as a "piece of metal," saying that he had fumbled an attempt to make a rhetorical point, and had been "disrespectful."

He also addressed the widespread player criticism that his punishments were weak by saying that he would think "long and hard" about granting player immunity in a future investigation.

This was the most serious challenge to his leadership that Manfred had yet faced, and might ever face. Players were questioning both his honesty in airing out all details of the Astros' cheating, and his enthusiasm for the game itself.

The next morning Manfred took an unplanned trip back to New York to deal with the crisis before it spiraled further out of control. There, he gathered all thirty team owners on a conference call to address the situation.

As *The New York Times* reported in a tough story headlined HE LET THE ASTROS PLAYERS SLIDE. NOW HE'S PAYING FOR IT, Manfred again issued a stern warning about electronic cheating. He also criticized baseball's omertà-like code of silence, which made it difficult to learn about any bad behavior.

The following day he stood in front of more than a thousand MLB employees in an atrium at the league's offices in midtown and held a town hall meeting about the scandal.

Back in West Palm, the story only got uglier. Josh Reddick had recently posted a photo on social media of his five-month-old twins. A commenter wrote, "I hope your kids get cancer."

The day after Manfred's town hall in Manhattan, Reddick told reporters that another Internet troll had told him, "I will kill your entire family."

The spring dragged on. Opposing fans booed the Astros with bloodlust in every spring-training park. Manfred and the league faced an unending torrent of criticism from players, fans, and opinion-makers in the media.

How would this end? Would it end?

Then, on March 12 at 3 p.m., a wave already gathering in the world washed over baseball and drowned the sign-stealing scandal. MLB announced the suspension of spring training due to COVID-19, which the day before had graduated from an epidemic to a pandemic.

Within weeks, thousands of Americans would be dead and the baseball season and its current scandal would be relegated to second-tier news. The season failed to begin on time. Players scattered around the country and world to shelter in place with their families and hide from the virus.

A. J. Hinch was at home in the Houston area, where he would have been anyway. Once one of the game's brightest young leaders, he was left to plot the beginnings of a plan to reconstruct his career.

He spent hours on the phone with old friends, agonizing day after day over how he could have failed to meet his own standards of leadership. With his daughters, he explained that once you messed up one time, once you lost the world's trust, people would believe everything bad about you. He hoped they would take that lesson forward into their own lives.

Shortly before the national quarantine, Jeff Luhnow had lunch with an old friend who had worked with him in St. Louis.

"The Cardinals weren't doing this stuff when we were there, were we?" the friend asked.

Luhnow laughed. "I don't know."

Despite all the innovation he pursued, all the brainpower he gathered in his front office—all his efforts to hack the game and run a more intelligent team than anyone else—Luhnow had to admit that the thread that took him down had largely eluded him. You just couldn't know everything.

In Puerto Rico, Alex Cora waited out not only the virus, but his punishment. MLB had largely completed its investigation into the 2018 Red Sox before the shutdown. That inquiry followed a January report in *The Athletic* that revealed how Boston had used the video-replay room to facilitate in-game sign stealing that season.

An easy narrative spread that Cora was the chief villain of the cheating era, and he took his evil methods from Houston to Boston. But Cora knew it wasn't that simple. The Red Sox had indeed violated the rules, just as the 2018 Astros had, by decoding sign sequences in the video room and transmitting them to the dugout and to base runners. Those violations, however, were nowhere near the infractions committed by the Astros.

On April 22, the MLB finally dropped its report on the Red Sox. The league suspended replay coordinator J. T. Watkins for one year and docked the team a second-round draft pick. The investigation found no evidence to implicate Cora in the rule-breaking that occurred in Boston. Manfred suspended him for the 2020 season—which itself had been suspended—and only for the Astros' cheating, not for what happened in Boston.

By this time Cora was deep into his first year as a stay-at-home dad in his hometown of Caguas, chasing his two-year-old twin boys around the yard. He was separated from the game that had consumed him since childhood—the one he loved so much that it had once left him face down in the grass, sobbing on national TV after losing the College World Series. Given the circumstances, it was a welcome break to reconnect with himself and his family.

He was having an easier time than his friend Carlos Beltrán, who had never gotten the chance to prove he could do it, like Hinch and Cora had. After losing his job with the Mets, Beltrán cut off contact with most of the friends and acquaintances he'd collected since signing with the Royals in 1995. Beltrán seemed to be retreating into the shell he'd worn as the introvert from Manatí all those years ago.

The version of him who, just months before, had sat for a long lunch at Manhattan's Antonucci Cafe, dazzling Omar Minaya and Allard Baird with a passion to manage that burned hotter than anyone would have guessed—that Beltrán was gone, at least for the time being.

He felt a deep resentment at being singled out for an era in which he believed cheating had been widespread. He felt that no one—not the Mets, not MLB, and not a Players Association that declined to provide him with an attorney because he was now a manager—had his back. The game he'd loved since boyhood had ended up treating him coldly.

For months, Beltrán wallowed in Manhattan, not far from the ballpark in Queens where he was supposed to manage—where he still wanted to manage. He stayed home during the worst of the pandemic's ravaging of New York City, then flew with his family to Puerto Rico. Finally he could begin to relax and heal.

"How's he doing?" a friend who'd been cut off asked Terry Collins that spring. Collins and Alex Cora were among the few in the game who'd been able to keep in touch.

"Not so good," Collins said.

Beltrán, Cora, Hinch, and Luhnow remained in exile. Baseball planned to resume without them, as it did on July 23, when a virus-truncated season finally commenced.

The game always leaves people behind and rolls on, though it does evolve. In this case, MLB officials were hard at work planning ways to make electronic sign stealing more difficult than ever, including limiting or even banning player access to live game video and blacking out the catcher's hands in postgame film.

The country had bigger problems than the Astros and their cheating in 2020, but that didn't mean opponents got over it. On July 29, the Astros and Dodgers engaged in an on-field brawl after L.A. reliever Joe Kelly threw up and in at Carlos Correa, and then taunted him with exaggerated crybaby faces.

Kelly was close with Cora, his manager on the 2018 Red Sox, and he was angry to see his friend punished while the Astros players skated.

"Nice swing, bitch," Kelly yelled at Correa after striking him out. This was all still raw and personal for the people affected.

The Astros avoided the wrath of opposing fans that year because the pandemic necessitated games in empty ballparks. But the rest of the league was far from ready to let go of its bitterness. In fact, many remained passionate about keeping the story alive, lest it be forgotten and repeated.

"People have to remember this," said one Yankees official in 2020. "Or else it will happen again."

EPILOGUE

After a long delay caused by the pandemic, Major League Baseball began its regular season on July 23, 2020, and played for the rest of the summer in empty ballparks across the country.

The Astros lost several key players to injuries during the shortened season, including ace pitcher Justin Verlander and 2019 American League Rookie of the Year Yordan Alvarez. Houston finished the regular season with a record of 29-31. Because of a newly expanded playoff field, the team earned a wild-card berth and advanced to the postseason.

The Astros defeated the Minnesota Twins in the wild-card series, the Oakland Athletics in the division series, then nearly upset the heavily favored Tampa Bay Rays—who finished the regular season with the best record in the league—in the American League Championship Series. But Tampa Bay won the decisive Game Seven.

Even through that 2020 postseason, the Astros could not escape their reputation. During the ALCS, the Rays used multiple sign sequences with no runners on base. While they had no evidence that Houston was still using cameras to cheat, they weren't going to take any chances.

The year brought a variety of outcomes for the four people who lost their jobs as a result of the scandal.

When their suspensions ended at the conclusion of the World Series, A. J. Hinch and Alex Cora were in immediate demand. To prospective employers, their skills and track records of success outweighed their transgressions in Houston. The Detroit Tigers hired Hinch to manage, and the Boston Red Sox gave Cora his old managing job back.

Carlos Beltrán remained with his family in Puerto Rico for most of 2020. He was not a candidate for any job openings in the game.

In November, Jeff Luhnow sued the Astros and owner Jim Crane, seeking the $22 million remaining on his contract. The lawsuit included Luhnow's vehement denials that he knew about the Astros' cheating.

"The Astros' termination of Luhnow is an attempt—like the Commissioner before them—to make Luhnow the scapegoat for the organization while the players and video-room staff who devised and executed the schemes went unpunished," the suit read. "The Astros concocted grounds to fire Luhnow 'for Cause' in order to save more than $22 million in guaranteed salary."

Luhnow went on to allege that Tom Koch-Weser, most recently the team's director of advance information, was the "ringleader" of the sign-stealing scheme. He further alleged that Rob Manfred had ignored evidence indicating that Luhnow was unaware of the cheating.

Major League Baseball declined to comment on Luhnow's lawsuit.

Luhnow also criticized the MLB investigation in an interview with the podcast *The Edge,* released in November 2020.

"This was not about a fact-finding mission," he told host Ben Reiter. "This was about satisfying the teams that were screaming for heads."

While continuing to deny knowledge of his team's cheating, Luhnow did express some regrets.

"I think from a leadership and philosophy standpoint, I should have paid more attention to rules compliance," he said. "I should have made it a higher priority. I trusted [that] the people under me were taking care of that, and that was wrong."

He went on to address the opponents who felt most victimized.

"We had a great team," Luhnow said. "We should have and could have won without it. I apologize for what the Astros did. I apologize to the Los Angeles Dodgers. I apologize to the New York Yankees. I apologize to the Boston Red Sox, and I apologize to any team that we might have gained an advantage on during the '17 and '18 season because we were breaking the rules. I really want that to be out there. I feel bad and I'm sorry. I really am sorry. I wish I had known about it. I would have stopped it. . . .

"I've had to accept consequences. I've had the most severe consequences of anybody, relative to what I did and what I knew. That's because I was the general manager."

The Yankees finished a strong 2020 season and went to the playoffs, losing to Tampa Bay in the five-game division series. Their title drought stretches to eleven seasons.

In the World Series, the Dodgers defeated the Rays in six games, and Clayton Kershaw finally got his championship.

Major League Baseball wanted nothing more than to return to normal, but the Astros scandal continued to echo three years later.

Bibliography

Note on Reporting and Dialogue

This book is the result of more than one hundred interviews with sources, many of whom were eyewitnesses to and/or participants in the events described. The vast majority of sources agreed to speak on the condition of anonymity. The story told in these pages is a result of those interviews, supplemented by the additional research cited below.

Where dialogue is re-created, it was either described to the author by direct eyewitnesses and/or participants or credited to previous reports.

Introduction: "I'm Gonna Kick His Fucking Ass!"
Baccellieri, Emma. "Sign Stealing Has Long Been a Part of MLB. It's Not Going Anywhere." SI.com, Nov. 13, 2019.

Chapter 1: How We Got Here
Dittmar, Joe. "A Shocking Discovery." *The Baseball Research Journal,* vol. 20, 1991.
Schuler, Ron. "Pearce Chiles." SABR.org.
Dickson, Paul. *The Hidden Language of Baseball: How Signs and Sign-Stealing Have Influenced the Course of Our National Pastime.* New York: Walker & Company, 2003.

Baccellieri, Emma. "Sign Stealing Has Long Been a Part of MLB. It's Not Going Anywhere." SI.com, Nov. 13, 2019.

Chapter 2: No, the 1951 Giants Don't Justify the Astros

O'Connor, Ian. "Story of Ralph Branca and Jackie Robinson Still Resonates." ESPN.com, Dec. 30, 2016.

Goldstein, Richard. "Ralph Branca, Who Gave Up 'Shot Heard 'Round the World,' Dies at 90." *The New York Times,* Nov. 23, 2016.

Anderson, Dave. "Branca Knew '51 Giants Stole Signs." *The New York Times,* Feb. 1, 2001.

Prager, Joshua. "A Final Twist in an Epic Baseball Swindle." *The Wall Street Journal,* Dec. 26, 2019.

Prager, Joshua. "'Why Me?' Echoed in Ralph Branca's World, Even Before a Doomed Pitch." *The New York Times,* Nov. 23, 2016.

Leib, Frederick G. "Cloak and Dagger Nothing New." *Sporting News,* July 13, 1960.

Chapter 3: The Advent of TV and Scouting Cameras

Lasorda, Tommy, with David Fisher. *The Artful Dodger.* New York: Avon Books, 1986.

Baccellieri, Emma. "Sign Stealing Has Long Been a Part of MLB. It's Not Going Anywhere." SI.com, Nov. 13, 2019.

Kurkjian, Tim. "Can You Read the Signs?" ESPN.com, Aug. 12, 2004.

Chass, Murray. "Opponents Claim the Mets are Stealing Signs Via Video." *The New York Times,* Aug. 17, 1997.

Chapter 4: The Path to Beltrán

Green, Shawn. *The Way of Baseball: Finding Stillness at 95 MPH.* New York: Simon & Schuster, 2012.

Morris, Peter. *A Game of Inches: The Stories Behind the Innovations That Shaped Baseball.* Chicago: Ivan R. Dee, 2010.

Hunter, Ian. "25 Years Ago, Alomar's Home Run Changed Everything for the Blue Jays." bluejayhunter.com, Oct. 11, 2017.

Turbow, Jason, and Michael Duca. *The Baseball Codes: Beanballs, Sign Stealing, and Bench-Clearing Brawls: The Unwritten Rules of America's Pastime.* New York: Anchor, 2011.

Chapter 5: The Education of A. J. Hinch

"A. J. Hinch" (documentary). *Our Stories*. Pac-12.com, May 30, 2019.

Drellich, Evan. "At the Heart of A.J. Hinch, a Baseball Player's Drive." *Houston Chronicle*, Oct. 25, 2014.

McTaggert, Brian. "Message Is Clear for Hinch: Mom Is Unique." MLB.com, May 8, 2015.

Gilbert, Steve. "Hinch and Davis Clear the Air." MLB.com, May 16, 2009.

Krasovic, Tom. "Byrnes Whiffed Firing Manager in '09." *The Baltimore Sun,* May 25, 2014.

Chapter 6: The Education of Carlos Beltrán

Castillo, Jorge. "Carlos Beltran Speaks Out Against Lack of Interpreters for Spanish-Speaking Major Leaguers." nj.com, Mar. 29, 2019.

Curry, Jack. "Beltran Brings Great Hope to 'New' Mets." *The New York Times,* Jan. 12, 2005.

Goold, Derrick. "Beltran Steps Up for Charity, New Hometown." *St. Louis Post-Dispatch*, Aug. 20, 2012.

Martinez, Hiram. "The Once and Future Carlos Beltran." ESPN.com, July 2, 2012.

Beltrán, Carlos. "How We Play Baseball in Puerto Rico." *The Players' Tribune,* May 31, 2016.

Rivera, Marly. "Carlos Beltran Academy in Puerto Rico Includes Academics." ESPNDeportes.com, July 1, 2015.

Sanchez, Jesse. "Beltran's Vision Realized with Translator Program." MLB.com, Jan. 14, 2016.

Chapter 7: Last Step Toward the Astros: Advent of the Replay Rooms

Nelson, Amy K. "Searching for Meaning in the Mistake." ESPN.com, Jan. 5, 2011.

Sherman, Joel. "Mark Teixeira: Yankees' Sign-Stealing Nothing like Carlos Beltran's Astros." *New York Post,* Feb. 21, 2020.

Rosenthal, Ken, and Evan Drellich. "MLB's Sign-Stealing Controversy Broadens: Red Sox Used Video Replay Room Illegally in 2018." *The Athletic,* Jan. 7, 2020.

Chapter 8: The Construction of the Astros

Reiter, Ben. *Astroball: The New Way to Win It All.* New York: Three Rivers Press, 2018.

Kaplan, Jake. "The Astros Overhauled Their Scouting Department. Are They a Step Ahead, or Will It Backfire?" *The Athletic,* May 31, 2018.

Rosenthal, Ken. "Astros, Luhnow at Center of Baseball's Scouts Versus Stats Debate." *The Athletic,* Sept. 5, 2017.

MacDougall, Ian. "How McKinsey Helped the Trump Administration Carry Out Its Immigration Policies." *The New York Times,* Dec. 3, 2019.

Rosenwald, Michael. "Drawing Pitchers." *The New Yorker,* Oct. 17, 2005.

Brown, Maury. "Why Jim Crane Could Become Baseball's Most Controversial Owner." *Forbes,* June 14, 2011.

Sandomir, Richard. "Jim Crane Approved as Astros Owner Despite Past Concerns." *The New York Times,* Nov. 21, 2011.

Kolhatkar, Sheelah. "McKinsey's Work for Saudi Arabia Highlights its History of Unsavory Entanglements." *The New Yorker,* Nov. 1, 2018.

Red, Christian. "Jailed Cardinals Hacker Chris Correa Points Finger at Astros for Scandal, Blasts Rob Manfred." New York *Daily News,* Jan. 31, 2017.

Anonymous. "McKinsey & Company: Capital's Willing Executioners." *Current Affairs,* Feb. 5, 2019.

Rosenthal, Ken. "Agent Calls Foul on Astros, MLB in Negotiations with No.1 Overall Pick." Foxsports.com, July 15, 2014.

Petchesky, Barry. "Leaked: 10 Months of the Houston Astros' Internal Trade Talks." Deadspin.com, June 30, 2014.

Drellich, Evan. "Radical Methods Paint Astros as 'Outcast.'" *Houston Chronicle,* May 23, 2014.

Chapter 9: The Yankees and the Dodgers Open Their Windows

Witz, Billy. "Solving the Yankee Equation, One Number at a Time." *The New York Times,* July 25, 2016.

Chapter 10: The Electronic-Sign-Stealing Era Kicks into High Gear

Verducci, Tom. "Why MLB Issued Historic Punishment to Astros for Sign Stealing." SI.com, Jan. 13, 2020.

Schmidt, Michael. "Boston Red Sox Used Apple Watches to Steal Signs Against Yankees." *The New York Times,* Sept. 5, 2017.

CBSN Boston, "Dombrowski, Manfred Downplay Seriousness of Red Sox Sign-Stealing Controversy." boston.cbslocal.com, Sept. 6, 2017.

Chapter 11: Enter Hinch and Cora

Olney, Buster. "How Joey Cora Pulled Alex Along After Their Father Died." ESPN.com, June 2, 2019.

Smith, Christopher. "Alex Cora, Boston Red Sox Manager, Learned to Lead from Dad Who Died of Colon Cancer and Mom Who Kept Family 'on Top,'" Masslive.com, Jan. 30, 2019.

Sumers, Brian. "ACC to Examine Claim That Miami Stole Signs." *Sun-Sentinel,* April 21, 2004.

Chapter 12: The Scheme Begins

Verducci, Tom. "From Trackman to Edgertronic to Rapsodo, the Tech Boom Is Fundamentally Altering Baseball." SI.com, Mar. 28, 2019.

Lemire, Joe. "Edgertonic Cameras Are the Tech Transforming Baseball by Accident." SportTechie.com, Feb. 5, 2019.

Diamond, Jared. "'Dark Arts' and 'Codebreaker': The Origins of the Houston Astros Cheating Scheme." *The Wall Street Journal,* Feb. 7, 2020.

Reiter, Ben. *Astroball: The New Way to Win It All.* New York: Three Rivers Press, 2018.

Barron, David. "Dallas Keuchel Disappointed in Astros' Lack of Big Moves." *Houston Chronicle,* Aug. 1, 2017.

Rosenthal, Ken, and Evan Drellich. "Astros Executive Asked Scouts for Help Stealing Signs and Suggested Using Cameras, Email Shows." *The Athletic,* Nov. 16, 2019.

Feinsand, Mark. "The Wild Night When Verlander Joined the Astros." MLB.com, Aug. 27, 2019.

Chapter 13: Yep, the Astros Used the Trash Can in the World Series

Nesbitt, Stephen J. "The Astros Told Chris Archer He Was Tipping Pitches. Now He Knows They Were 'Willing to Do Anything to Win.'" *The Athletic,* Feb. 13, 2020.

Benz, Tim. "Ex–White Sox Catcher, Pitt Star Kevan Smith at Center of

Astros' Sign-Stealing: 'We Knew They Had Something.'" TribLive.com, Jan. 17, 2020.

Jomboy. "Astros Using Cameras to Steal Signs, a Breakdown." Jomboy Media, Nov. 12, 2019.

Rosenthal, Ken. "Carlos Correa Rips Bellinger, Passionately Defends Altuve and Says the Astros Deserve Their 2017 title." *The Athletic,* Feb. 15, 2020.

Rollins, Khadrice. "Astros Owner Sends Planes to Puerto Rico for Aid." SI.com, Oct. 3, 2017.

Verducci, Tom. "Why MLB Issued Historic Punishment to Astros for Sign Stealing." SI.com, Jan. 13, 2020.

Verducci, Tom. "From Trackman to Edgertronic to Rapsodo, the Tech Boom Is Fundamentally Altering Baseball." SI.com, Mar. 28, 2019.

Chapter 14: The Astros' Front Office Starts to Come Apart

Perez, A. J. "Roberto Osuna Won't Be Tried for Domestic Violence Arrest as Part of Deal with Prosecutors." *USA Today,* Sept. 25, 2018.

USA Today. "Aroldis Chapman Accepts 30-Game Suspension from MLB for Domestic Violence Incident." Mar. 1, 2016.

Rome, Chandler. "Full Transcript of Discussion with Astros GM Jeff Luhnow, Reliever Roberto Osuna." *Houston Chronicle,* Aug. 5, 2018.

Chapter 15: Mass Paranoia

Sherman, Joel. "Paranoid Astros Falsely Accuse Yankees of Using Camera to Cheat." *New York Post,* Oct. 17, 2018.

Passan, Jeff. "Sources: Red Sox Were Warned by Indians About Astros Attempting to Steal Signs and Information." *Yahoo! Sports,* Oct. 16, 2018.

Chapter 16: The Final Stand

Verducci, Tom. "Exclusive: MLB Set to Pass New Rules Designed to Crack Down on Sign Stealing." SI.com, Feb. 19, 2019.

Davidoff, Ken. "Alex Cora's Wink to Carlos Beltran Isn't as It Seems, but It Is Telling." *New York Post,* Jan. 15, 2020.

Rosenthal, Ken. "'Wow, This Is Impressive.' How a Lunch with Old Colleagues Put the Mets on a Path to Hire Carlos Beltrán." *The Athletic,* Nov. 4, 2019.

Apstein, Stephanie. "Astros Staffer's Outburst at Female Reporters Illustrates MLB's Forgive-and-Forget Attitude Toward Domestic Violence." SI.com, Oct. 21, 2019.

Passan, Jeff. "Inside the Astros' Culture That Bred Brandon Taubman's Comments." ESPN.com, Oct. 25, 2019.

Svlurga, Barry, and Dave Sheinin. "The World Just Learned of the Astros' Cheating. Inside Baseball, It Was an Open Secret." *Washington Post,* Feb. 11, 2020.

Chapter 17: It All Falls Apart

Rosenthal, Ken, and Evan Drellich. "The Astros Stole Signs Electronically in 2017—Part of a Much Broader Issue for Major League Baseball." *The Athletic,* Nov. 12, 2019.

Lee, Joon. "How the Internet Helped Crack the Astros Sign-Stealing Case." ESPN.com, Jan. 17, 2020.

Speier, Alex. "Inside Alex Cora's Departure from the Red Sox." *The Boston Globe,* Jan. 19, 2020.

Chapter 18: "Fuck You. "

Rosenthal, Ken, and Evan Drellich, with Marc Carig. "Details Emerge About Carlos Beltrán's Role in the 2017 Astros Clubhouse and the Team's Sign-Stealing Scheme." *The Athletic,* Feb. 11, 2020.

Martin, Dan. "Carlos Beltran Was Relentless 'Godfather' in Astros' Sign-Stealing Scheme." *New York Post,* Feb. 11, 2020.

MLB Network. "Exclusive Interview with A .J. Hinch." Feb. 7, 2020.

Rosencrans, C. Trent. "Trevor Bauer Was Asked About the Astros. He Didn't Hold Back on His Answer." *The Athletic,* Feb. 14, 2020.

Waldstein, David. "He Let the Astros Players Slide. Now He's Paying for It." *The New York Times,* Feb. 22, 2020.

Wells, Adam. "Astros' Josh Reddick Says He's Gotten Death Threats After Cheating Scandal." Bleacherreport.com, Feb. 21, 2020.

Acknowledgments

Reporting is in many ways an unintentional collaboration among competitors, as we engage in the never-ending process of answering and building on one another's work. In this case, I'm particularly indebted to the reporting of Ken Rosenthal and Evan Drellich at *The Athletic* and Jeff Passan of *Yahoo! Sports* and ESPN. Without their scoops, we wouldn't know about the trash can, and there would be no book. I'm also just a grateful reader and fan.

There are numerous people whose love or patience or indulgence or encouragement made it possible for me to attempt a writing career at all.

I want to especially thank Sean Casey, Chris Burruto, Dave Alfieri, Catherine Lewis at the creative writing program at Purchase College, SUNY, Charlie Ponce de Leon, Lynn Mahoney, Josiah Signor, Stephen Canino, Justin Martin, Amy (Sokal) Gazley, Michael Cardinali, the late Teri Young, Scott Henstrand, Sandy Padwe, T. J. Quinn, Jim Rich, Teri Thompson, Jim Cohen, John Quinn, Omar Minaya, Jim Salisbury, R. A. Dickey, Kristie Ackert, Gary Cohen, Terry Collins, Dan Warthen, Joe Angio, Bruce Diamond, Chris Carlin, Sandy Alderson, and Tim Brown.

A special wink to Paul Auster and Siri Hustvedt for welcoming me into your lives and treating me like a real writer (and for the honor of Coach Martino in 4 3 2 1).

Kevin Burkhardt: Boy, do I owe you one.

While I reported this book, Jim Duquette, Todd Zeile, Anthony Recker, and Ron Darling provided essential insight into the inner workings of the game, not to mention friendship that I value deeply. Duq in particular worked overtime as a sounding board for this project.

Derrick Goold, John Thorn, Nick Piecoro, Dylan Hernandez, Peter Gammons, Andy McCullough, Jorge Arangure, Jorge Castillo, David Wright, George Henn, and Hannah Keyser helped me to understand and frame important passages. Tony Adams contributed vital research.

Many people who asked not to have their names dragged into this sat for coffee, meals, long phone conversations, and text exchanges with me. They helped because of a commitment to seeing this story told accurately. Thank you for your time and trust. You know who you are.

At SNY, thanks to Steve Raab, Curt Gowdy Jr., Brad Como, Matt Dunn, and all the *Baseball Night in New York* talent, crew, and producers—a group captained by Doug Williams, Dave Mandel, Michael Flynn, and Gerard Guilfoyle—for support and camaraderie.

At ICM, thank you to Brian Jacobs and Esther Newberg for your advocacy. At Doubleday, thanks to Jason Kaufman for making the work better.

Love you to Liv, Matt, Clementine, Jesse, and Warner.

Ruby and Henry, you were in the room when I completed the first draft. You hugged and kissed me. Now that was a moment. I love you both.

My mom and dad are my readers, friends, and heroes. This book—and really everything I do, every day—is dedicated to them. Dad, this is your Parenthood speech. Finally.

K: A HISTORY OF BASEBALL IN TEN PITCHES
by Tyler Kepner

The baseball is an amazing plaything. We can grip it and hold it so many different ways, and even the slightest calibration can turn an ordinary pitch into a weapon to thwart the greatest hitters in the world. Each pitch has its own history, evolving through the decades as the masters pass it down to the next generation. From the earliest days of the game, when Candy Cummings dreamed up the curveball while flinging clamshells on a Brooklyn beach, pitchers have never stopped innovating. In *K: A History of Baseball in Ten Pitches*, Tyler Kepner traces the colorful stories and fascinating folklore behind the ten major pitches.

Sports

CASEY STENGEL
Baseball's Greatest Character
by Marty Appel

As a player, Charles Dillon "Casey" Stengel's contemporaries included Babe Ruth, Honus Wagner, and Christy Mathewson. As a legendary manager, he formed indelible, complicated relationships with Yogi Berra, Joe DiMaggio, Mickey Mantle, and Billy Martin. For more than five glorious decades, Stengel was the undisputed, quirky, hilarious, and beloved face of baseball—and along the way he revolutionized the role of manager. But for a man who spent so much of his life in the limelight, Stengel remains an enigma. In *Casey Stengel*, acclaimed New York Yankees' historian and bestselling author Marty Appel digs into Casey Stengel's quirks and foibles, unearthing a tremendous trove of baseball stories, perspective, and history.

Biography

TED WILLIAMS
The Biography of an American Hero
by Leigh Montville

The Kid. The Splendid Splinter. Teddy Ballgame. One of the greatest figures of his generation and arguably the greatest baseball hitter of all time. But what made Ted Williams a legend—and a lightning rod for controversy in life and in death? Still a gangly teenager when he stepped into a Boston Red Sox uniform in 1939, Williams's boisterous personality and penchant for towering home runs earned him adoring admirers and venomous critics. In 1941, the entire country followed Williams's stunning .406 batting average season, a record that has not been touched in eight decades. Then at the pinnacle of his prime, Williams left Boston to train and serve as a fighter pilot in World War II, missing three full years of baseball, making his achievements all the more remarkable. With unmatched verve and passion, and drawing upon hundreds of interviews, bestselling author Leigh Montville brings to life Ted Williams's superb triumphs, lonely tragedies, and intensely colorful personality in a biography that is fitting of an American hero and legend.

Biography

ANCHOR BOOKS
Available wherever books are sold.
anchorbooks.com